URBAN SYSTEMS MODELS

By WALTER HELLY

A Volume in the OPERATIONS RESEARCH
AND INDUSTRIAL ENGINEERING Series

1975, 195 pp. / ISBN 0--12--339450--3

FROM A REVIEW:

"Urban analysis professionals incr̶e̶a̶s̶
to diversify their
models. Their
Some b

ECONOMIC THEORY AND THE CITIES

This comprehensive statement of theory in urban economics reflects the emerging unity and integration of the many themes encountered in the field. *Economic Theory and the Cities* achieves generality with no sacrifice of rigor in its presentation of urban economic theory. Designed for a professional and graduate student audience, it is both an ideal text for advanced courses in urban economics and an excellent reference for practitioners in the field. The book covers the most important aspects of theory in urban economics, using basic economic models and principles to analyze urban problems, the spatial aspect of urban organization, and the economic relationships among urban areas.

The book presents equilibrium models of the internal structure of a city and a system of cities, depicting cities as they evolve in a free market economy. The internal allocations of resources within and between cities by the market are then subjected to normative analysis to determine if they are Pareto-efficient. Also covered are:

- environmental problems and policies (in a spatial setting)
- the housing market and landowner decisions
- transportation (in both static and dynamic contexts)
- local public finance
- suburbanization.

Researchers, practitioners, graduate students, and teachers in urban economics, city planning, regional science, and geography will welcome this new account of urban economic theory.

Economic Theory and the Cities

STUDIES IN URBAN ECONOMICS

Under the Editorship of

Edwin S. Mills
Princeton University

Norman J. Glickman. ECONOMETRIC ANALYSIS OF REGIONAL SYS-
TEMS: Explorations in Model Building and Policy Analysis

J. Vernon Henderson. ECONOMIC THEORY AND THE CITIES

Economic Theory and the Cities

J. VERNON HENDERSON
DEPARTMENT OF ECONOMICS
BROWN UNIVERSITY
PROVIDENCE, RHODE ISLAND

ACADEMIC PRESS   New York   San Francisco   London   1977

A Subsidiary of Harcourt Brace Jovanovich, Publishers

036296

ACADEMIC PRESS, INC.
111 Fifth Avenue, New York, New York 10003

United Kingdom Edition published by
ACADEMIC PRESS, INC. (LONDON) LTD.
24/28 Oval Road, London NW1

Library of Congress Cataloging in Publication Data

Henderson, J   Vernon.
    Economic theory and the cities.

    (Studies in urban economics)
    Bibliography: p.
    1.   Urban economics.   I.   Title.   II.   Series.
HT321.H397   330.9'173'2   76-42970
ISBN 0–12–340350–2

HT
321
. H397
1977

Contents

Foreword

It is fruitless to try to date the birth of an applied specialty such as urban economics. But it is not unreasonable to claim that modern urban model building started with the 1964 publication of Alonso's *Location and Land Use*. There were important contributions to urban economics before then, but almost nothing that can be identified as an ancestor of modern urban land use models.

If it is accepted that urban land use modeling reached puberty in 1977, it is a remarkably healthy and energetic child. Dozens of high quality books and papers appear each year, with no sign of slackening. It is likely that no applied specialty in economics ever developed so quickly and successfully. Much of the best work in urban land use modeling meets as high technical standards of careful use of economic theory as does work in any applied specialty. The subject has produced important theoretical and empirical insights and a framework for careful applied work. Perhaps most important, the subject has developed without losing contact with the central corpus of microeconomic theory. Careful communication with micro theory has permitted urban model building to obtain a level of professional acceptance that other specialties took decades to achieve. Especially impressive is the number of economists who move easily back and forth between urban modeling and work on other subjects.

Vernon Henderson's book illustrates these points. The first three chapters summarize and extend existing urban land use models. The models analyzed are careful and thorough technical developments. Most important, they show the richness of the work he and others have done. The models can be used and modified to provide insights into many urban issues. Then, Chapters 4–10 apply and extend the basic models to study a range of urban problems, including housing, transportation, city-size distribution, pollution, and local public finance. These chapters are a tour de force. They provide insights into nearly all the important urban problems of the time, carefully staying close to what can be demonstrated with formal models.

The following pages can be read with profit by both those interested in basic positive model development and those interested in the use of formal models to analyze important practical problems.

EDWIN S. MILLS
PRINCETON UNIVERSITY

Preface

In this book I present what I believe to be the most important aspects of theory in urban economics. Since urban economics is a rather undefined and diffuse field, any presentation is necessarily selective, reflecting personal tastes and opinions. Given that, I note on what basis I chose the material that is presented and developed.

First, the basic spatial model of a monocentric city is presented, since it is the starting point of most rigorous work in urban economics. This model is then expanded into a general equilibrium model of a system of cities. I thought it was essential to develop a model of a system of cities that is based upon normal general equilibrium concepts and that yields results consistent with the basic international trade and growth theorems. This preserves the link between spatial models of cities and mainstream economic theory. Finally, I chose to present models of what I consider to be the most important subtopics or problem areas in urban economics—externalities, housing, transportation, local public finance, and suburbanization. Poverty is excluded on the basis that it is too broad a topic incorporating large sections of labor economics, income distribution theory, and public finance.

This book is written primarily for people in the profession. However it is also designed for use in graduate urban economics courses. Recommended prerequisites are an undergraduate urban economics course and a year of graduate level microeconomic theory. It is possible that the book can be used in very advanced undergraduate courses if the students are well versed in microeconomics and are quantitatively oriented.

Acknowledgments

I developed the material in this book over the last few years, both in journal articles and for graduate urban economics courses at Queen's University, The University of Chicago, and Brown University. Most of this material has been presented at some stage in its development in the Urban Economics Workshop at The University of Chicago. The comments of George Tolley as well as Charles Upton and the students in that workshop have been instrumental in shaping my view of what is relevant and important in urban economics. Finally, during this time, I benefited from many discussions with Peter Mieszkowski on a variety of issues in urban public economics.

With respect to the manuscript itself, Edwin Mills read and commented on the entire manuscript and has been a helpful and encouraging editor. Herbert Mohring, who was a most patient correspondent, provided detailed and very useful comments on Chapters 5, 7, and 8. Karl Donenwirth provided detailed expositional comments on Chapters 1, 3, and 4 that were very important in rewriting and revising the manuscript. Peter Mieszkowski gave detailed comments on Chapters 9 and 10, providing helpful direction on the content of these chapters.

Marion Anthony patiently and skillfully typed the entire manuscript (several times). Finally, I thank my wife, Margaret, for her support and encouragement.

Introduction

Urban economics is the application of the methodology of economics to the study of man's activities and residence in cities. Cities are viewed as well-ordered entities with basic characteristics and empirical relationships that can be understood, explained, and predicted by using simple economic models and principles. Similarly, systems of cities are well-defined economic entities that function as part of a total economy and are tied to the development of the economy through trade, migration, and investment patterns. As such, chaos hypotheses concerning the indiscernible nature of cities and the application of models from physics and biology depicting cities as organisms subject to their own laws of motion or of birth, growth, sickness, and death are rejected from the start.

Cities have theoretically and empirically robust patterns of population and employment density, land and housing prices, and commuting patterns. Urban land and housing markets, urban transportation, environmental problems, urban decay, and the effects of urban fiscal arrangements and policies can be analyzed using the traditional tools of the economist. This is important because in applying economic analysis to cities not only can we attain a firm grasp of the nature of cities, but we can identify many of the underlying causes of urban problems and prescribe (or not prescribe) policies to deal with these problems. At the same time we can understand and predict the impact of such policies on the welfare and composition of urban residents.

However, urban economics is not just the ad hoc application of existing economic models and tools to an urban setting. There is a consistent underlying basis for these applications and a set of considerations that persist from problem to problem. The analysis of cities emphasizes the spatial aspects of economic organization. First there is the role of transport costs in moving goods between production sites, retail outlets, and homes, and in moving people between homes, job sites, and recreation sites. Second, there are the spatial aspects of people crowding together in urban areas and the resulting neighborhood, environmental, and congestion externalities. Because of the necessary inclusion of spatial dimensions in the examination of urban problems, urban economics stands apart from mainstream economics, which largely ignores the spatial and crowding aspects of man's activities. It has required the development of special, spatial models to deal with the particular conceptual problems involved.

While much of the recent theoretical work in urban economics has emphasized the development of spatial models that are specific to an urban setting, these spatial models can also be utilized to yield the basic propositions found in mainstream spaceless models. This book emphasizes this fact and examines the nature of economies composed of a system of cities.

Throughout the book, the focus is on the long-run equilibrium properties of cities and a system of cities, as well as on the forces moving city economies to equilibrium. The long-run model serves to highlight the basic characteristics, nature, and tendencies of cities and a system of cities. Long-run effects are also the primary basis for government policymaking, since it is difficult to formulate policies to deal with the multitude of various economic shocks that are invariably moving city economies temporarily away from long-run equilibrium. In the book the analysis of disequilibrium or successions of short-run temporary equilibria is not emphasized. Disequilibrium in a system of cities is a topic urban economists have yet to properly deal with.

What Is a City or Urban Area?

Ironically, one difficult conceptual task in writing this book has been to define precisely what an urban area or city is, from an economic, as opposed to legal or fiscal, point of view. With an urban area of 100,000 placed in the midst of an agricultural plain with one distinct Central Business District (CBD) surrounded by residences, there is no problem. But for a metropolitan area such as Chicago, there is a problem. Is the metropolitan area of Chicago, including Evanston, Cicero, and East Chicago, one urban area and economic unit or is it a set of units? If it is a set of units, to define the number of urban areas in the Chicago area, we must decide when a "suburb" becomes an urban area in its own right as opposed to a bedroom community or appendage to another area. We define when communities become urban areas in their own right by means of the following scenario, leaving the definition of an urban area intentionally imprecise.

Consider a monocentric city of 100,000 people that is growing over time. As the urban area grows, suburbs, or bedroom communities, start to form for fiscal purposes (see Chapter 10). Most people continue to commute to the CBD. With the development of the expressway system and trucking industries in the city, employment starts to decentralize to the suburbs. The decentralized employment remains integrated with the main industrial activities of the city, with goods being shipped back and forth in the intermediate stages of production. The CBD remains by far the most important employer, drawing commuters from *all* parts of the urban area. The metropolitan area is still just a single economic unit or urban area.

At some point as the urban area continues to grow, several changes may occur. Another part of the area may become a major employer, drawing commuters from the area adjacent to it and all points beyond it (away from the CBD). Residents adjacent to that business district and beyond in general no longer commute to the CBD. At this point, we may want to call this area an economic unit or urban area in its own right, with its own rent gradient, source of scale economies, and possibly fiscal jurisdiction.

However, the industry of this area may still be strongly linked to the core city, using a common labor market and/or experiencing a common source of scale economies. In that case, it may be more useful to define the metropolitan area as still a single economic unit, but one with two employment centers. The two centers relieve commuting and congestion pressures relative to having only one center while permitting the continued common development of scale economies. Moreover, people throughout the area may continue to use the original center for cultural and shopping activities. Under these stricter guidelines, a new urban area can only be said to arise when its industry becomes separate from that of the core city. Separate means that, although the industries may trade, their scale economies are not linked and they draw upon different labor and other primary input markets.

Content of the Book

The first three chapters present equilibrium models of the internal structure of a city and a system of cities, depicting cities as they will evolve in a free-market economy. In Chapter 1, from simple profit and utility maximization problems in space, the familiar rent, density, and building-height gradients of cities are derived. Many of the concepts illustrated in this chapter were originally developed in Alonso's (1964) and Muth's (1969) pioneering works. Chapter 2 draws together the commercial and residential sectors analyzed in Chapter 1 to present an aggregative model of a city.

For a city facing a fixed borrowing rate on capital and an exogenous supply curve of labor, we examine the determination of city size, given the behavior of land developers and city governments. This approach is similar to the usual partial equilibrium models of city size developed in the literature, although our emphasis is somewhat different.

Chapter 3, I believe, is one of the most important chapters in the book. It ties the monocentric models of a city into a general equilibrium framework for a total economy, where city size is determined in a system of cities among which factors flow freely and cities trade freely. City sizes are determined from investment behavior of capital owners, migration decisions of laborers, and entrepreneurial actions of land developers and city governments. The model of a system of cities is then related to general aggregate models of economies to show that it yields results consistent with basic propositions in international trade and economic growth theory. The chapter is based upon previous work of mine (Henderson, 1974a), but the treatment of the determination, stability, and uniqueness of equilibrium is considerably more sophisticated.

The first three chapters are a positive analysis of a system of cities; the next two chapters deal with the normative aspects of analyzing a system of cities. Chapter 4 is a normative analysis describing problems in the national allocation of factors among cities, given the existence of either external economies of scale in production or public goods. Tax-subsidy solutions for achieving an optimal allocation of population are described. This chapter is based on work by Flatters, Henderson, and Mieszkowski (1974), and it extends their results derived from a regional Ricardian model to a spatial urban model.

Chapter 5 contains a normative analysis illustrating problems concerning the internal allocation of resources in cities. The most common example in the literature used to illustrate this problem is the road congestion externality problem, which is concerned with the spatial arrangement of residents in cities and the allocation of land to roads in cities. We choose to illustrate the problem of efficient internal allocation of resources with a different example, for several reasons. In the later chapters on transportation it is suggested that an adequate analysis of congestion problems requires a much more sophisticated transportation model than is usually considered in this literature. Moreover, since this example is so pervasive in the literature and since there are many competent discussions of it, it seemed sensible to choose a different problem. The problem chosen is the effect on resource allocation of air pollution. We study the problem in a spatial framework which brings to light several new considerations in the analysis of externalities. We show that a comprehensive environmental policy must deal with land use problems and problems in the distribution of pollution tax proceeds, as well as imposing a set of Pigouvian taxes. This chapter is based on Henderson (1977).

Chapter 6, on housing, besides examining the usual externality, zoning, and segregation questions, looks at models of housing depreciation and filtering down. A problem in writing the chapter was that sophisticated models of the housing market are complicated and difficult to cover rigorously in a concise way. Therefore, although the housing assignment problem and Sweeney's (1974b) work on filtering down are described, the reader is referred to the literature for a complete presentation of these subjects. In Chapter 6, we concentrate on relating the models of housing depreciation and the housing market to traditional models of investment by the firm. In particular we investigate what conditions must be imposed on housing technology or the economic environment of housing producers to get filtering down in the housing market and whether filtering down is likely to be primarily a supply- or demand-induced phenomenon.

Chapters 7 and 8 examine transportation. In the literature there are a variety of quite different traffic models and ways of depicting traffic situations, some of which are static and some dynamic. Accordingly, at the beginning of Chapter 7 I attempt to give a clear specification of the different ways of modeling traffic situations and flows so that the implications of using various types of models may be understood. Chapter 7 then goes on to present a standard pricing and investment model in transportation, where a traffic planner may face a variety of pricing and investment constraints when formulating policy. In particular, the issue of subsidizing rapid transit is examined, and we determine when it is efficient to set rapid transit fares below marginal and/or average costs.

In Chapter 8 a rush-hour or peak-period traffic situation is modeled and the varying pattern of traffic flows throughout the rush hour is analyzed. This chapter should provide insights into the nature of traffic demand and peak-period situations, and possible ways of efficiently regulating peak-period traffic. We also examine the impact of the imposition of optimal congestion pricing on the evaluation and provision of optimal capacity levels on roads. This chapter is based on previous work I have done (Henderson, 1974b), but the modeling of the technical nature of transportation is more sophisticated.

Finally, the book ends with a survey of issues in local public finance such as property taxation, revenue sharing, and fiscal federalism. A separate chapter is devoted to the subject of suburbanization. Static and dynamic models of suburbanization are examined, with an emphasis on the conflicts that arise among initial residents, developers, excluded residents, and later residents of a suburb in planning and regulating the development of that suburb.

1

Spatial Equilibrium and the Spatial Characteristics of a Simple City

In this chapter a simple model of a city is developed, with the following guidelines in mind. In specifying the model, we want to incorporate the basic features of the economic structure of cities. Thus the model should capture the essence of spatial interaction between producers and consumers in a city, and it should yield theoretical results that correspond to the basic empirical facts about cities. For example, the model should show that land rents, population density, and building heights decline with distance from the city center, as demonstrated in empirical work (e.g., Muth, 1969). It should be able to explain why higher-income people tend to live farther from city centers than lower-income people and why wages vary spatially within a city. When different cities with similar transportation technologies are compared, the level of rents, population density, and building heights should increase with city size. We also want a model of a city that can be adapted to enable us to analyze a system of cities and to describe equilibrium city sizes, factor movements, and trade patterns among the cities of an economy. Finally, the model should be consistent with the models and analyses of later chapters on housing, transportation, and public finance, which detail different aspects of urban living and are useful in analyzing specific urban problems.

In specifying the nature of cities in the model, the following assumptions are made. The economy consists of a flat featureless plain. Instead of the population spreading evenly over the plain, concentrations of population, or cities, form because it is assumed there are scale economies in production. Exploitation of these scale economies requires that there be concentrations of employment in production activities. These scale economies result from scale efficiencies in input markets, marketing, communications, transportation, and/or public service provision. Concentration of employment results in concentration of residences occupied by people who commute to the employment centers.

In cities most or all commercial activity occurs in the Central Business District (CBD), which is located in the central part of the city. This central location of all commercial activity results from businesses outbidding residents for this central land. The desire for businesses to be located together at the city center follows from several assumptions. First, if firms are located together, the advantages of scale economies may be more fully realized. Second, it is assumed that all goods produced in the city are shipped to a retailing and transport node at the very center of the city where they are sold to city residents and exported to other cities. This node could be a railway station, trucking terminal, or harbor (in a semicircular city). Firms minimize the costs of shipping goods to the node by locating around the node. Finally, we note that because the business district is at the center of the city, the total costs of commuting to work for all residents are minimized relative to the business district's being at a noncentral location.[1]

Surrounding the CBD is the residential sector where all city residents live. From their home sites residents commute to the city center and then disperse to their work sites. It is this feature of most or all residents commuting to work in the CBD that distinguishes a simple city from more complicated cities, where only part of the city's labor force commutes to the CBD. At various points in the book the impact of non-CBD employment on the basic results of the model will be considered.

Finally, we note that, in a stable equilibrium solution, both the CBD and the total city will be symmetric circles. As shown later, this result follows when there is only one business district because the plain on which cities are located is featureless.

In the first section of the chapter the residential sector of the city is examined. Equilibrium of a household in space is analyzed. Then, building upon the properties of a household's equilibrium, we study long-run equi-

---

[1] Being at the center of a circle minimizes the distance involved in traveling to all points in the circle. Since our city will be a circle, the central location of the CBD minimizes total commuting costs, given there can be only one business district. With two or more business districts, this proposition is no longer correct.

librium in the housing and land markets. Finally, aggregate demand and supply relationships in the residential sector are derived. Throughout, the general concepts developed are illustrated with a simple example using specific functional forms. In the second section of the chapter, the commercial sector of the city is examined. Building upon the individual producer's profit maximization problem, aggregate relationships describing the commercial sector's use of labor, capital, and land are developed. These aggregate relationships will be used to determine equilibrium levels of employment and prices in Chapter 2.

1. THE RESIDENTIAL SECTOR

1.1 Consumer Residential Choice and Equilibrium in the Residential Sector

Residents in the city maximize utility defined over market goods and amenities subject to a budget constraint and the amenity choices facing them. Market goods are the city's own traded good x produced in the CBD, the city's import good z, and housing services h, which are rented from housing producers. The prices of the traded goods, p_x and p_z, do not vary within the city, since these goods are all purchased from the same market at the center of the city. The rental price of housing may vary spatially; and, in fact, housing and housing prices are distinct items in the model.

Housing represents both a consumer good and a particular spatial location in the city. Associated with each spatial location in the residential sector is a level of amenities consumed by residents. The only amenity we consider in this chapter is leisure consumption, which is directly related, through commuting times, to access to the CBD. The rental on housing implicitly prices both housing services and access, or leisure consumption; and thus the unit price of housing $p(u)$ will vary spatially as leisure varies. This amenity formulation is perfectly general and can be expanded to include a vector of goods such as park and recreational services and clean air (see Chapter 5).[2]

With respect to leisure, we assume that residents work a fixed number of hours. Leisure is the fixed number of nonworking hours T less time spent commuting. We assume that the time it takes to commute a *unit* distance (there and back) to work is t; and t is the same everywhere in the city. (This assumption implies there is no congestion; or as the number of commuters accumulates as we approach the CBD, travel speeds are unchanged.) Therefore, a consumer at distance u from the city center has leisure consumption

---

[2] I first came across the general formulation in Hartwick (1971). Diamond (1976) also uses a similar formulation.

$e(u)$ equal to

$$e(u) = T - tu.$$

Note that time costs are the only form of commuting costs in this chapter.[3]

Given these assumptions, we can now formally state the consumer optimization problem. Where $V(u)$ is utility at location u and y is income, the consumer

$$\max_{\text{w.r.t. } x,z,h,e,u} V(u) = V'(x(u), z(u), h(u), e(u)) \tag{1.1}$$

subject to

$$y - p_x x(u) - p_z z(u) - p(u)h(u) = 0,$$
$$T - e(u) - tu = 0.$$

For the consumer this is essentially a simultaneous two-stage maximization problem. He must pick an optimal location in space, given the spatial set of amenities and housing prices; and at the optimal location, he must choose an optimal consumption bundle. For a consumer *at location u*, his optimal consumption bundle is chosen according to the budget constraint and the usual first-order conditions equating price ratios with marginal rates of substitution in consumption. Given these conditions and assuming that V' is a regular utility function,[4] we can then specify demand equations for all market goods as a function of income, all output prices, and leisure. For example, for housing

$$h(u) = h(y, p(u), p_x, p_z, e(u)), \tag{1.2}$$

where h is increasing in y and decreasing in $p(u)$.

The question we are primarily concerned with is how the consumer comes to choose a particular u or distance from the city center. Maximizing equation (1.1) with respect to $e(u)$ and u yields the first-order conditions that $\partial V'/\partial e(u) - \gamma = 0$ and $-\lambda h(u)(\partial p(u)/\partial u) - \gamma t = 0$ where γ and λ are Lagrange multipliers and are, respectively, the marginal utility of leisure and that of income. Combining to solve out γ yields the condition that holds when a consumer is at his optimal location

$$h(u) \frac{\partial p(u)}{\partial u} = -\frac{\partial V'/\partial e(u)}{\lambda} t \equiv -p_e(u)t. \tag{1.3}$$

The term $p_e(u)$ is the monetized value of the marginal utility of leisure, where we have defined

$$p_e(u) = (\partial V'/\partial e(u))/\lambda.$$

---

[3] I first came across this formulation in Beckmann (1974).
[4] V' should be a continuous, nondecreasing, and strictly quasi-concave function.

This term measures the marginal evaluation of leisure, which is the opportunity cost of travel time.

At his optimal location, if the consumer moves an infinitesimal distance farther from the city center, he experiences a loss in leisure. The value of this lost leisure is the marginal evaluation of leisure $p_e(u)$ multiplied by the reduction in leisure $-t$. Equation (1.3) states that he is exactly compensated for this lost leisure by reduced housing costs $h(u)(\partial p(u)/\partial u)$, such that utility is unchanged.[5] That is, at an optimal location he cannot improve his welfare by moving. This implies that $\partial p(u)/\partial u < 0$, where this decline in housing rents is necessary to compensate consumers for lost leisure time as they move farther from the city center. Otherwise, consumers could not be induced to live farther from the center and we could not have an equilibrium set of locations. If housing rents rose or stayed constant as consumers moved away from the city center, a consumer would always be better off moving inward, since leisure would be increased with unchanged or lower housing costs.

Equation (1.3) describes a relationship between equilibrium housing rents and distance that must hold for an individual household to be in equilibrium. The next step is to derive the properties of the set of equilibrium housing prices that occurs along a ray from the city center. This set of prices is called the rent gradient. The rent gradient is defined by its height and slope, or by the level of prices at each distance from the CBD and the change in these prices as distance changes. In the next section we derive these properties and in the following section we show how the rent gradient must be consistent with equilibrium in the residential housing and land markets.

The Rent Gradient with Identical Consumers

If all residents in a city have identical incomes and tastes, then deriving the properties of the residential rent gradient is straightforward. If consumers are identical, in a stable spatial equilibrium all residents must have the same utility level at their different locations. Otherwise residents in locations with lower utility levels will bid for locations with higher utility levels, driving up prices at those locations and/or causing spatial movements. The situation is only stable when all identical residents are equally well off.

To derive the properties of the rent gradient, we introduce the concept of an indirect utility function. As indicated earlier, for a consumer at location u, there exists a set of demand equations for market goods where demand is a function of income, prices, and leisure. When these demand equations for

---

[5] That is, at the optimal location we are at a stationary point where infinitesimal changes in location bring no utility changes, or $dV/du = 0$, given the constraints of the problem. This formulation involves certain continuity and smoothness assumptions about how utility varies over space, as will become clearer later.

market goods are substituted into the direct utility function, utility indirectly becomes a function of income, prices, and leisure. We may then define the indirect utility function, or

$$V = V(y, p(u), p_x, p_z, e(u)) \qquad (1.4)$$

where V is increasing in y and e, decreasing in prices, and homogeneous of degree zero in income and prices. One interesting property of the indirect utility function utilized at various points in the book is that the demand for housing (and similarly for other goods) may be represented as[6]

$$h(u) = -\frac{\partial V/\partial p(u)}{\partial V/\partial y}. \qquad (1.5)$$

Equation (1.5) is often referred to as Roy's identity.

With identical residents the rent gradient must be such that utility in equation (1.4) is the same everywhere in the city. Therefore, housing prices must vary such that $dV/du = 0$. Accordingly we could differentiate equation (1.4) and do appropriate substitutions to find the slope of the rent gradient.[7] Alternatively we note that since equation (1.3) specifies a relationship between actual housing prices and distance that must hold for individuals to be in equilibrium, it must also define the slope of the rent gradient that holds in a stable-market equilibrium. Rearranging equation (1.3) yields the slope of the rent gradient

$$\partial p(u)/\partial u = -h(u)^{-1}p_e(u)t < 0. \qquad (1.6)$$

We can solve for the height of the rent gradient at any point using the indirect utility function. To demonstrate this we examine Figure 1.1a, in which a residential rent gradient between u_0 and u_1 is illustrated. u_0 and u_1 are, respectively, the CBD and city radii; thus the residential area lies between u_0 and u_1. The basic reference point on the gradient is at the city edge u_1. Consumers at the city edge have utility $V(u_1)$ defined in equation (1.4) by leisure $e(u_1)$ given commuting time tu_1, by income and traded good prices, and by the known price of housing at u_1. The price of housing at u_1, or $p(u_1)$, equals the known price received from producing housing on land

---

[6] An intuitive explanation why equation (1.5) holds is simple. $-\partial V/\partial p(u)$ is the marginal utility obtained from a dollar decline in housing prices. This equals the marginal utility of a dollar ($\partial V/\partial y$) multiplied by the change in dollars available to the consumer, which equals the number of housing units $h(u)$ multiplied by the dollar change in price (or 1). Rearranging terms yields (1.5).

[7] We differentiate equation (1.4), set $dV = 0$, divide by $\partial V/\partial y$, and substitute in equation (1.5) and the expression for $p_e(u)$. Rearranging terms yields equation (1.6). Equation (1.4) can also be used to derive the consumer's spatial equilibrium condition where at a utility-maximizing location $\partial V/\partial u = 0$ and $\partial^2 V/\partial u^2 \leq 0$.

at u_1, which borders on agricultural land. (As we will see later, $p(u_1)$ is determined by known agricultural rents and the price of capital.) Given that all consumers have identical tastes, $V(u_1)$ defines utility throughout the city. Then from equation (1.4), for any u_i, given the known values of V and $e(u_i)$ we should be able to solve for $p(u_i)$, the height of the rent gradient at that point. While this discussion demonstrates a method for deriving the equilibrium rent gradient, we still need to know how u_1 and hence $V(u_1)$ are determined. We turn to that topic in the next section when we examine equilibrium in the housing and land markets, but first we comment on several other properties associated with the equilibrium rent gradient.

So far we have described the equilibrium change in rents for consumers moving along a ray from the city center. To determine the equilibrium pattern of rents throughout the city, circumferential movements by consumers must also be considered. Equilibrium with respect to circumferential movements occurs when along all rays from the CBD the rent gradient is the same as P_1 in Figure 1.1a, so that at a given radius from the city center all rents on that circumference are equalized. Since commuting costs to the CBD are the same from any point on that circumference, consumers will then have no incentive to switch locations circumferentially. For this reason cities on a flat featureless plain must be circular or else people will bid to fill out a circle.

Finally we note that because $p(u)$ declines, for discrete spatial moves the consumer's housing consumption will change in response to the changing price. Since with identical consumers, utility remains constant as locations and prices change, the housing demand response is described by the Hicks pure substitution effect where $\partial h(u)/\partial p(u) < 0$. Therefore, housing consumption increases with distance as price declines. This relation is illustrated in Figure 1.1b.

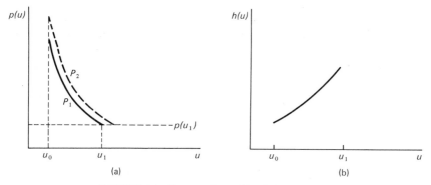

FIGURE 1.1   Rent gradients: identical consumers.

This increase in housing consumption is also the reason the rent gradient is pictured as convex.[8] Convexity implies that $\partial p(u)/\partial u$ in equation (1.6) declines with distance, or $\partial^2 p(u)/\partial u^2 > 0$. This decline in $\partial p(u)/\partial u$ in equation (1.6) occurs because h is increasing as u increases which causes the right-hand side of equation (1.6) to decline, providing $p_e(u)$ does not vary much with discrete spatial moves. Alternatively stated, with convexity, as we move out the rent gradient and leisure declines, the approximately equal compensating decline in housing expenditures at each point, which is $h(u)\,\partial p(u)/\partial u$, is achieved with smaller and smaller changes in unit prices, $\partial p(u)/\partial u$, given that housing consumption $h(u)$ is continuously increasing.

The Rent Gradient and Housing Market Equilibrium

The height and length of an equilibrium rent gradient like that pictured in Figure 1.1a must be consistent with conditions defining housing market equilibrium in the residential sector of the city. This equilibrium is determined by demand and supply conditions in the housing market and in factor markets underlying the housing market. Although most of the properties that define a stable equilibrium in the housing market are quite obvious, we state them here for emphasis because it is important to have them firmly in mind for the discussion that follows and when we analyze more sophisticated situations in the housing and land markets in Chapter 5.[9] Since the housing market equilibrium cannot be entirely isolated from conditions in factor markets, we also briefly describe the supply of housing here. It is analyzed in Section 1.2.

Consumers rent housing from housing producers.[10] Housing producers produce housing according to the usual profit-maximization conditions with rented capital and land. Capital is perfectly malleable and mobile and is rented by housing producers at a fixed price in local or national capital markets. Land is owned either by a class of people called rentiers or collectively by city residents through the operation and management of the city government (see Chapter 2). We have distinguished four groups of people—consumers, producers, capital owners, and rentiers. However, the specification is general and we can collapse these people into three, two, or even one group. Consumers could produce their own housing by renting inputs;

---

[8] This convexity is not necessary. It implies that $\partial^2 p(u)/\partial u^2 = ((-\partial h/\partial p)(\partial p/\partial u)^2 h^{-1} + (\partial p_e(u)/\partial e)t^2 h^{-1}) > 0$. If $\partial p_e(u)/\partial e$ is small (or positive), this condition is met.

[9] For an analysis of the attainment of residential spatial equilibrium, the reader should consult Alonso (1964), Chapters 4 and 5 and Appendix A.

[10] We assume consumers rent rather than purchase, since that fits in with the structure of a single-period model and comparative statics. If consumers own housing, we would have to employ a multiperiod model, use a wealth constraint, and consider capital gains/losses.

rentiers or capital owners could produce the housing; consumers could be the rentiers and own their own land; and so on.

Given this situation, four conditions define a stable equilibrium in the housing market. Although the conditions are specific to the housing market, with the land market being discussed separately in Section 1.2, since the two markets are not independent, in some of the conditions the land market is referred to.

(1) In equilibrium, on the supply side, suppliers of housing rent to the consumer who is willing to pay the most for that housing; and thus housing producers have no incentive to switch customers or tenants. In Figure 1.1a, since all consumers have equal utility along the rent gradient P_1, at any location no other consumer would be willing to pay more for that housing than the current resident.

(2) On the demand side, each consumer rents the housing and location that maximizes utility, given the equilibrium set of prices; and thus no renter has an incentive to move. In Figure 1.1a, since all residents have equal utility, given P_1, a consumer cannot improve his welfare by bidding away, and thus raising, the price of the housing of another resident.

(3) The boundaries of the residential area are the CBD radius u_0 and the city radius u_1. At these boundaries the price of residential housing equals its opportunity cost, or the cost of producing housing on land in the alternative competing use at the boundary. If the residential price exceeds [is less than] that cost, housing producers and land owners have an incentive to increase [decrease] the residential area. Since the price of capital is everywhere the same, we will show that higher [lower] housing prices directly reflect higher [lower] land prices. Then for example, if the cost of producing housing on land in the alternative use at u_1 is lower than the current price of housing there, this means the price of land in the alternative use is lower than the residential price. Landowners will individually profit by increasing the allocation of land to urban use, until land prices and hence housing costs and prices are equalized at the border of competing uses. Then the city's spatial area will be stable.

(4) All housing and locations supplied are rented; and given u_0, u_1, and the rent gradient, all residents consume their desired level of housing. That is, demand equals supply and there are no holes in the city or misplaced residents. If the city population were to increase, in aggregate more housing and hence more land would be demanded. u_1 would increase, and to accommodate the new population for the same $p(u_1)$ the rent gradient would shift up to, say, P_2 in Figure 1.1a for the same income and prices. The fact that the rent gradient shifts up is proved formally in Section 1.3. The degree to which P_2 shifts up depends on both the increase in population and the

partially offsetting decline in per person housing and derived land demands
at each point as housing prices rise. Note that with the increase in population
and rise in P_2, consumers will all be worse off if their incomes are unchanged.
For example, in the indirect utility function, for the person on the new city
edge (which is our reference point for defining utility levels in the city) leisure,
or $e(u_1)$, declines while all other variables are unchanged.

The Rent Gradient and Nonidentical Consumers

To derive the equilibrium rent gradient when consumers are not identical
is more complicated. We assume that consumers differ only by income. To
solve for the gradient, the concept of a bid rent function is utilized. A bid
rent function describes what unit rents a particular consumer would be
willing to pay for housing services in different locations, such that he is
indifferent among these locations.

To define a bid rent function we use the indirect utility function $V = V(y, p(u), p_x, p_z, e(u))$ defined in equation (1.4). Taking the inverse of this
function, we have

$$p^0(u) = p(V, y, p_x, p_z, e(u)). \tag{1.7}$$

Equation (1.7) is a bid rent function, where $p^0(u)$ is a hypothetical bid price,
not a market equilibrium price. This function describes the variation in the
amount a consumer is willing to pay for housing as leisure $e(u)$ varies.

To determine the properties of equation (1.7), we differentiate the indirect utility function, holding income and other prices fixed. If we set
$dV = 0$, divide by the marginal utility of income, and substitute in equation
(1.5) and the expression for $p_e(u)$, the result is

$$\partial p^0(u)/\partial u = -h(u)^{-1}p_e(u)t. \tag{1.8}$$

Equation (1.8) defines the slope of a bid rent curve and it indicates how a
person's bid rent will vary along a ray from the city center. A set of bid rent
curves is pictured in Figure 1.2a. The height of the bid rent curves is defined
by the utility level in (1.7), where along any curve utility is fixed and the
curves shift up [down] as utility falls [rises]. This property is expressed by
the negative relationship in the indirect utility function between V and
$p^0(u)$ for $e(u)$ fixed. Bid rent curves for the same individual do not cross, just
as indifference curves do not cross.

In general, bid rent curves and in particular the slope of bid rent curves
vary as income varies among individuals. As income changes, $h(u)$ and
$p_e(u)$ will vary; hence, at each location u, from equation (1.8), the slope of the
bid curves should either increase or decrease. We choose to illustrate an equilibrium where the slope decreases as income increases. In equation (1.8) this

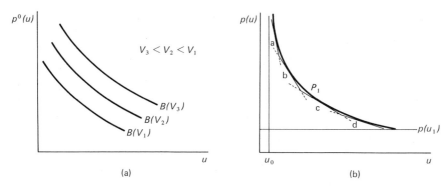

FIGURE 1.2 Bid rents and gradients for nonidentical consumers.

means that the quantity of housing consumed $h(u)$ increases *relative* to the marginal evaluation of leisure $p_e(u)$ as income increases. This assumption is discussed in detail after we illustrate the nature of an equilibrium rent gradient.

For the illustration, we first rank *groups* of equal-income consumers by the steepness of their bid rent curves. We place the steepest near the CBD and the least steep near the city edge. In Figure 1.2b we draw four bid rent curves labelled a, b, c, and d, one for each of the four different groups of consumers. As just assumed, the steepest bid rent curve belongs to the lowest-income consumers. The equilibrium rent gradient P_1 is an *envelope* of bid rent curves and is composed of a segment for each income group where within each segment the bid rent curve and rent gradient are coincident. Each point on the gradient represents how much each person has to pay to bid his house and location away from other users in his or other income groups. At the points of junction of the rent gradient segments, the dashed extensions of the bid rent curves that do not lie on the rent gradient represent what people in a particular income group would be willing to pay to live in another part of the city such that their utility is unchanged. The properties of the equilibrium rent gradient are as follows.

From equation (1.18), the slope of a bid rent function which is also the slope of the rent gradient specifies the same price–distance relationship as equation (1.3). This implies that along the equilibrium rent gradient consumers are at their utility-maximizing location.

The ordering of people by the steepness of their bid rent curves is necessary for stability and satisfies the market equilibrium conditions that:

(1) producers are renting to the highest bidders—for example, we can see by comparing the rent gradient and the dashed extensions of the bid rent curves that type b consumers would not outbid type a consumers interior to

the point of junction of their equilibrium bid rent curves and rent gradient segments; and

(2) consumers are at their utility-maximizing location—for example, type b consumers would be worse off, or on a higher bid rent curve, if they paid the prices type a people paid.

Any other spatial configuration, such as b people living interior to type a people, would be unstable, since then type a people would be willing to pay higher prices than b people to live in b's segment of the city. (We can see this by redrawing Figure 1.2b with less steep bid rent curves nearest the city center.[11])

In Figure 1.2b, the height of the rent gradient, the size of the residential area, and the size of the segments within which each income group lives are such that all people are housed, all land and housing is rented in the city, and all people consume their desired level of housing given their location and the prices on the rent gradient. As with a city of identical consumers, an increase in population will shift up the rent gradient and extend u_1.

If the underlying reasons for how the slopes of bid rent curves vary are examined, the ordering of consumers by the steepness of their bid curves turns out to be intuitively appealing. If slopes decrease at each point as income increases, this means, from equation (1.8) where $\partial p^0(u)/\partial u < 0$, that $d(\partial p^0(u)/\partial u)/dy > 0$. Differentiating equation (1.8) with respect to y for u fixed, we know

$$d(\partial p^0(u)/\partial u)/dy = h(u)^{-1}y^{-1}p_e(u)t[\eta_{h,y} - \eta_{p_e,y}] \gtrless 0, \qquad (1.9)$$

where $\eta_{p_e,y}$ is the income elasticity of the marginal evaluation of leisure and $\eta_{h,y}$ is the income elasticity of demand for housing. Whether equation (1.9) is positive or negative depends on whether the expression in brackets is positive or negative, and hence it depends on whether $\eta_{h,y} \gtrless \eta_{p_e,y}$. For the assumption made earlier that the slopes of rent curves decrease as income increases, or $d(\partial p^0(u)/\partial u)/dy > 0$, $\eta_{h,y} > \eta_{p_e,y}$. From the definition of elasticities, this means that for a 1% increase in income, the percentage increase in housing is greater than the percentage increase (if any) in the marginal evaluation of leisure. In these circumstances lower-income people live closest to the CBD and have the most leisure.

This makes sense, since lower-income people who end up nearest the CBD are those people who value leisure the most *relative* to housing. Thus they are the people who are willing to pay the highest price per unit of housing near the CBD to housing producers. A simple numerical example can be

[11] If the rent gradient is smooth at the points of overlap (i.e., income changes minutely), this ordering of people satisfies the second-order condition of optimization for any individual, and at the point of overlap $\partial^2 V/\partial u^2 < 0$.

used to illustrate this point. Suppose higher- and lower-income people would consume 10 and 5 units, respectively, of housing given current prices at a location u. At that location lower-income people would be willing to pay \$5 per week more (indirectly through higher housing prices and hence payments) to move slightly closer to the CBD and have a unit increase in leisure. Suppose higher-income people are only willing to pay \$9 a week more (through larger housing payments) for a unit increase in leisure. Then the percentage by which higher-income people's housing consumption is larger than lower-income people's is greater than the percentage by which higher-income people's marginal evaluation of leisure is larger (i.e., 100% > 80%). This means that the increase in price bid per unit of housing to move closer to the CBD for higher-income people is less than for lower-income people (i.e., \$9/5 < \$5/5) and housing producers will accept the higher bids of lower-income people for high-access land. On the other hand, if higher-income people are willing to pay \$11 for a unit increase in leisure, they will outbid lower-income people for high-access land (i.e., \$11/5 > \$5/5). The problem for higher-income people trying to live next to the CBD is that even if they are willing to pay more than lower-income people in absolute terms for increased leisure, their percentage difference in housing consumption relative to lower-income people cannot be greater than their percentage difference in leisure evaluation or the effect of their greater leisure evaluation on unit housing prices is dissipated through their higher housing consumption. This type of argument can also be used to explain why high- or low-income people tend to live in more polluted or higher-crime areas.

The assumption that $d(\partial p^0(u)/\partial u)\,\partial y > 0$ is a rather arbitrary theoretical assumption. This assumption was made in the foregoing discussion and is made in the literature since it yields results consistent with the empirical observation that higher-income people tend to live farther from the city center in the United States. However, that empirical phenomenon could be explained on other grounds and in more sophisticated models not considered until later in the book. For example, in the housing filtering-down models in Chapter 6, higher-income people tend to live in the newest housing, which, given the age and development of American cities, generally is built on the outskirts of cities. In Chapter 10, we note that higher-income people have a fiscal incentive to suburbanize and hence to move farther away from the city center than lower income people.

Non-CBD Local Employment. In deriving these rent gradients it has been assumed that all people commute to the CBD. This need not be so. Suppose in Figure 1.2b that on the segment of the P_1 rent gradient where type a people live, some of the type a people work in a grocery store in that area. Providing that most people still work in the CBD, the shape of the rent gradient is still determined by the same equilibrium conditions for CBD commuters and is unchanged. That is, their bidding determines the competitive price of land. Identical type a people who work locally pay the same market rents as commuters but have more leisure. To maintain equilibrium in labor markets and choice of occupation, the local wages of noncommuters will be lower than those of commuters by the value of their increased leisure. If, however, the ratio of local to CBD workers becomes too large, then the gradient will change. For example, if beyond a certain point no one commutes to the CBD, the rent gradient would be radically different.

An Illustration of Housing Rent Gradients in a Simple City

It is useful to illustrate the foregoing discussion with a simple example using specific functional forms. This example and the specific functional forms will also be used later to derive explicit aggregate relationships for a city. Consumers maximize a logarithmic linear utility function subject to a budget constraint and a leisure constraint.

Therefore, the consumer maximization problem is to

$$\max_{\text{w.r.t. } x,z,h,e,u} V = A'x(u)^a z(u)^b h(u)^c e(u)^d, \qquad a + b + c = f \qquad (1.1a)$$

subject to

$$y - p_x x(u) - p_z z(u) - p(u)h(u) = 0,$$
$$T - e(u) - tu = 0.$$

The first-order conditions are $aV/x(u) - \lambda p_x = 0$, $bV/z(u) - \lambda p_z = 0$, $cV/h(u) - \lambda p(u) = 0$, $dV/e - \gamma = 0$, and $-\lambda h (\partial p(u)/\partial u) - \gamma t = 0$ where λ is the marginal utility of income and γ is the marginal utility of leisure time. Substituting the first-order conditions with respect to the consumption of market goods into the budget constraint, we can get demand equations. For example, from the first-order conditions we know that $p_x x(u) = (a/c)p(u)h(u)$ and $p_z z(u) = (b/c)p(u)h(u)$. Substituting these in the budget constraint and solving, we find

$$h(u) = (c/f)yp(u)^{-1}. \qquad (1.2a)$$

The other demand equations are $x(u) = (a/f)yp_x^{-1}$ and $z(u) = (b/f)yp_z^{-1}$.

By combining and arranging the first-order conditions for e and u we find

$$h(u)\frac{\partial p(u)}{\partial u} = -t\frac{Vd/e(u)}{\lambda} = -tp_e(u). \qquad (1.3a)$$

As a consumer moves farther away from the city center, the value of lost leisure is compensated by reduced housing costs. By substituting $e(u) = T - tu$ and $\lambda = cV/(p(u)h(u))$ from the first-order conditions into equation (1.3a) we can rewrite this equation to get the slope of bid rent curves and rent gradients.

$$\partial p(u)/\partial u = -(td/c)p(u)(T - tu)^{-1}. \tag{1.6a}$$

The alternative way to derive equation (1.6a) is to use the indirect utility function. To derive the indirect utility function we substitute the consumer demand equations and $e = T - tu$ into the direct utility function to get

$$V = Ay^f p_x{}^{-a} p_z{}^{-b} p(u)^{-c}(T - tu)^d \tag{1.4a}$$

where $A = A'(a/f)^a(b/f)^b(c/f)^c$. Maximizing V in (1.5a) with respect to u yields equation (1.6a).

In this illustrative example, the slope of the bid rent curve and rent gradient in equation (1.6a) is independent of income and hence holds for all income levels. Therefore, equation (1.6a) also describes the slope of the rent gradient in a city where people have either equal incomes or differing incomes. To find the height of the rent gradient we write equation (1.6a) in logarithmic form, integrate, and then take antilogarithms to get

$$p(u) = C_0(T - tu)^{d/c}$$

where C_0 is the constant of integration.

The most general way to evaluate C_0 for a particular city is the following. We know the opportunity cost of land in agriculture (which can be zero) that the city must pay to get land at the border of the city. Therefore, we can determine urban housing prices at the city edge (see Section 1.2), or $p(u_1)$ in Figure 1.1b. Evaluating at the city edge, we have $p(u_1) = C_0(T - tu_1)^{d/c}$. Solving for C_0 and substituting into the rent gradient expression, we get

$$p(u) = p(u_1)(T - tu_1)^{-d/c}(T - tu)^{d/c}. \tag{1.10}$$

This is the residential rent gradient for a city of either identical or multi-income people. The height of this gradient at any location is determined by the housing rent at the city edge, the endogenous spatial size of the city as measured by u_1 (which is solved for later in the chapter), and the parameters of the model. A rent gradient is illustrated in Figure 1.1b or 1.2b by P_1.

Another common way to evaluate C_0 is to assume that

(1) all people have identical tastes and income and hence in equilibrium have identical utility levels, and

(2) the utility level in the city is fixed at a level $\overset{*}{V}$, which is given by an infinitely elastic supply curve of labor to the city at utility level $\overset{*}{V}$ (see Chapter 2).

If we know $\overset{*}{V}$, then by rearranging equation (1.4a) we know

$$p(u) = (\overset{*}{V})^{-1/c} A^{1/c} y^{f/c} p_x^{-a/c} p_z^{-b/c} (T - tu)^{d/c}$$

or

$$C_0 = (\overset{*}{V})^{-1/c} A^{1/c} y^{f/c} p_x^{-a/c} p_z^{-b/c}.$$

1.2   Production of Housing

So far, we have investigated and illustrated consumer spatial equilibrium, housing rent gradients, and equilibrium in the housing market. We still have to investigate fully the supply side of housing, land rent gradients, and equilibrium in the land and capital markets.

Housing is produced under constant returns to scale with land l and capital k where

$$h(u) = h(k(u), l(u)). \tag{1.11}$$

Producers seek to maximize profits $\pi(u) = p(u)h(u) - p_k k(u) - p_l(u)l(u)$ where p_k is the spatially invariant price of capital and $p_l(u)$ is the price of land at location u. At a given location, inputs are employed according to the usual first-order conditions describing marginal productivity conditions, or $p_l = p(u)(\partial h/\partial l)$ and $p_k = p(u)(\partial h/\partial k)$. It often is convenient to alternatively describe production technology by the unit cost function where the unit cost of production $c = p(p_k, p_l)$. p is linear homogeneous, increasing in input prices, and subsumes efficient factor usage by the firm.[12] If there is perfect competition, so that retail price equals unit production costs, the unit cost relationship can be expressed as

$$p(u) = p(p_k, p_l). \tag{1.12}$$

In the previous section we saw that housing prices must vary spatially to maintain consumer equilibrium. This means the gross revenue from producing a unit of housing will vary spatially. Hence, in addition to choosing optimal input combinations at any location, producers are concerned with choosing a profit-maximizing location. A producer's profit-maximizing location is one where $\partial \pi / \partial u = 0$ or

$$h(u)(\partial p(u)/\partial u) = l(u)(\partial p_l(u)/\partial u). \tag{1.13}$$

Equation (1.13) states that when a producer moves an infinitesimal distance from his optimal location, his change in land costs exactly equals his change

---

[12] In general, for the existence of unit cost functions with or without scale as an argument, h should be nondecreasing in its arguments, a right-continuous function, and quasi-concave.

in housing revenue. That is, given that his original location is optimal, he cannot be made better off by moving.

The next step in the analysis is to derive the characteristics of the set of equilibrium land prices, which is the land rent gradient. First we note that if producers are identical in terms of their technology and entrepreneurial ability, profits from building housing must be everywhere equal. If housing is a competitive industry, profits are zero. Zero profits are realized by housing producers bidding up [down] the rent paid on land in locations where nonequilibrium profits are positive [negative], until profits are zero. Zero profits also imply that unit costs in equation (1.12) must always vary through land costs to equal output prices. Given these assumptions, the slope of the land rent gradient may be found in several ways. We can differentiate the profit function and rearrange terms, given $d\pi/du = 0$; or we can differentiate the unit cost function and, after appropriate substitutions, rearrange terms to get the slope.[13] Alternatively, since equation (1.13) specifies a land rent–distance relationship that must hold for individual producers to be in equilibrium, it must also indicate the slope of the land rent gradient that must hold in a stable-market equilibrium. Rearranging equation (1.13) yields the slope

$$\partial p_l(u)/\partial u = h(u)l(u)^{-1}(\partial p(u)/\partial u). \qquad (1.14)$$

The unit cost function can be used to solve for the height of the rent gradient at each point, because given $p(u_i)$ and p_k, equation (1.12) can be solved for $p_l(u_i)$.

A land rent gradient is pictured in Figure 1.3 and is consistent with equilibrium in land markets. Equilibrium in land markets satisfies the four types of conditions listed for housing. All land supplied will be rented at a nonnegative price, or there are no holes or vacant areas in the city; and all housing producers will rent their desired quantity of land given prices (condition 4). Land rents at the borders of competing uses, such as agricultural or commercial uses, will be equalized (condition 3). Landowners in equilibrium receive the maximum rent anyone is willing to pay for their land (condition 1). Demanders of land, such as housing producers, receive their maximum possible profits (zero) at their equilibrium land site, relative to other sites that they could rent and build housing on (condition 2).

[13] Differentiating the unit cost function yields $\partial p(u)/\partial u = \partial p/\partial p_l(u)\, \partial p_l(u)/\partial u$. To interpret this condition we note a useful property of unit cost functions. From Shephard's lemma (Diewert, 1974) $k(u)/h(u) = \partial p/\partial p_k$ and $l(u)/h(u) = \partial p/\partial p_l(u)$; or the derivative of the unit cost function equals the per unit demand for the respective factor. This may be explained intuitively as follows. $\partial p/\partial p_k$ is the increase in unit costs if the price of capital rises by \$1. This increase in unit costs equals the number of units of capital employed multiplied by \$1 divided by the number of housing units, or it equals $k(u)/h(u)$. Substituting the equation for $\partial p/\partial p_l(u)$ into the spatial equilibrium condition on unit costs yields equation (1.14).

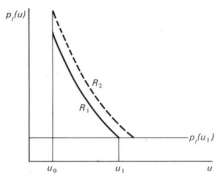

FIGURE 1.3   Land rent gradients.

Spatial Characteristics Implied by the Equilibrium Rent Gradient

Several important results follow directly from equation (1.14). In equation (1.3) we showed that changes in housing costs, $(\partial p(u)/\partial u)h(u)$, due to infinitesimal spatial moves exactly equal the change in leisure multiplied by the marginal evaluation of leisure, $-tp_e(u)$. From equation (1.14) we can see that changes in land rents paid by housing producers exactly equal changes in housing costs and hence they also equal the value of marginal leisure losses. That is,[14]

$$l(u)\frac{\partial p_l(u)}{\partial u} = h(u)\frac{\partial p(u)}{\partial u} = -p_e(u)t.$$

Second, equation (1.14) may be written as

$$\frac{\partial p_l(u)/\partial u}{p_l(u)} = \rho_l^{-1}\frac{\partial p(u)/\partial u}{p(u)} \tag{1.15}$$

where ρ_l is land's factor share in output revenue, or $\rho_l = p_l l/(ph)$. Equation (1.15) states that the percentage change in unit rents equals the percentage change in housing prices *magnified* by the inverse of land's factor share. Since land prices alone (i.e., not capital rentals) reflect housing price changes, their percentage change will always magnify those of housing prices. Thus as we approach the city center, land rents should rise much more quickly

[14] Note that this statement is only true for infinitesimal spatial moves. For discrete spatial moves, as the price of housing changes, housing and land consumption also change. In that case, changes in housing costs holding utility constant reflect not just amenity differences but also housing consumption differences. This suggests that changes in land or housing rents can only be used to directly value amenity differences, such as the value of differential access, for infinitesimal changes in these amenities. For discrete changes one can use differences in rent expenditures to measure the value of amentity differences only if lot size is fixed.

than housing rents. ρ_l is usually estimated to be around 0.1 (Muth, 1969) and therefore a 1% rise in housing rents should induce about a 10% rise in residential land rents.

From the information on price changes in equation (1.14) we can demonstrate how the intensity of land use varies in a city and how population density varies. There are two measures of the intensity of land use in a city. The first is the ratio of capital to land in producing a unit of housing. We define the direct elasticity of substitution as $\sigma = d \log(k/l)/d \log(p_l/p_k)$. In the city only p_l varies with distance, so we may state, using the definition of σ and equation (1.15),

$$\frac{\partial \log(k(u)/l(u))}{\partial u} = \sigma \, \partial \log p_l(u)/\partial u = \frac{\sigma}{\rho_l} \, \partial \log p(u)/\partial u. \qquad (1.16)$$

Equation (1.16) indicates that a 1% increase in housing prices as we approach the city center leads to a σ/ρ_l percent increase in the use of capital relative to land per unit of housing. σ is estimated to be about 0.7 (Muth, 1971) and, from above, $\rho_l = 0.1$. Therefore, a 1% change in $p(u)$ will lead to about a 7% increase in the capital-to-land ratio. This strong increase in the capital/land ratio as we approach the city center will be reflected in higher buildings. This change in the k/l ratio is illustrated in Figure 1.4a. If the rent gradient shifts up because, say, population increases, for the same rent on capital the k/l ratio will shift up, as illustrated in Figure 1.4a. Buildings at the same location will be higher in larger cities. The increase in the k/l ratio also implies that the physical marginal product of capital is declining as we approach the CBD. Given that housing producers everywhere use capital according to the marginal productivity condition $p_k = p(u)MP_k$, this decline in MP_k matches the rise in $p(u)$, so in net the *value* of the marginal product of capital is unchanged.

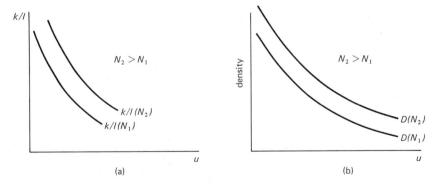

FIGURE 1.4   Capital-to-land ratios and population density.

The second measure of how land use intensity changes is the value of housing per unit of land. If housing production is competitive, $p(u)h(u) = p_l(u)l(u) + p_k k(u)$ or $p(u)h(u)/l(u) = p_l(u) + p_k k(u)/l(u)$. Differentiating, we get

$$\partial(p(u)h(u)/l(u))/\partial u = \partial p_l(u)/\partial u + p_k \partial(k(u)/l(u))/\partial u.$$

Substituting in from equations (1.14) and (1.16) we obtain

$$\frac{\partial \log(p(u)h(u)/l(u))}{\partial u} = \left(1 + \frac{\rho_k}{\rho_l} \sigma\right) \partial \log p(u)/\partial u \qquad (1.17)$$

where $\rho_k = p_k k(u)/(p(u)h(u))$ is capital's factor share in production revenue. Equation (1.17) states that a 1% rise in housing prices as we approach the city center will lead to a $(1 + (\rho_k/\rho_l)\sigma)$ percent rise in the value of housing per unit of land. For $\rho_k = 0.9$, $\rho_l = 0.1$, and $\sigma = 0.7$, a 1% rise in housing prices would lead to a 7.3% rise in the value of housing per unit of land. This is clearly a significant rise in the intensity of land use.

In terms of population density, there are two reasons why the number of people per square unit, or population density, rises as we approach the city center. First, housing consumption for equal-income people declines with higher housing prices as we approach the city center. Second, corresponding to the increasing housing prices are increasing land rents, which means, as seen in Figure 1.4a, that less land relative to capital will be used in housing production. Both these facts indicate that per person use of land will decline as we approach the city center. Hence, population density will increase as we approach the city center. This is pictured in Figure 1.4b. Note that the density gradient will shift up if the rent gradient shifts up.

An Illustration of Land Rent Gradients

By specifying a particular production function for housing and using the results on consumption relationships from the specific utility function used in the previous section, we can illustrate a land rent gradient as well as spatial variations in density and the per person use of land. We use the production function

$$h(u) = B'l(u)^\alpha k(u)^{1-\alpha}. \qquad (1.11a)$$

The first-order conditions for profit maximization are

$$p_l(u) = p(u)\alpha h(u)/l(u) \qquad \text{and} \qquad p_k = p(u)(1 - \alpha)h(u)/k(u).$$

Rearranging the first condition, we get the demand for land and capital functions, or

$$l(u) = \alpha h(u)p(u)p_l(u)^{-1} \qquad \text{and} \qquad k(u) = (1 - \alpha)h(u)p(u)p_k^{-1}.$$

Substituting in the demand equation for housing from equation (1.2a), where $h(u) = (c/f)yp(u)^{-1}$, we can write the demand for land and capital as

$$l(u) = (\alpha c/f)yp_l(u)^{-1} \quad \text{and} \quad k(u) = (1 - \alpha)(c/f)yp_k^{-1} \quad (1.18)$$

Thus the derived demand for factors is a function of income and own prices. In equation (1.18), as we approach the CBD and land rents rise, the use of land declines and density rises. Substituting into the production function for $l(u)$ and $k(u)$ from the first-order conditions, we obtain the unit cost function

$$p(u) = Bp_l(u)^{\alpha}p_k^{(1-\alpha)} \quad (1.12a)$$

where $B = B'\alpha^{-\alpha}(1 - \alpha)^{\alpha-1}$.

The land rent gradient may be found by differentiating profits with respect to u, setting $d\pi = 0$, substituting in demand equations for $l(u)$ and $k(u)$, integrating, and then substituting in equation (1.10) for $p(u)$. Alternatively, the housing rent gradient may be found by substituting the cost function (1.12a) into the housing rent gradient (1.10) to obtain

$$p_l(u) = p_l(u_1)(T - tu_1)^{-d/c\alpha}(T - tu)^{d/c\alpha} \quad (1.19)$$

where $p_l(u_1)$ is the land rent at the city edge in agriculture. The slope of the land rent gradient is $-td/c\alpha$ and is steeper than the housing rent gradient of slope $-td/c$, as was indicated would be the case in equation (1.15). The height of this gradient is a function of city spatial size and $p_l(u_1)$.

1.3 Aggregate Relationships in the Residential Sector

In the previous two sections, using basic consumer utility and producer profit maximization models, we examined the spatial variation in housing and land prices, housing consumption, the capital/land ratio, and density. With this information we can derive aggregate market relationships for the residential sector. These relationships are the usual ones describing aggregate demand for land and capital in the residential sector as a function of prices, income, and other variables. It is assumed that housing is a normal good with a positive income effect and a negative own-price effect; that capital and land are normal inputs with positive output effects and negative own-price effects; and that equilibrium rent gradients satisfy the four properties of market equilibrium discussed earlier. After examining general aggregate demand relationships, we illustrate these demand functions and market equilibrium using the specific functional forms for utility and production functions from Sections 1.1 and 1.2. We also use these functional forms to illustrate calculations of residential population, rents, and use of factor inputs.

The aggregate demand for residential land given the area of the CBD is measured by the radius of the city u_1. This measures the urban demand for agricultural land. We hypothesize the following demand function.

$$u_1 = u(p_l(u_1), N_1, N_2, N_3, \ldots, y_1, y_2, y_3, \ldots, t, u_0, p_k) \qquad (1.20)$$

where $p_l(u_1)$ is the price of agricultural land, N_i the number of people earning income y_i, t the unit time cost of travel, u_0 the radius of the CBD, and p_k the price of capital. If the supply of agricultural land to the city is infinitely elastic at a given $p_l(u_1)$, then, given that $p_l(u_1)$, the demand equation (1.20) specifies the radius of the city.

The demand function has these properties:

(1) $\partial u_1/\partial N_i > 0$. If population rises, more agricultural land is demanded at the same price. This will occur if the urban land rent gradient shifts up at the initial edge of the city and the city expands farther into agriculture to take advantage of the relatively lower rents. At the new expanded city edge, land rents will again be equalized. Such a shift is depicted by the shift from R_1 to R_2 in Figure 1.3. If the rent gradient shifts up at the initial u_1 (or at any point), it is fairly easy to demonstrate that it must shift up at all points interior to that u_1.[15]

Then to show that, as population rises, more agricultural land is demanded, it is sufficient to show that the land rent gradient must shift up as population increases. That the rent gradient shifts up can be demonstrated by showing that the contrary cannot be true. Suppose population rises and the rent gradient and spatial area of the city remain unchanged. This implies either that new people consume no land and demand no housing, or that initial residents were not maximizing utility before and are now satisfied with less land (so that new people are able to get some) at the same price. This contradicts either or both the assumptions that utility and profits are always maximized in equilibrium and that land and housing are normal economic goods. If we suppose that the rent gradient falls, the foregoing inconsistencies are even more pronounced. Therefore, the rent gradient must shift up with population and hence the city area will expand.

---

[15] The general proposition is that if the rent gradient shifts up at one point, it must shift up at all points. At the point where the rent gradient shifts up, we examine the neighborhood around that point where in that segment of the rent gradient people have identical tastes and income. Given that rents have risen at one point, they must rise at all points on the segment to maintain stable equilibrium and equal utility for identical people. If land rents rise in one segment, either they rise in other segments to equalize land rents at the border of competing uses or the area of this segment will expand into other segments, reducing their size. This reduction in size in itself will drive up prices in these other segments to equate demand with the reduced supply.

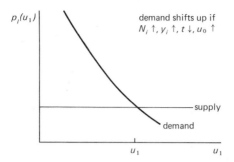

FIGURE 1.5   Urban demand for agricultural land. Demand shifts up if N_i and y_i shift up and t and u_0 shift down.

(2)   Using the same type of argument, it is possible to show the following: $\partial u_1/\partial p_l(u_1) < 0$, the normal own-price effect on factor demand; $\partial u_1/\partial y > 0$, the normal income effect on derived demand for a factor; $\partial u_1/\partial u_0 > 0$, or, *ceteris paribus*, the whole urban area expands if the CBD expands.

(3) $\partial u_1/\partial p_k \gtrless 0$.   If the price of capital rises, it is unclear what happens to the demand for land. While the demand for land relative to capital rises, the relative consumer demand for housing and both factors falls, since housing is now more costly to produce and purchase.

(4) $\partial u_1/\partial t < 0$.   This indicates that increased cost of access to the CBD causes people to crowd closer to the CBD. If t rises, people farthest from the CBD, say at u_1, have a greater absolute increase in commuting time than people nearer the CBD because they travel greater distances. Therefore people nearer the CBD relative to those farther away must experience an increase in land rents to offset their increased relative access advantage. This maintains a stable spatial equilibrium between those near the CBD and those farther away. This upward rotation in the rent gradient will reduce demand for land everywhere. Hence, u_1 will decline.

The urban demand curve for agricultural land is illustrated in Figure 1.5. The supply curve of agricultural land is also pictured and an equilibrium illustrated. Although the supply of land is drawn as infinitely elastic at $p_l(u_1)$, it could be upward sloping. For example, if the city buys agricultural produce from its hinterland and there are costs to the farmers of shipping to the city market, then agricultural land rents will vary with relative market access or distance to the city center. In certain circumstances, if the radius of agricultural production rises with city size, so will the level of agricultural land rents.[16] Then the opportunity cost of land to the city will rise.

---

[16] As the city expands, if in the agricultural area the *difference* in access between the farmers closest and those farthest from the CBD increases, then agricultural rents should increase.

The aggregate demand for residential capital has the normal properties of aggregate demand functions.

$$K_{\text{res}} = K(p_k, N_1, N_2, \ldots, N_3, y_1, y_2, y_3, \ldots, p_l(u_1)). \qquad (1.21)$$

By the usual arguments, $\partial K/\partial p_k < 0$, $\partial K/\partial N_i > 0$, $\partial K/\partial y_i > 0$, and $\partial K/\partial p_l(u_1) \gtreqless 0$. Given that p_k is fixed to the residential sector, these demand function properties also describe properties of equilibrium levels of K.

Specific Functional Forms

These aggregative relationships are illustrated using the logarithmic linear production and utility functions specified earlier. These illustrations will be used later in presenting an aggregative model of a city. For the illustration it is assumed that *all* consumers have *identical tastes and incomes*. To illustrate aggregate relationships is very complicated when incomes and/or tastes vary (see Montesano, 1972). The basic problem is in integrating over space when there are different types of consumers whose location is endogenous. Since the objective here is to illustrate an aggregative model, we choose to simplify and assume that consumers are identical.

We start by calculating the residential population of a city. At each distance from the city center the population $N(u)$ equals the total amount of land at that location, $2\pi u$, divided by per person consumption of land. Total population N is the sum of populations at all locations or

$$N = \int_{u_0}^{u_1} N(u) \, du = \int_{u_0}^{u_1} 2\pi u l(u)^{-1} \, du.$$

Using our logarithmic linear utility and production functions, we substitute into this equation for $l(u)$ from the demand for land equation (1.20) where $l(u) = (\alpha c/f) y p_l(u)^{-1}$, and then we substitute for $p_l(u)$ from the rent gradient equation (1.19) where $p_l(u) = p_l(u_1)(T - tu_1)^{-d/c\alpha}(T - tu)^{d/c\alpha}$. This yields

$$N = \int_{u_0}^{u_1} 2\pi u (\alpha c/f y)^{-1} p_l(u_1)(T - tu_1)^{-d/c\alpha}(T - tu)^{d/c\alpha} \, du.$$

Integrating, we get

$$N = C_1 p_l(u_1) y^{-1} t^{-2} s(t, u_0, u_1) \qquad (1.22)$$

where

$$C_1 = 2\pi \left(\frac{f}{c\alpha}\right)\left(\frac{d}{c\alpha} + 2\right)^{-1}\left(\frac{d}{c\alpha} + 1\right)^{-1}$$

and

$$s(t, u_0, u_1) = (T - tu_1)^{-d/c\alpha}(T - tu_0)^{1 + d/c\alpha}\left[T + tu_0\left(\frac{d}{c\alpha} + 1\right)\right]$$
$$- (T - tu_1)\left[T + tu_1\left(\frac{d}{c\alpha} + 1\right)\right] > 0.^{17}$$

An inverse of equation (1.22) is an equation for u_1, the urban demand for agricultural land, where $u_1 = u(p_l(u_1), N_i, y_i, t, u_0, p_k)$. The properties of this function may be illustrated by differentiating (1.22) and rearranging terms to get

$$e_1 \, du_1 = (dN/N) + (dy/y) - (dp_l(u_1)/p_l(u_1)) - e_2 \, dt + e_3 \, du_0 \quad (1.23)$$

where $e_1, e_2, e_3 > 0.^{18}$ Equation (1.23) illustrates the properties of the urban demand function for agricultural land that were discussed earlier. $\partial u_1/\partial p_l(u_1) < 0$, the own-price relationship. $\partial u_1/\partial N, \partial u_1/\partial y > 0$, the aggregate demand relationships for population and income. $\partial u_1/\partial t < 0$ and $\partial u_1/\partial u_0 > 0$.

The aggregate demand for capital is the demand for capital per house summed over all households. The amount of capital per house is $k(u)$ and the population at each distance from the CBD is $2\pi u l(u)^{-1}$. Therefore at

---

[17] Clearly, for $N > 0$, $s > 0$. If $u_0 = u_1$, $s = N = 0$, since there is no residential area. For $u_1 > u_0$ we assume that parametric values are such that $s > 0$. For any reasonable parametric values, $s > 0$.

[18] $e_1 = \dfrac{td}{c\alpha} s(t, u_0, u_1)^{-1}\left\{(T - tu_1)^{-(d/c\alpha) - 1}(T - tu_0)^{(d/c\alpha) + 1}\left[T + tu_0\left(\dfrac{d}{c\alpha} + 1\right) - T\right]\right.$
$$\left. + 2tu_1\left(1 + \frac{c\alpha}{d}\right)\right]\right\} > 0,$$

$e_2 = e_1 t^{-1} u_1 - 2t^{-1} - t^{-1} u_0 e_3 > 0$,

$e_3 = u_0 t^2 s(t, u_0, u_1)^{-1}(T - tu_1)^{-(d/c\alpha)}(T - tu_0)^{(d/c\alpha)}\left(\dfrac{d}{c\alpha} + 1\right)\left(\dfrac{d}{c\alpha} + 2\right) > 0.$

These variables are unambiguously positive, except for e_2, providing $s > 0$. As for s, $e_2 > 0$ for reasonable parametric values. For future reference, note that it is possible to show that $(T - tu_1)e_1 c\alpha/(td) > 1$ or that $(T - tu_1)$ multiplied by the bracketed part of e_1 and $s(t, u_0, u_1)^{-1}$ is greater than one. This latter expression reduces to

$$\frac{g(u_1) + (T - tu_1)2tu_1(1 + c\alpha/d)}{g(u_1) - (T - tu_1)tu_1(d/c\alpha + 1)}$$

where $g(u_1)$ is some positive expression and both numerator and denominator are positive. As long as $T > tu_1$ or leisure is positive, this expression is greater than one.

each radius the demand for capital is $k(u)2\pi u l(u)^{-1}$. From equation (1.18) we can substitute into this relationship $k(u) = (1 - \alpha)c/fyp_k^{-1}$ and $l(u) = \alpha c/fyp_l(u)^{-1}$. Therefore the aggregate demand for capital is[19]

$$K = \int_{u_1}^{u_0} 2\pi u k(u)/l(u) \, du = \int_{u_1}^{u_0} 2\pi u \alpha/(1 - \alpha)p_k^{-1} p_l(u) \, du.$$

To evaluate this, we can substitute in equation (1.19) for $p_l(u)$ and integrate. Alternatively, we can employ other information to solve for K. Given logarithmic linear utility functions, each consumer spends a fixed fraction of his income on housing, or from (1.2a), $p(u)h(u) = (c/f)y$. From equation (1.18) we also know that the share of any factor is a fixed proportion of housing costs. Specifically, $p_k k(u) = (1 - \alpha)p(u)h(u)$. Combining these relationships, we see that each consumer buys $k(u) = (1 - \alpha)(c/f)yp_k^{-1}$. This expression contains no spatial variables and, therefore, aggregate demand is simply

$$K = (1 - \alpha)(c/f)yp_k^{-1}N. \tag{1.24}$$

As before, this aggregate demand function has the normal properties that $\partial K/\partial p_k < 0$ for the own-price effect and $\partial K/\partial y$, $\partial K/\partial N > 0$ for the income and population effects.

Finally, we note that total rents at each location are the unit rent $p_l(u)$ multiplied by the amount of land at each location $2\pi u$. Therefore, total residential rents are

$$\text{Rents}_{\text{res}} = \int_{u_0}^{u_1} 2\pi u p_l(u) \, du.$$

We can substitute in equation (1.19) for $p_l(u)$ and integrate. Alternatively we note that per person land rents are a fixed proportion α of housing costs, which in turn are a fixed proportion of income c/f. Therefore, per person rents are $(\alpha c/f)y$ and total residential rents are

$$\text{Rents}_{\text{res}} = (\alpha c/f)yN. \tag{1.25}$$

2.   THE BUSINESS SECTOR

2.1   Firms and Spatial Equilibrium in the CBD

Firms in the CBD produce the city's traded or export good. Each firm ships its output to the transport–retailing node at the city center where the good is either exported or sold to city residents. In return for its exports the city imports z from other cities or countries.

---

[19] Alternatively, the aggregate demand for capital equals the demand for capital per unit of land summed over all units of land. From footnote 14, the amount of capital and land per unit of housing are, respectively, $\partial p/\partial p_k$ and $\partial p/\partial p_l$. Therefore $K = \int_{u_0}^{u_1} 2\pi u(\partial p/\partial p_k)/(\partial p/\partial p_l(u)) \, du$. To solve this we substitute in from equation (1.12a), which then gives us the equation in the text.

The firm production function is

$$x(u) = G(N)x(k(u), n(u), l(u)). \tag{1.26}$$

$G(N)$ is a Hicks neutral shift factor indicating economies of scale that are dependent on city employment in x activity (the only employment source in the city). $\partial G/\partial N \geq 0$. These scale economies are the basis for agglomeration of population in the city. They are at the industry level and may be experienced by any entering firm. Each firm behaves as though $G(N)$ were exogenous. The x function denotes the firm's own technology, where output, given $G(N)$, is a function of capital $k(u)$, labor $n(u)$, and land $l(u)$. The x function is linear homogeneous and hence $G(N)x$ is homothetic.

In the shipping of products to the marketing–transport node at the city center, transport services are produced with units of x, which corresponds to the evaporation formulation of transport costs in international trade. It costs firms t_x of a unit of x to ship one unit of x one unit distance. The quantity of x actually sold in the city center is $x(u)(1 - t_x u)$ or the revenue received for each unit of x produced is $p_x(1 - t_x u)$.

These assumptions about production have a number of implications. First, in maximizing profits, the firm pays factors the value of their perceived marginal product or, for wages, $p_n = p_x(1 - t_x u)G(N)\, \partial x/\partial n$. Total factor payments then are $p_x(1 - t_x u)G(N)((\partial x/\partial n)n + (\partial x/\partial k)k + (\partial x/\partial l)l)$, which, from Euler's theorem, equals $p_x(1 - t_x u)G(N)x$ if the x function is linear homogeneous. Therefore, firm factor payments exhaust firm revenue. This fact plus the fact that $G(N)$ is an external scale effect that affects all firms equally ensures that perfect competition is stable and feasible.

Second, production technology may be alternatively described by the unit cost function $p(N, p_n, p_k, p_l(u))$. This function is nonincreasing in N, increasing and linear homogeneous in prices, and subsumes efficient usage of factor inputs. With perfect competition, the firm's net price should equal unit costs or[20]

$$p_x(1 - t_x u) = p(N, p_n, p_k, p_l(u)). \tag{1.27}$$

Finally, as long as $G(N)$ increases with N, for the same factor ratios the marginal products of factors increase continuously. Moreover, because $G(N)$ is a Hicks neutral shifter, the marginal products of factors increase by the same proportion for the same factor ratios. If, on the other hand, the scale effect were relatively labor saving compared to capital, this would imply that the marginal product of capital would be more beneficially affected than the marginal product of labor as a city grows. Then, for example, either capital rentals would rise relative to wages if city factor supplies are fixed (and factor prices variable) or the city's relative demand for labor would fall

---

[20] See footnote 12 on the existence of unit cost functions.

if factor prices are fixed (and factor supplies are variable). Clearly, assuming $G(N)$ is Hicks neutral or nonneutral has important implications for the relative use of capital and labor in various size cities. Normally, scale efficiencies are assumed to be neutral in aggregate.

A firm's spatial equilibrium is described as follows. Firm profits are $\pi = p_x(1 - t_x u)x(u) - p_l(u)l(u) - p_k k(u) - p_n n(u)$. At the firm's profit-maximizing location, $\partial \pi / \partial u = 0$ or

$$l(u)\, \partial p_l(u)/\partial u = -x(u)p_x t_x < 0. \tag{1.28}$$

Unit land rents decline with distance from the city center, as transport costs increase. The change in total rents exactly equals the increase in transport costs $(x(u)p_x t_x)$ of moving a unit distance. Therefore, firm profits are unchanged and the firm does not benefit by moving.

To find the slope and height of the commercial land rent gradient, we first note that if all producers are identical in technology and ability, profits from producing x must be everywhere equal. If the x industry is competitive, profits will be everywhere zero and net price will always equal unit production costs. Therefore, to find the slope of the rent gradient, we can differentiate the unit cost function and do appropriate substitutions, or we can differentiate the profit function and set $d\pi = 0$.[21] Alternatively we observe that since equation (1.28) specifies a relationship that must hold for individual producers to be in equilibrium, it also gives the slope of the equilibrium rent gradient. The height of the rent gradient at any u can be solved directly from equation (1.27) given p_x, t_x, and other variables.

In long-run equilibrium in the urban land market, land rents in the residential sector at u_0, the boundary of the CBD, equal land rents at u_0 in the business sector, or

$$p_l(u_0)_{\text{res}} = p_l(u_0)_{\text{bus}}. \tag{1.29}$$

For this equilibrium to be stable, as indicated in the discussion of residential equilibrium with different types of consumers (p. 18), businesses must be able to outbid residences for land interior to u_0. (This is the stability condition implicit in the rent gradients in Figure 1.2.) Therefore, the slope of the bid rent curve for businesses must exceed that for residences at u_0, or

$$\left| \partial p_l(u_0)_{\text{res}}/\partial u \right| \le \left| \partial p_l(u_0)_{\text{bus}}/\partial u \right|,$$

or, using (1.14) and (1.28), with one firm at u_0

$$N(u_0)tp_e(u) \le x(u_0)p_x t_x \tag{1.30}$$

---

[21] Differentiating the unit cost function gives us $-p_x t_x\, du = \partial p/\partial p_l(u)\, \partial p_l(u)/\partial u\, du$. From Shephard's lemma (footnote 13) $l(u)/x(u) = \partial p/\partial p_l(u)$. Substituting this in yields equation (1.28)

Specific Functional Forms

The foregoing points are illustrated with a logarithmic linear production function of the form

$$x(u) = G(N)C'l(u)^\gamma k(u)^\beta n(u)^\delta, \qquad \gamma + \beta + \delta = 1. \qquad (1.26a)$$

From the first-order conditions for profit maximization, we get the marginal productivity conditions, which may be rewritten as factor demand equations where, for $\tilde{p}_x = p_x(1 - t_x u)$,

$$l(u) = \gamma\tilde{p}_x x(u)/p_l(u), \quad n(u) = \delta\tilde{p}_x x(u)/p_n, \quad k(u) = \beta\tilde{p}_x x(u)/p_k. \quad (1.31)$$

The unit cost function corresponding to this production function is obtained by substituting into the production function for $l(u)$, $k(u)$, and $n(u)$ from equation (1.31) to get

$$p_x(1 - t_x u) = G(N)^{-1}Cp_n{}^\delta p_k{}^\beta p_l(u)^\gamma \qquad (1.27a)$$

where $C = (C')^{-1}\delta^{-\delta}\beta^{-\beta}\gamma^{-\gamma}$. Rearranging equation (1.27a) yields a rent gradient of

$$p_l(u) = p_x^{1/\gamma}(1 - t_x u)^{1/\gamma}C^{-1/\gamma}G(N)^{1/\gamma}p_n^{-\delta/\gamma}p_k^{-\beta/\gamma}. \qquad (1.32)$$

If we employ the condition that $p_l(u_0)_{res} = p_l(u_0)_{bus}$, we may write business rents as a function of $p_l(u_0)$ and distance from the city center. Substituting u_0 for u in (1.32), dividing the result by (1.32), and rearranging terms yields

$$p_l(u) = p_l(u_0)(1 - t_x u_0)^{-1/\gamma}(1 - t_x u)^{1/\gamma}. \qquad (1.33)$$

The height of the business rent gradient is determined by the rent at the edge of the residential sector $p_l(u_0)$, the size of the CBD u_0, and transport costs t_x.

2.2 Aggregate Relationships in the CBD

Having examined equilibrium conditions for the individual producer and in the general land market, we can now determine aggregate employment of capital and labor, total output, and income from the rent of land in the CBD. Because of scale economies, general aggregate relationships for factor inputs cannot be proved by contradiction proofs. Therefore, we proceed directly to illustrating the problem with a logarithmic linear production function.

At each location from the city center the aggregate employment of labor is the employment of labor per unit of land, $n(u)/l(u)$, summed over all units of land, $2\pi u$. From the factor demand equations (1.31), $n(u)/l(u) = \delta/\alpha p_l(u)/p_n$. Therefore total employment in the CBD is[22]

$$N = \int_0^{u_0} 2\pi u \left(\frac{\delta}{\gamma}\right)\left(\frac{p_l(u)}{p_n}\right) dN.$$

Substituting in (1.32) for $p_l(u)$ and integrating, we get

$$N = C_2 p_x^{1/\gamma} G(N)^{1/\gamma} p_n^{-1-\delta/\gamma} p_k^{-\beta/\gamma} t_x^{-2} f(t_x, u_0) \qquad (1.34)$$

where

$$C_2 = C^{1/\gamma} 2\pi \left(\frac{\delta}{\gamma}\right)\left(\frac{1}{\gamma} + 2\right)^{-1}\left(\frac{1}{\gamma} + 1\right)^{-1}$$

and

$$f(t_x, u_0) = \left\{1 - (1 - t_x u_0)^{1/\gamma + 1}\left[1 + t_x u_0\left(\frac{1}{\gamma} + 1\right)\right]\right\}.$$

Equation (1.34) describes total employment of labor in the x industry. It is sometimes interpreted as an aggregate demand function for labor in the x industry. Interpreting it as a demand function must be done with care since it characterizes neither the demand of individual producers nor the city's demand for labor (even though the x industry is the only employer in the city). As we will see in Chapter 2 to find the *city's* demand for labor, we have to incorporate information from the residential sector of the city to obtain a city demand function for population.

To examine the x industry's employment of labor, we differentiate (1.34) to obtain

$$\frac{dN}{N} = \frac{1}{\gamma - \varepsilon}\frac{dp_x}{p_x} - \frac{\gamma + \delta}{\gamma - \varepsilon}\frac{dp_n}{p_n} - \frac{\beta}{\gamma - \varepsilon}\frac{dp_k}{p_k} + \frac{e_4}{1 - \varepsilon/\gamma} du_0 - \frac{e_5}{1 - \varepsilon/\gamma} dt_x \quad (1.35)$$

where $\varepsilon = (dG(N)/dN)N/G(N)$ is the elasticity of the scale economy shift factor with respect to N and $e_4 > 0$, $e_5 \lessgtr 0$.[23] A term we will use frequently

---

[22] Note that from the formulation of the production function, firm size is indeterminate, so that production activity is summed over locations rather than firms. The aggregate demand for labor may also be derived as follows. From footnote 21 the demand for labor per unit of output is $\partial p/\partial p_n$ and the unit demand for land is $\partial p/\partial p_l(u)$. Hence total employment at location u is $2\pi u(\partial p/\partial p_n)/(\partial p/\partial p_l(u))$. Evaluating these derivatives using the unit cost function in equation (1.27a) yields the expression above for N.

[23] $e_4 = f(t_x, u_0)^{-1}(1 - t_x u_0)^{1/\gamma}\left(\frac{1}{\gamma} + 1\right)\left(\frac{1}{\gamma} + 2\right)t_x^2 u_0 > 0,$

$e_5 = 2t_x - t_x^{-1} u_0 e_4 > 0.$

in the next three chapters, ε indicates the extent of scale economies at the *margin* of additional employment. In general, we will assume that ε is declining with city size, or $\partial \varepsilon / \partial N < 0$, indicating that scale economies are larger at the margin when cities are small.

In examining equation (1.34), we see that if $\varepsilon < \gamma$ or ε is relatively small, this equation will possess normally expected properties. An increase in employment is associated with a rise in output price, a decline in own input price, an increase in CBD area, and in some cases a decline in transport costs.[24] A rise in p_k, for p_x fixed, is associated with a decline in both capital and labor employment, although labor employment can be shown to increase relative to capital employment (compare the dp_k / p_k coefficients in equations (1.35) and (1.37) for $\gamma > \varepsilon$).

If marginal scale effects are large, such that $\varepsilon > \gamma$, equation (1.35) has seemingly unusual properties. For example, a rise in wages is associated with an increase in labor employed. However, if one interprets equation (1.35) as stating that when scale effects are large, wages can rise as employment increases (for the same size CBD), then that makes sense.

At each location from the city center the aggregate employment of capital is $k(u)$ which can also be stated as the employment of capital per unit of land, $k(u)/l(u)$, summed over all units of land $2\pi u$. From the factor demand equations (1.31), $k(u)/l(u) = (\beta/\gamma)p_l(u)/p_k$. Therefore total employment in the CBD is

$$K = \int_0^{u_0} k(u)\, du = \int_0^{u_0} 2\pi u k(u)/l(u)\, du = \int_0^{u_0} 2\pi u (\beta/\gamma)p_l(u)/p_k\, du.$$

To evaluate this we can substitute in equation (1.32) for $p_l(u)$ and integrate. Alternatively, from equation (1.31) two first-order conditions are $p_n = \delta \tilde{p}_x x(u)/n(u)$ and $p_k = \beta \tilde{p}_x x(u)/k(u)$. Combining and solving out $p_x x$, we get $k(u) = (\beta/\delta)p_k^{-1}p_n n(u)$. Since $N = \int_0^{u_0} n(u)\, du$, we may then state

$$K_{\text{bus}} = \int_0^{u_0} k(u)\, du = (\beta/\delta)p_n p_k^{-1} N. \tag{1.36}$$

Differentiating (1.36) yields the properties of the employment function for capital.

$$\frac{dK}{K} = \frac{dp_n}{p_n} - \frac{dp_k}{p_k} + \frac{dN}{N}.$$

To make this comparable with the function for labor, we substitute in

---

[24] For the same u_0, if t_x increases, rents should rise nearer the city center relative to farther away due to increased premiums on access to the transport node. This increase in rents will lead to a greater use of N relative to land but a potentially offsetting reduction in demand for all factors.

equation (1.35) for dN/N to get

$$\frac{dK}{K} = \frac{1}{\gamma - \varepsilon}\frac{dp_x}{p_x} - \frac{\delta + \varepsilon}{\gamma - \varepsilon}\frac{dp_n}{p_n} - \frac{\beta + \gamma - \varepsilon}{\gamma - \varepsilon}\frac{dp_k}{p_k}$$

$$+ \frac{e_4}{1 - \varepsilon/\gamma}\,du_0 - \frac{e_5}{1 - \varepsilon/\gamma}\,dt_x. \tag{1.37}$$

When scale effects are small, the properties of this employment of capital equation will be similar to those of the properties of the labor equation. Increases in capital usage are associated with increases in output price and CBD area and declines in own price. An increase in the price of labor is associated with an absolute decline in capital usage, but a rise relative to labor usage (compare the coefficients of dp_n/p_n in (1.35) and (1.37) if $\gamma > \varepsilon$). As before, if scale effects are large, the properties of equation (1.37) may seem unusual, but are plausible.

For future reference we define expressions for total CBD rents and total output actually retailed at the transport–marketing node.

$$\text{Rents}_{\text{bus}} = \int_0^{u_0} 2\pi u p_l(u)\,du,$$

$$X = \int_0^{u_0} x(u)(1 - t_x u)\,du$$

To solve these equations we can do appropriate substitutions and integrate. Alternatively, we note from the labor marginal productivity condition that $x(u) = p_n n(u)\,\delta^{-1}\tilde{p}_x^{-1}$ and therefore using equation (1.34), where

$$N = \int_0^{u_0} n(u)\,du = \int_0^{u_0} 2\pi u\,\delta/\gamma p_l(u)/p_n\,du,$$

it is possible to evaluate both equations directly in terms of labor employment. Doing this, we find

$$\text{Rents}_{\text{bus}} = (\gamma/\delta)p_n N, \tag{1.38}$$

$$X = \delta^{-1}p_x^{-1}p_n N. \tag{1.39}$$

These expressions for CBD rents and output plus the expressions for CBD employment of capital and labor define the primary aggregate relationships in the CBD.

2

An Aggregative Model of a Simple City

In this chapter an aggregative model of a city is presented and analyzed. The purpose of developing an aggregative model is to solve for the city's total demand for population, factor incomes, and equilibrium city size, and to show how various economic characteristics of the city vary with city size. In addition to being used to solve for equilibrium city size, the model that is developed can be used to do comparative static analyses of the long-run effect on city size and other economic characteristics of changes in commuting costs, property taxes, and other variables.

In the previous chapter we developed a model of the residential and business sectors of a city and derived functions describing aggregate demands for labor, capital, and land in those sectors. The aggregative model combines these two sectors to find the city's total demand for factors, factor income, and city size given the supply functions of factors available to the city. The model is solved using the specific functional forms introduced in Chapter 1. In doing this it is assumed that city residents have identical incomes and tastes. In a sense a partial equilibrium framework is assumed, since the city is treated as a small entity relative to the rest of the economy and world. As such, the city borrows capital at a fixed rental rate in national or international markets; it buys and sells traded goods at fixed prices or at least faces a given demand function for its exports; and it has an exogenous supply function of labor.

Given that the basic objective is to solve for city size, the initial goal is to express variables such as rents, wages, and spatial area of the city in terms of city size. With this information, since the indirect utility function is a function of income, rents, and commuting distance, utility can then be solved for as a function of city size. Reflected in the indirect utility function are the facts that a city is both a place to work (earn wages) and live (pay rents and commuting costs). For example, we will show under certain conditions that as city size increases, initially utility rises as wages rise due to scale economies in production. Eventually, however, as city size continues to grow, increasing commuting costs and declining leisure offset the benefits of higher wages and people's welfare starts to decline with increasing city size. Given this analysis, we can determine what utility levels a city can offer and thus we will have a city demand function for population. Combining this demand function with a supply function, we will be able to solve for city size.

In solving for city size, it is essential to identify economic actors in the model and their sources of income. Laborers receive wages and incur urban costs of living by working in the city. City land rents are collected by the city government or by a city land bank company in which all city residents own equal shares. Collected land rents are then divided up equally among city residents and are a second source of income. This method avoids introducing a separate class of people, or rentiers. For capital, there is a separate group of people, or capital owners, who we assume in this chapter do not live in the city. The city borrows all of its capital in national or international markets.

In this chapter the final group of actors are city governments. Their activities are, first, to restrict city size through various zoning or land use regulations so as to maximize their particular objective functions, and second, to act as a collector and distributor of urban land rents. In the partial equilibrium model in this chapter the existence of city governments that are able to limit city sizes may produce conflicts between the city size that is best for initial residents, any excluded residents, and possibly the economy as a whole.

In Chapter 3, which examines a general equilibrium model of a system of cities, we consider alternative and sometimes more sophisticated specifications of the nature of our actors. In particular, we detail more precisely the nature of capital owners, land developers, and land bank companies.

1. THE AGGREGATIVE MODEL

In Chapter 1 we specified logarithmic linear utility and production functions of the form $V = A'x(u)^a z(u)^b h(u)^c e(u)^d$ and $x = G(N)B'l(u)^\gamma k(u)^\beta n(u)^\delta$ where $a + b + c = f$ and $\gamma + \beta + \delta = 1$. Residents consume $x(u)$, the city's produced good; $z(u)$, its import good; $h(u)$, housing; and $e(u)$, leisure. $l(u)$, $k(u)$, and $n(u)$ are firm employment of land, capital, and labor; and $G(N)$ is a Hicks neutral production function shifter where N is city population. Given these functional forms and the analysis of spatial equilibrium, we developed expressions describing city population, business employment of labor, and residential and business employment of capital and land. We use these aggregative relationships here to develop and solve a model of city size. The basic equations of the model describe full employment in the labor, capital, and land markets, demand and supply of the city's output, and income in the city.

Basic Aggregative Equations

From equation (1.34) there is the business employment of labor

$$N = t_x^{-2} C_2 P_x^{1/\gamma} G(N)^{1/\gamma} p_n^{-1-\delta/\gamma} p_k^{-\beta/\gamma} f(t_x, u_0) \tag{2.1}$$

where p_x, p_n, and p_k are the prices of x, n, and k; t_x is the cost of shipping x a unit distance; and u_0 is the radius of the CBD. Labor is fully employed, so business employment equals residential population, or from equation (1.22)

$$N = C_1 p_l(u_1) y^{-1} t^{-2} s(t, u_0, u_1) \tag{2.2}$$

where $p_l(u_1)$ is land rent at the edge, y is income, t is unit distance commuting costs, and u_1 is city radius.

The city's total usage of capital K equals the sum of its residential and business uses or, summing equations (1.24) and (1.36),

$$K = (1 - \alpha)(c/f) y p_k^{-1} N + (\beta/\delta) p_n p_k^{-1} N$$

or

$$K/N = p_k^{-1}[(1 - \alpha)(c/f)y + (\beta/\delta)p_n]. \tag{2.3}$$

A supply function of capital is not separately specified because the supply of capital to the city will be infinitely elastic at the current capital rental rate determined in national and international markets.

In terms of the urban land market, there are two aggregative relationships. When the market is in equilibrium, residential rents at the city edge will equal farm rents and residential rents at the edge of the CBD will equal business rents at that point. For the latter condition, from equations (1.19) and (1.32)

$$p_l(u_0) = p_l(u_1)(T - tu_1)^{-d/c\alpha}(T - tu_0)^{d/c\alpha}$$
$$= p_x^{1/\gamma} C^{-1/\gamma} G(N)^{1/\gamma} (1 - t_x u_0)^{1/\gamma} p_n^{-\delta/\gamma} p_k^{-\beta/\gamma}. \tag{2.4}$$

If p_x and p_z are assumed fixed or set in national markets, we do not need to separately specify demand functions for city output. However, if p_x is variable to the city and is determined by, say, the potential export market area of the city, then we could write p_x as

$$p_x = p(X). \tag{2.5}$$

Then it would be necessary to introduce the expression for total city output from equation (1.39) or

$$X = \delta^{-1} p_x^{-1} p_n N. \tag{2.6}$$

The final relationship needed to determine equilibrium in a city of a given size is the income equation for people living in the city. Laborers are the only city residents and, for now, we assume that they are paid their wage income plus their share of income from urban land use. Essentially each resident holds an equal share in a city land bank company. From equation (1.25) total residential rents are $(\alpha c/f)yN$ and from equation (1.38) total business rents are $(\gamma/\delta)p_n N$. However, the city pays out to the federal government (or farmers) the opportunity cost of the urban land, which is the rental value of land removed from agricultural production or the urban land area πu_1^2 multiplied by the opportunity cost of agricultural land $p_l(u_1)$. For algebraic simplicity we assume that these rental payments to the federal government are transferred back to the city, so the net loss of rental income is zero.[1] Therefore, per person labor income is

$$y = p_n + \left(\frac{\alpha c}{f}\right)y + \left(\frac{\gamma}{\delta}\right)p_n$$

or, rearranging terms,

$$y = \left(1 - \frac{\alpha c}{f}\right)^{-1}\left(1 + \frac{\gamma}{\delta}\right)p_n. \tag{2.7}$$

Equations (2.1)–(2.7) provide sufficient information to enable us to solve for wages, incomes, rents, capital employment, and spatial dimensions of the city as a function of city size or population. In terms of equation counting, holding t, t_x, $p_l(u_1)$, and p_k fixed, we have seven equations; seven unknowns, p_n, y, u_0, u_1, K, p_x, and X; and one variable, N. From the way in which the aggregative equations are derived, any solutions subsume perfect competi-

---

[1] This implies there is an inefficiency in the urban land market, since people at the city edge are still charged $p_l(u_1)$, even though the effective cost of agricultural land to the city is zero (see Chapter 4). We are faced with an algebraic dilemma. If we subtract average agricultural rents from equation (2.7), our model becomes an algebraic and expositional nightmare (although it can be solved). On the other hand, we cannot let $p_l(u_1) = 0$, given the form of our utility function and rent gradient. (If $p_l(u_1) = 0$, at the city edge the demand and use of land is infinite, or u_1 is indeterminate, and the rent gradient $p_l(u) = p_l(u_1)(T - tu_1)^{-d/c\alpha}(T - tu)^{d/c\alpha}$ has no useful interpretation in our model.)

tion, equalization of factor prices and private marginal products, equalization of price ratios and consumer marginal rates of substitution, and efficient land use by consumers and producers within the city.

Unfortunately, equations (2.1)–(2.7) are sufficiently complicated that they cannot be solved directly through substitution. However, we can develop the properties of the solution by showing how the variables in the system change with city size.

Demand and Supply Relationships for City Population

Although we can show how the variables in the system vary with city size, what we really want is to determine equilibrium city size. To do this we must derive the city demand function for labor, which describes the utility levels the city can offer as its size varies, and combine it with a supply function of labor. Since, by the nature of spatial equilibrium, all identical residents of the city have equal utility levels, we examine how the utility of a representative individual changes as city size changes to determine the demand function. We choose the person at the city edge. Using the indirect utility function, or equation (1.4a), after substituting in the unit cost function, or equation (1.12a), for the price of housing, we have

$$V(u_1) = (A_1 p_x^{-a} p_z^{-b} p_l(u_1)^{-c\alpha}) y^f p_k^{-c(1-\alpha)}(T - tu_1)^d \qquad (2.8)$$

where $A_1 = AB^{-c}$. Since all these variables can be solved for in terms of city size or population, V, or utility, can be expressed as a function of city size; this then is the demand function.

The supply function of labor in a partial equilibrium model is exogenously given and is of the form

$$N^s = N(V), \qquad \infty > \partial N/\partial V \geq 0. \qquad (2.9)$$

The supply curve is upward sloping for two reasons. First, laborers are imperfectly mobile. Potential residents will incur moving and information costs if they decide they want to leave their location in other cities. To attract more people from farther away, having higher information and moving costs, the city must offer higher benefits or utility levels. Second, and more directly in the realm of the model, the city must compete with other cities for labor, and to attract more and more laborers from other cities it may be necessary to offer higher and higher competitive utility levels (see Chapter 3).

To determine solutions for city size, we differentiate the equations of the model to see how key variables vary with city size. This differentiation is the key to solving for city size and for doing any comparative statics, as well as for developing the properties of a simple growth model of a city. In developing our solutions, to simplify the exposition, we make two assumptions in the textual presentation of the model, both of which are relaxed for interested readers in footnotes to the text. We first assume that the relative prices of traded goods are fixed, or that the city faces an infinitely elastic demand curve for its export. This assumption is in line with the partial equilibrium view of the city in this chapter.

The second assumption is that the area of the CBD is fixed or zoned with the result that u_0 becomes an exogenous variable. This has the effect of eliminating equation (2.4) for equilibrium in the land market, which equates residential and business rents at u_0. Since u_0 is fixed, there is no reason to expect rents to be equalized at the border. This assumption greatly simplifies the algebra and interpretation of results.

2.   PARTIAL EQUILIBRIUM CITY SIZE

To proceed to solve for city size, we differentiate the equations of the model and investigate how wages, city spatial area, the K/N ratio, and utility levels vary as city size increases, given the parameters of the model. Besides the terms of trade and borrowing rate, variables held fixed are the rent in agriculture, those describing transportation technology, and, in the textual presentation, the size of the CBD, u_0.

2.1   Wage, Capital Intensity, and Utility Rates

To find out how wages vary, we differentiate the labor employment equation (2.1) where $N = C_2 p_x^{1/\gamma} G(N)^{1/\gamma} p_n^{-1-\delta/\gamma} p_k^{-\beta/\gamma} t_x^{-2} f(t_x, u_0)$. Differentiating and rearranging terms yields[2]

$$\frac{dp_n}{p_n} = \frac{\varepsilon - \gamma}{\gamma + \delta} \frac{dN}{N}. \tag{2.10}$$

[2] If u_0 is endogenous, we must differentiate both the population and labor employment equations to get

$$\frac{dN}{N} = -\frac{\gamma + \delta}{\gamma - \varepsilon} \frac{dp_n}{p_n} + \frac{\gamma e_4}{\gamma - \varepsilon} du_0, \tag{2.10a}$$

$$\frac{dN}{N} = -\frac{dy}{y} + e_1 du_1 - e_3 du_0 \tag{2.12a}$$

where $e_4, e_3 > 0$ are as defined in Chapter 1. There is also an additional differential equation for equilibrium in the urban land market. Differentiating equation (2.4), we get

$$\frac{td}{\alpha c}(T - tu_1)^{-1} du_1 - \frac{td}{c\alpha}(T - tu_0)^{-1} du_0 = -\frac{t_x}{\gamma}(1 - t_x u_0)^{-1} du_0 - \frac{\delta}{\gamma}\frac{dp_n}{p_n} + \frac{\varepsilon}{\gamma}\frac{dN}{N}. \tag{a}$$

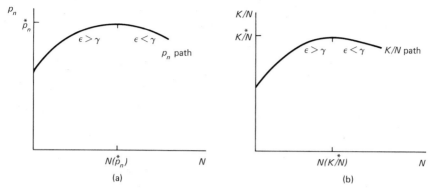

FIGURE 2.1 Wage and capital demand paths.

ε, which equals $(dG/dN)/(N/G)$, is the elasticity of the scale effect with respect to city population. In general it is assumed that

$$d\varepsilon/dN < 0, \tag{2.11}$$

or that the elasticity of scale effects declines monotonically with city size. The reason for assuming this will become clear later.

In equation (2.10) if $\varepsilon > \gamma$, the coefficient of dN/N is positive and p_n increases with city size; if $\varepsilon < \gamma$, p_n decreases with city size. We assume that ε *starts out larger than γ and declines strictly monotonically*, so that p_n has a unique maximum, or $dp_n/p_n = 0$ when $\varepsilon = \gamma$. This is graphed in Figure 2.1a. If ε does not decline monotonically but jumps up and down, there may be several local maxima to the p_n path. Second, if ε does not decline past γ for a finite N, p_n will not have a local maximum and it will either rise or fall continuously. We choose to concentrate on the situation in Figure 2.1a.

We solve (2.10a) for du_0 and substitute into (2.12a) to get

$$du_1 = (e_1\gamma e_4)^{-1}\left\{[e_3(\gamma - \varepsilon) + \gamma e_4]\frac{dN}{N} + [e_3(\gamma + \delta) + \gamma e_4]\frac{dp_n}{p_n}\right\}.$$

Substituting for du_1 and du_0 in equation (a), we get

$$\frac{dp_n}{p_n} = \frac{\varepsilon(1 + e_6) - \gamma e_6 - e_7}{e_6(\gamma + \delta) + \delta + e_7}\frac{dN}{N} \tag{b}$$

where

$$e_6 = e_4^{-1}\left[\frac{t_x}{\gamma}(1 - t_x u_0)^{-1} - \frac{td}{c\alpha}(T - tu_0)^{-1} + \frac{e_3 e_7}{\gamma}\right] > 0,$$

$$e_7 = \gamma e_1^{-1}\frac{td}{c\alpha}(T - tu_1)^{-1} > 0.$$

Intuitively the following forces are at work on p_n. ε represents scale economies and as long as ε is relatively large, given a fixed p_x, with increasing efficiency firms can afford to pay higher wages.[3] However, as city size increases, so do CBD rents. With u_0 fixed, more firms and labor and capital employment are competing for the fixed amount of land, thus driving up land rents. If u_0 is variable and market determined, as city size grows, residential commuting distances and u_1 rise, driving up rents in the residential area and at u_0.[4] This forces up the level of land rents businesses have to pay to bid CBD land away from residences. In equation (2.10) these land rent effects are represented by the share of land in x production, γ. Once $\gamma > \varepsilon$, to meet their rising unit land rent obligations firms must offer lower p_n. Thus a firm's ability to pay both higher land rents and wages out of the fixed p_x as city size increases is limited by efficiency increases or the size of ε.

To find how the spatial area of the city changes as N increases, we first differentiate the residential population equation (2.2) where

$$N = C_1 p_l(u_1) y^{-1} t^{-2} s(t, u_0, u_1)$$

to get, from equation (1.23),

$$dN/N = -dy/y + e_1 \, du_1. \tag{2.12}$$

By differentiating the income equation (2.7) where

$$y = (1 - c\alpha/f)^{-1}(1 + \gamma/\delta)p_n,$$

we see that

$$dy/y = dp_n/p_n. \tag{2.13}$$

Substituting equation (2.13) into (2.12) and then substituting in equation (2.10), where wage changes are a function of population changes, we can

---

[3] If p_x is variable, substituting the differential form of equations (2.5) and (2.6) into the differentiated form of (2.5) for dp_x/p_x, we obtain for equation (2.10)

$$\frac{dp_n}{p_n} = \frac{\varepsilon - \gamma + \eta/(\eta + 1)}{\gamma + \delta - \eta/(\eta + 1)} \frac{dN}{N}$$

where the elasticity of demand $\eta < 0$. If $|\eta| < 1$, or demand is inelastic, this reduces city size where p_n is maximized. If $|\eta| > 1$, it increases it. These are intuitively appealing results.

[4] From footnote 2, the condition for a maximum with u_0 endogenous from equation (b) is $\varepsilon(1 + e_6) - \gamma(e_1^{-1}(td/c\alpha)(T - tu_1)^{-1} + e_6) = 0$. From the definition of e_1 in Chapter 1 it can be shown that $e_1^{-1}(td/c\alpha)(T - tu_1)^{-1} < 1$. Therefore, as long as ε is initially greater than γ, p_n will initially rise. As ε declines, at some point where $\varepsilon < \gamma$ (given that the coefficient of ε is greater than that of γ), p_n will reach a maximum at $N(\overset{*}{p}_n)$. This implies that $N(\overset{*}{p}_n)$ for u_0 variable is greater than for u_0 fixed. This makes sense given the inefficiencies implied in fixing u_0.

solve for u_1 where

$$du_1 = e_1^{-1} \frac{\varepsilon + \delta}{\gamma + \delta} \frac{dN}{N}. \tag{2.14}$$

Therefore, the spatial area of the city increases continuously as population grows.

To find out how the demand for capital varies with city size, we differentiate the capital employment equation (2.3) where

$$K/N = p_k^{-1}[(1 - \alpha)(c/f)y + (\beta/\delta)p_n]$$

to get

$$\frac{dK}{K} - \frac{dN}{N} = \frac{dp_n}{p_n}. \tag{2.15}$$

Substituting in equation (2.10) for wage changes and rearranging terms yields

$$\frac{dK}{K} = \frac{\delta + \varepsilon}{\delta + \gamma} \frac{dN}{N}. \tag{2.16}$$

Capital employment rises with city population, but the K/N ratio varies as the city grows. It is interesting to note how and why.

The K/N ratio rises as long as the coefficient of dN/N in equation (2.16) is greater than 1 and hence as long as $\varepsilon > \gamma$. However, once $\varepsilon < \gamma$, K/N must decline. The explanation underlying these conditions is as follows. p_k is fixed in this partial equilibrium situation; therefore, as city size grows, firms at the various locations will employ factors such that their marginal products of capital (MP_k) remain constant. From the assumptions of Chapter 1, for any firm, MP_k can be defined as being an increasing function of the scale effect N and, by diminishing return arguments, a decreasing function of $k(u)/n(u)$ and $k(u)/l(u)$. Here as long as $\varepsilon > \gamma$ firms can pay a constant MP_k, even with the individual $k(u)/n(u)$ and hence K/N rising, which has a negative effect on MP_k, because of the relatively large scale effect. The rising K/N also makes possible the payment of higher wages when $\varepsilon > \gamma$ as city size increases. However, once $\varepsilon < \gamma$, to meet escalating land rental and marginal product of land conditions given a reduced degree of marginal scale economies, for all firms the use of $k(u)$ and $n(u)$ to $l(u)$ must increase. Then to maintain a given p_k and MP_k with the adverse effects of a rising $k(u)/l(u)$ and of a declining degree of marginal scale economies, in addition to N rising, the individual $k(u)/n(u)$ and hence K/N must decline. These changing factor ratios also result in wages declining (i.e., both $k(u)/n(u)$ and $l(u)/n(u)$ are declining).

This variation in K/N is graphed in Figure 2.1b. Note that as a city grows, the usual notion is that it uses more and more capital relative to other factors. However, beyond the point where wages that firms can offer are at a maximum, the city cannot maintain this growth in capital usage.

Having determined how wages, spatial area, and the K/N ratio vary with city size, we can now determine city size by deriving a city demand for population function. If we differentiate equation (2.8) for the utility of a representative individual, where $V(u_1) = (A_1 p_x^{-a} p_z^{-b} p_l(u_1)^{-c\alpha}) y^f p_k^{-c(1-\alpha)} (T - tu_1)^d$, we get

$$dV/V = f(dy/y) - td/(T - tu_1) \, du_1. \tag{2.17}$$

Substituting in equation (2.13), where $dy/y = dp_n/p_n$, and then in equations (2.10) and (2.14) for dp_n/p_n and du_1, respectively, we get[5]

$$
\frac{dV}{V} = (\gamma + \delta)^{-1} \Big\{ \varepsilon [f - td(T - tu_1)^{-1} e_1^{-1}]
$$

$$
- \gamma \Big[f + \Big(\frac{\delta}{\gamma}\Big) td(T - tu_1)^{-1} e_1^{-1} \Big] \Big\} \frac{dN}{N}. \tag{2.18}
$$

Given the definition of e_1 in Chapter 1, it can be shown that $c\alpha > tde_1^{-1}(T - tu_1)^{-1}$ and therefore the coefficient of ε is positive, given that $f = a + b + c > c$ and $\alpha < 1$. If ε is sufficiently larger than γ, the bracketed expression will be positive and V will increase with population. However, as ε declines toward γ with increasing city size, utility will reach a maximum, or $dV = 0$ when ε is still greater than γ, given that the coefficient of ε in equation (2.18) is less than that of γ. Then with further growth, utility will start to decline. Thus, comparing equation (2.18) for dV/V with equation (2.10) for dp_n/p_n, we find that utility reaches a maximum before p_n does (at $\varepsilon = \gamma$). Since as city size grows, utility changes are the value of wage changes *deflated* by leisure losses from increased commuting time, this result is intuitively appealing. The city size that maximizes utility is smaller than that which maximizes wages. Of course, if ε is always less than γ, the V path

---

[5] For u_0 varying dV/V may be obtained by substituting into equation (2.17) the expressions for du_1 and dp_n/p_n from footnote 2. This yields

$$
\frac{dV}{V} = \Big(\varepsilon \Big[f(1 + e_6) - \frac{td}{(T - tu_1)e_1} \Big(1 + e_6 + \frac{\gamma e_3 - e_7 e_3}{e_4 \gamma} \Big) \Big] - \gamma \Big\{ f e_6
$$

$$
+ \frac{td}{(T - tu_1)e_1} \Big[f + \frac{\delta}{\gamma} \Big(1 + e_6 + \frac{e_3}{e_4} - \frac{e_7 e_3}{e_4 \gamma} \Big) \Big] \Big\} \Big) [e_6(\gamma + \delta) + \delta + e_7]^{-1} \frac{dN}{N}.
$$

Comparing this equation when u_0 is variable with equation (2.17) for u_0 fixed, we see that the coefficient of ε increases, while the change in the coefficient of γ is unclear. Thus it seems likely that $dV = 0$ at a larger N (lower ε) for u_0 variable than for u_0 fixed.

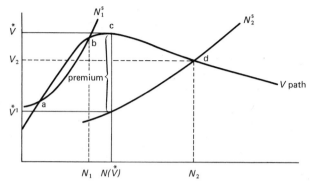

FIGURE 2.2   Utility path and city size.

declines over all ranges of N; and if ε is always sufficiently greater than γ, the V path rises over all ranges of N. A utility path with a unique maximum is graphed in Figure 2.2.

The situation where ε starts out larger than γ and then declines past γ is meant to capture the notion that as a unit cities have declining efficiency as their sizes become larger and larger. Instead of assuming that the degree of marginal scale economies declines with city growth, one can simulate this effect of declining efficiency in a simple model of a city by assuming that congestion and the average unit costs of commuting increase with city size. Dixit (1973) uses this assumption.

2.2 Solving for City Size

The Simple Solution.   To determine equilibrium city size, Figure 2.2 is used. The utility path derived from equation (2.18) is interpreted as a city demand function for population, showing the various utility levels a city can offer under the market equilibrium constraints of equal utility levels for all residents. The supply function of labor is given by equation (2.9). Two alternative supply curves of labor to the city are shown.

If city size is determined by the intersection of demand and supply curves, then for supply curve $N_1{}^s$ [$N_2{}^s$], market city size is N_1 [N_2] at point b [d]. The equilibria at b and d are stable. The equilibrium for $N_1{}^s$ at a is unstable given the relative slopes of the demand and supply curves. A random increase in population from a would result in further factor inflows until point b is reached. If the V path rises or declines continuously, a stable equilibrium is always achieved as long as the slope of the V path is less than the slope of the supply curve.

In our model finite city sizes are achieved by the limiting effects on utility levels of declining leisure and a lessening of the degree of scale economies as city sizes increase. However the decline in leisure in part follows from the assumption that cities have only a single center. If new centers were allowed to form, this would alleviate commuting pressures and mitigate (although not eradicate) this effect. However, one can think of a variety of other variables that also work to limit city sizes, such as diseconomies of scale in production, pollution levels, crime rates, and health problems from crowding.[6] The choice of leisure losses as the limiting factor has partly been for algebraic reasons. However, no matter what effect is chosen to limit city size, the basic concepts used to determine city sizes in this chapter hold.

Problems with a Simple Solution

If the supply curve is $N_2{}^s$, there exists the possibility that the city government will attempt to restrict city size to $N(\mathring{V})$ where utility levels for all residents actually in the city will potentially be maximized. Then residents actually in the city could be made better off by the difference between $\mathring{V}$ and V_2 in Figure 2.2. The city government is elected by residents in the city in a competitive political situation where there are a variety of candidates for office. In order to be (re)elected and to maximize votes, a potential city government seeks to formulate policies that will make city residents best off. Whether they attempt to restrict city size to $N(\mathring{V})$ depends on two considerations. First, city governments and residents must have information about how utility levels vary with city size. This problem is discussed at length in Chapter 3; but in the following discussion we assume this information is known. Second, it is not always the case that city residents are best off restricting city size.

To see this, we first examine how city governments restrict city size in a market economy. There are at least two ways to restrict city size. One is to zone lot sizes to be at the market levels underlying the solution to $\mathring{V}$ and $N(\mathring{V})$ and to limit the city area to be the $\mathring{u}_1$ underlying the solution. The latter part of this policy could be realized by zoning adjacent farm land for only agricultural use or refusing to supply any residents beyond $\mathring{u}_1$ with essential services (such as connecting roads to the city center). The second way to restrict city population in the context of the assumptions stated at the beginning of the chapter is to limit the number of shares issued by the city government or land bank company, where each resident must own a fixed share in order to live in the city and collect land rental income.

---

[6] See Dixit (1973) on congestion, Tolley (1974) on pollution, and Yellin (1974) on the interaction of social prejudice and density.

Suppose the city government limits city size to $N(\mathring{V})$ by one of these methods. Given that people are excluded from the city, there should be a premium on entry into the city. For the supply curve $N_2{}^s$ in Figure 2.2 and city size $N(\mathring{V})$, we have marked the premium in utility terms that the marginal entrant would be willing to pay to live in the city, given his alternative opportunities as indicated by the $N_2{}^s$ curve. How is this premium expressed in the marketplace? To see this, we must informally introduce dynamic considerations.

If the key to entry is owning a share, this premium will be reflected by an increase in share prices corresponding to the capitalized monetary value of the utility premium. Who benefits from this increase in share prices and restrictions on city size? $N(\overset{*}{V})$ presents a long-run solution. If over time people have previously entered the city by their order on the supply curve (given that those to the left of $N(\mathring{V})$ in Figure 2.2 benefit the most from moving to the city) and if prior to reaching $N(\overset{*}{V})$ shares are simply given away to new residents until at $N(\overset{*}{V})$ shares and population are frozen, then the residents of the city benefit both from the current high utility levels of $\mathring{V}$ from restricting city size and a potential capital gain on the value of their share.[7] To realize this gain they would have to sell their share, as, for example, when they retire. They, therefore, would be in favor of policies that tend to restrict city size. As should be obvious, in general, the extent of the potential capital gain accruing to current residents depends on the magnitude of the utility premium, which people were originally in the city, the way in which shares are distributed, and people's expectations about future restrictions on city size when city size is less than $N(\overset{*}{V})$ and premiums on entry to the city created by these expectations.

If city size is restricted through zoning and people own their own homes, the situation is similar. The key to entering the city is a purchase of a home. If city size is restricted, initial residents will benefit from both high current utility levels and potential capital gains on their homes.

However, in a model where there are a group of people called rentiers or landowners who own the urban housing, and lot size is zoned to restrict city population to $N(\overset{*}{V})$, housing rents would be bid up by the monetized value of the utility premium in Figure 2.2. This would shift the realized utility path down to $\mathring{V}^1$, given the high rents rentiers could charge as a key to entering the city. Essentially any premium from restricting city size is transferred to rentiers. In that case, the city government would make its

---

[7] Note that in equilibrium at $N(\mathring{V})$, those on the supply curve to the left of $N(\mathring{V})$ must be the people in the city. They would be willing to pay more for shares than people to the right of $N(\mathring{V})$, whose alternatives are better. That is, a person to the left of $N(\mathring{V})$ would always be willing to buy out (pay a higher premium than) a person to the right of $N(\mathring{V})$. I am grateful to Robert Sinche for pointing this out to me.

residents better off by letting city size expand to N_2 with utility level V_2. Note that in the case where city size is restricted, there is also a conflict between landowners who own land interior to $\mathring{u}_1$, the city radius for population $N(\mathring{V})$, and those who own land exterior to $\mathring{u}_1$. The second group would favor a land development policy that is expansionary.

From this discussion, we can get a picture of the political conflicts between renters, home owners, residential landowners, and owners of undeveloped land. A potential city government running for (re)election faces these conflicts in seeking both votes and campaign funding. These conflicts in a suburban context are elaborated on in Chapter 10.

3.   COMPARATIVE STATICS

Suppose a city is initially in equilibrium in Figure 2.2, either at the intersection of the demand and supply curves or at the point where the utility path achieves a maximum. Comparative static analysis is used to find out what happens to this equilibrium in the long run in terms of city size, wages, rents, etc., if the value of an exogenous variable changes by a small amount. In our model the exogenous variables are t, t_x, p_x, p_k, $p_l(u_1)$, and u_0 (if it is fixed).

The usual comparative statics exercise in urban models is to vary the commuting cost variable t to determine the effect on city size. We examine the effect of a change in t on city size here briefly; and then consider a second example. Suppose we are currently at equilibrium as determined by the intersection of a demand and supply function as at point d in Figure 2.2. Then, commuting costs t exogenously increase. What happens to city size?

To see this we differentiate the equations in our model, allowing both city size and t to vary, where the change in t is given exogenously. Differentiating the employment and income equations, we still get $dp_n/p_n = (\varepsilon - \gamma)/(\gamma + \delta)\, dN/N$ and $dy/y = dp_n/p_n$, respectively. Differentiating the residential population equation, we have $dN/N = -dy/y + e_1\, du_1 + e_2\, dt$. Substituting into this for dy/y and then dp_n/p_n, we find $du_1 = e_1^{-1}(\varepsilon + \delta)/(\gamma + \delta)\, dN/N - e_2/e_1\, dt$. Differentiating the utility equation, we now have $dV/V = f(dy/y) - td/(T - tu_1)\, du_1 - u_1 d/(T - tu_1)\, dt$. Substituting into this for dy/y and then dp_n/p_n and du_1, we obtain

$$dV/V = e_8\, \frac{dN}{N} + \left[\left(\frac{e_2}{e_1}\right)td - u_1 d\right](T - tu_1)^{-1}\, dt$$

where

$$e_8 = f\left(\frac{\varepsilon - \gamma}{\gamma + \delta}\right) - e_1^{-1}\left(\frac{\varepsilon + \delta}{\gamma + \delta}\right)td(T - tu_1)^{-1}.$$

From the definitions of e_1 and e_2 in footnote 18, Chapter 1, we can show that $e_2 < t^{-1}u_1e_1$ and hence that the coefficient of dt is negative. From the labor supply equation (2.9) we know by differentiation that $dN/N = \xi \, dV/V$. Combining the demand and supply equations yields

$$\frac{dN}{N} = -\frac{e_1^{-1}(T - tu_1)^{-1}(e_1u_1d - e_2td)}{1/\xi - e_8} \, dt.$$

The numerator of this expression is negative. If city size is beyond $N(\overset{*}{V})$, from equation (2.18) we can show that $e_8 < 0$ and hence the denominator is always positive. In that case, for $dt > 0$, $dN/N < 0$; or city size declines as t increases. For city sizes less than $N(\overset{*}{V})$, we can show that for a stable equilibrium $1/\varepsilon - e_8 > 0$, or dN/N is also negative for $dt > 0$. Therefore, an increase in t leads to a decline in population. By substituting back into the change in utility equation, we can see that utility declines if both components of the equation are negative.

In the remaining part of the chapter we examine another comparative statics exercise, the results of which will be used later in the book in discussions of the property tax.

3.1 Property Tax Incidence

The property tax is a tax on residential and commercial structures, commercial capital facilities, consumer durables (sometimes), and urban land. Therefore, in the model in this chapter the property tax is viewed as a consumption tax on residential housing and a factor usage tax on business inputs of capital and land. It is assumed the effective tax rate is the same for residential and commercial applications and is spatially invariant. For simplicity we assume all assets are valued at 100% of market value, so that the quoted tax rate is the effective tax rate.

In terms of a comparative statics exercise we want to investigate who will bear the burden or effectively pay the cost of increases in property taxes. For example, for housing, will increases in taxes be borne by housing consumers in the form of higher gross housing prices; or will they be passed back to owners of land and capital in the form of lower rents? For businesses, will increases in taxes be passed forward to consumers, borne by capital owners, or shifted to landowners? These questions are comprehensively examined in Chapter 9. The presentation that follows tends to dwell on the mechanical aspects of analyzing the problem, as a way of illustrating the range of applications of the aggregative model in this chapter.

In analyzing property tax incidence, we start by examining how the property tax nominally affects housing and land prices and the demand for these goods. With a property tax, for residents the price of housing is

$p(u)(1 + r)$ where r is the property tax rate defined for net rental, not gross asset, prices and $p(u)$ is the before-tax cost of housing or the housing rent paid to competitive housing producers. The indirect utility function and demand for housing function must be adjusted to account for the new price, or equations (1.2a) and (1.4a) become

$$h(u) = (c/f)yp(u)^{-1}(1 + r)^{-1}, \tag{2.19}$$
$$V(u) = Ay^f p_x^{-a} p_z^{-b} p(u)^{-c}(1 + r)^{-c}(T - tu)^d. \tag{2.20}$$

Housing consumption is distorted by the introduction of a wedge between price $p(u)(1 + r)$ and cost $p(u)$ that does not occur for other goods x and z. The slopes of the after-tax rent gradients $p(u)$ and $p_l(u)$ are unaffected since r is spatially invariant (or the differential of (2.20) with respect to u does not contain r). The net of tax unit cost function for housing is unchanged since the tax is factor neutral, or $p(u) = Bp_l(u)^x p_k^{1-x}$. However, the demand for land (and capital) reflects the reduced demand for housing, or

$$l(u) = (\alpha c/f)yp_l(u)^{-1}(1 + r)^{-1}. \tag{2.21}$$

For businesses the tax is on land and capital but not on labor inputs. As such, firm profits are now

$$p_x(1 - t_x u)G(N)l(u)^\gamma k(u)^\beta n(u)^\delta - p_k(1 + r)k(u) - p_n n(u) - p_l(u)(1 + r)l(u);$$

and the first-order conditions of consumer maximization yield

$$p_n = p_x(1 - t_x u)(\delta x(u)/n(u))$$

while

$$p_k(1 + r) = p_x(1 - t_x u)(\beta x(u)/k(u)).$$

Therefore, the new unit cost function is

$$p_x(1 - t_x u) = G(N)^{-1}Cp_n^\delta(p_k(1 + r))^\beta(p_l(u)(1 + r))^\gamma. \tag{2.22}$$

Note that the choice of production inputs is distorted by raising the price of k and l but not n above opportunity cost. The inverse of (2.22) yields the new rent gradient, or

$$p_l(u) = G(N)^{1/\gamma}p_x^{1/\gamma}(1 - t_x u)^{1/\gamma}C^{-1/\gamma}p_n^{-\delta/\gamma}p_k^{-\beta/\gamma}(1 + r)^{-(\gamma+\beta)/\gamma}. \tag{2.23}$$

This reflects a shift down in rents firms can pay out with a property tax relative to a no-tax situation and the same other prices.

In a partial equilibrium model the city faces fixed prices of traded goods and a fixed rental rate on capital. In this situation our concern is what will happen to city size and other endogenous variables, such as wages and rents, if either we impose a property tax where there is no property tax or we raise an existing tax rate. This question ignores the global or economy-wide incidence of the property tax, which may affect the national rental on capital (see Chapter 9). It takes the national rental as given and focuses on the incidence question from the narrow perspective of one city. As such, the incidence question is simplified. The tax on factor inputs cannot be passed on to purchasers of the city's export good x, since the city faces an infinitely elastic demand curve for its product. Nor can the tax be passed back to capital owners, since the city faces an infinitely elastic supply curve of capital. Therefore, the tax or increases in the tax must be borne by city residents and/or landowners in the form of lower wages or land rents. In the unit cost function in equation (2.22) as r rises either $p_l(u)$ or p_n, or both, must fall, given fixed p_x and p_k.

Before examining the effect of the tax on wages, rents, and city size, we need an expenditure side to the public sector that receives the property tax revenue. We do not discuss optimal provision of public goods until Chapter 10. Therefore, we assume that *full equal* benefits for all citizens arise from property tax expenditures. This is accomplished by redistributing tax dollars as an equal income supplement to all residents. For the city taken as a whole there are no income losses or effects due to the tax, only pure substitution effects and welfare losses due to housing consumption distortions and commercial factor usage distortions.

The Incidence of Local Deviations in the Property Tax: The Informal Analysis

Suppose in the city an existing property tax is increased. Given the preceding discussion it is apparent that in the business sector, in order to pay the tax, for the same population, wages and rents decline given that the same retail price and net capital rentals must be maintained. If the commercial area of the city is fixed and there is the same labor N supplied, then to maintain the same relative demands and employment of these two factors, wages and rents should decline by similar proportions. At the same time the demand for and use of capital declines given its increase in gross price.

In the residential sector, the increased gross price of housing leads to a reduced demand for housing, capital, and land. In equilibrium for the same population this should result in the city area u_1 shrinking and hence a shift down in the net of tax housing price and land rent gradients, as urban land is converted back to agricultural land (given that net rents at the old u_1 fall below agricultural rents). This shift down partially offsets the effect of the increased tax on the gross price of housing. (Note that it can only partially offset the tax effect; or the gross price of housing must rise. If the gross price of housing falls, the demand for land and u_1 will rise, removing the basis for the decline in net of tax rents.)

For the same population, the city residents are worse off. Intuitively, the basic notion is that increases in the property tax result in increased distortions in the housing and factor markets. In terms of market variables, taking the representative person at the city edge, the loss due to reduced wages, reduced land rental income, and increased gross price of housing exceeds the gains from reduced commuting distance, or city radius u_1, and increased income from property tax proceeds.

This change in welfare for a given population is demonstrated in Figure 2.3. The utility path is initially V. With an increase in the property tax it shifts down everywhere to the new path V'. Suppose the initial equilibrium is at point a, the intersection of the V path and a supply curve; and the new equilibrium is at b, the intersection of the V' path and the supply curve. City population and welfare levels will decline. The welfare loss will be the decline in utility for remaining residents plus the smaller losses in utility for out-migrants whose opportunities are represented along the supply curve between a and b.

This analysis assumes that equilibrium city size is determined by the intersection of utility paths and supply curves. Suppose this is not so, but city size is determined by the actions of the city government that restrict city size to be that which maximizes utility on the utility path. As explained earlier, this results from the behavior of a city government elected by majority vote of residents in the city, where people directly or indirectly (through a land bank company) own their own homes. City size is initially at c. Where the new city size will be depends on whether the population where utility is maximized increases or decreases with the increased property tax. In Figure 2.3 we show the maximum point of the utility path shifting right to d, or $N(\overset{*}{V}) < N(\overset{*}{V'})$. This indicates that although utility declines with the

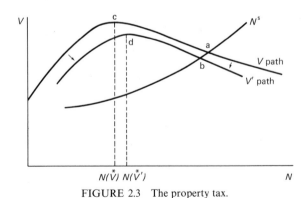

FIGURE 2.3 The property tax.

increase in the property tax, city size increases if city size is determined by the optimizing behavior of the city government.

The maximum point of the utility path may shift right for the following reason. The property tax increase reduces the demand for land, causing city area and average commuting distances to decline for the same population. This means that for the same level of scale economies commuting costs are less. It may also imply at the initial city population that, after the tax, marginal scale economy benefits from increasing city size now exceed the marginal costs of increased commuting time and leisure losses. Therefore, it is efficient to expand city size.

The Algebra behind the Results

With the property tax, the aggregate equations for a city change. In the residential sector, given the same net of tax rent gradient but a reduced demand for land in equation (2.21), the new expression for population from equation (1.22) is

$$N = C_1 p_l(u_1) y^{-1} t^{-2} s(t, u_0, u_1)(1 + r), \qquad (2.24)$$

or the no-tax expression for city population multiplied by $(1 + r)$. With the introduction of a tax, the use of residential capital relative to population declines with the reduced housing demand, or from equation (1.24)

$$K_{res} = (1 - \alpha)(c/f) y p_k^{-1} N(1 + r)^{-1}. \qquad (2.25)$$

Similarly, with a tax, net-of-tax residential rents decline relative to N, or from equation (1.25)

$$Rents_{res} = (\alpha c/f) y N(1 + r)^{-1}. \qquad (2.26)$$

Residential property taxes collected are r multiplied by housing expenditures net of taxes, or for logarithmic linear utility functions

$$Taxes_{res} = r(c/f) y N(1 + r)^{-1}. \qquad (2.27)$$

In the business sector, given the new factor demand relationships illustrated by equation (2.21), from equation (1.34) labor employment equation is

$$N = \int_0^{u_0} 2\pi u \, \frac{n(u)}{l(u)} \, du = \int_0^{u_0} 2\pi u \left(\frac{\delta}{\gamma}\right)\left(\frac{p_l(u)(1 + r)}{p_n}\right) du$$

$$= C_2 p_x^{1/\gamma} G(N)^{1/\gamma} p_n^{-1 - \delta/\gamma} p_x^{-\beta/\gamma} t_x^{-2} f(t_x, u_0)(1 + r)^{-\beta/\gamma}. \qquad (2.28)$$

With a tax the use of capital relative to labor falls, or

$$K_{bus} = (\beta/\delta) p_n p_k^{-1} N(1 + r)^{-1}. \qquad (2.29)$$

Gross business rents ($(1 + r)$ Rents) are proportional to other factor payments, or net business rents are

$$\text{Rents} = (\gamma/\delta)p_n N(1 + r)^{-1}. \tag{2.30}$$

Business taxes are r multiplied by rents in equation (2.30) and capital payments from equation (2.29), or

$$\text{Taxes}_{\text{bus}} = \left(\frac{r}{1 + r}\right)\left(\frac{\beta + \gamma}{\delta}\right)p_n N. \tag{2.31}$$

The only remaining part of the aggregate model to respecify is income, which now includes average tax collections in equations (2.27) and (2.31). Therefore, the new income equation is

$$y = \frac{f(\delta + \gamma + r)}{\delta(f(1 + r) - \alpha c - cr)}p_n. \tag{2.32}$$

Shifts in the Utility Path

To find out how the utility path shifts and city size changes with an increase in the property tax, we want to know what happens to utility V *for each N* as r increases. To determine this we see what happens to wages, income, and city area as r increases for the same N.

Differentiating the labor employment equation, we get

$$\frac{dN}{N} = -\frac{(\gamma + \delta)}{(\gamma - \varepsilon)}\frac{dp_n}{p_n} - \frac{\beta}{(\gamma - \varepsilon)}\frac{dr}{(1 + r)}. \tag{2.33}$$

From equation (2.33) for $dN = 0$

$$\frac{dp_n}{p_n} = -\frac{\beta}{(\gamma + \delta)}\frac{dr}{(1 + r)} < 0, \tag{2.34}$$

or wages decline with the tax increase. To show how the city area changes, we differentiate the income equation (2.32) and the residential population equation (2.24) to get[8]

$$\frac{dy}{y} = \frac{dp_n}{p_n} + e_9 \frac{dr}{(1 + r)}, \tag{2.35}$$

$$\frac{dN}{N} = -\frac{dy}{y} + e_1 \, du_1 + \frac{dr}{(1 + r)}. \tag{2.36}$$

[8] $e_9 = \dfrac{(1 + r)(f - \alpha c) - (1 + r)(\gamma + \delta)(f - c)}{(\gamma + \delta + r)(f - \alpha c) + (\delta + \gamma + r)r(f - c)} < \dfrac{1}{\gamma + \delta}.$

e_9 may also be less than 1, depending on parametric values.

Substituting into equation (2.36) for dy/y and then dp_n/p_n for $dN = 0$, we find

$$du_1 = e_1^{-1}[-1/(\gamma + \delta) + e_9]\, dr/(1 + r) < 0. \tag{2.37}$$

Given $e_9 < 1/(\gamma + \delta)$, u_1 declines as r increases. Differentiating the utility equation (2.20), we get

$$dV/V = f(dy/y) - c[dr/(1 + r)] - td/(T - tu_1)\, du_1. \tag{2.38}$$

Substituting into equation (2.39) for dy/y, dp_n/p_n, and u_1, we get

$$\frac{dV}{V} = \left[-f\left(\frac{\beta}{\gamma + \delta} - e_9\right) - c - \frac{td}{(T - tu_1)e_1}\left(e_9 - \frac{1}{\gamma + \delta}\right)\right]\frac{dr}{1 + r}. \tag{2.39}$$

The last expression in the square brackets is positive given that $e_9 < 1/(\gamma + \delta)$, whereas the second and probably the first expressions are negative. Given that $td(T - tu_1)^{-1}e_1^{-1} < c\alpha$ from footnote 18, Chapter 1, it seems likely that $dV < 0$ in equation (2.39). It may be possible, however, that $dV > 0$. The reason is that there is already a distortion because u_0 is fixed. If u_0 is fixed to be too small relative to an optimal u_0, a property tax would reduce the demand for business land, reducing the inefficiencies caused by u_0 being fixed. In general, however, this will not be true and dV/V will decline. Therefore, in Figure 2.3, we draw the V path shifting down at each point as r increases.

The final question concerns the direction in which the maximum point of the V path shifts with an increase in r. To find this out, we examine the determinants of the maximum point for *any* r. For any (fixed) r from equation (2.38), after substituting in $du_1 = e_1^{-1}(dN/N) + e_1^{-1}(dy/y)$ from equation (2.36) and $dy/y = dp_n/p_n = -(\gamma - \varepsilon)/(\gamma + \delta)\, dN/N$ from (2.33) and (2.35), the maximum point occurs when

$$\frac{dN}{N}\frac{f(\varepsilon - \gamma)}{\gamma + \delta} = \frac{td}{(T - tu_1)e_1}\frac{(\varepsilon + \delta)}{\gamma + \delta}\frac{dN}{N} \tag{2.39a}$$

where f, γ, t, d, T, and δ are all parameters and ε is a fixed function of N. The left-hand side of equation (2.39a) is the marginal benefits of increasing city size and the right-hand side is the marginal cost. For the same N, only $(T - tu_1)$ and e_1 vary with r. For the same N, if $(T - tu_1)e_1$ increases with r, the right-hand side of equation (2.39a) declines, indicating a reduction in marginal leisure losses, while the left-hand side, or marginal benefits, remains unchanged. In that case an increase in r will lead to an increase in the city size where utility is maximized, or equation (2.39a) will be satisfied at a higher N and a lower ε. Under what conditions will this happen and hence will the maximum point of the V path shift right?

An increase in r will lead to a decrease in u_1 (equation (2.36)). Therefore, $(T - tu_1)e_1$ increases with r if $\partial(T - tu_1)e_1/\partial u_1 < 0$. Using the definition of e_1 in footnote 18, Chapter 1, $\partial(T - tu_1)e_1/\partial u_1$ may be positive or negative but will generally be negative if d, the exponent of leisure in the utility function, is not small.[9] Therefore, in Figure 2.3, we show the maximum of the utility path shifting to the right as r increases.

[9] For example, if α, or land's share in housing output, is 0.1; if c/f, or housing's share in the budget, is 0.2; and if f is 1, then d should be greater than 0.04.

3

The System of Cities in an Economy

In Chapters 1 and 2 we examined equilibrium in a single city, where that city faces fixed terms of trade, a fixed rental rate on capital, and an exogenous supply curve of labor. The fundamental question left unanswered by this analysis is how equilibrium in the total economy is determined; or how the terms of trade, capital rental rates, and cost of labor facing an individual city are set in national markets. How does any city fit into the system of cities in an economy? How and why are factors allocated to any city from national factor markets; or how do cities compete with each other for factors? Why are some cities large and others small? Why do some grow and others decline?

In this chapter we examine the system of cities in an economy. First, a general equilibrium model of a static system of cities is described where all resources are ubiquitous and cities in the economy are situated on a flat featureless plain where there is no agriculture. We assume that the economy endowments of capital and labor are fixed and capital and labor are perfectly mobile among cities. This specification allows us to isolate fundamental problems in the evolution of a system of cities, even before complications such as growth and natural resources are considered. Then we consider the effect on a system of cities of growth, international trade, and natural resources.

In the chapter the long-run equilibrium numbers and sizes of cities are solved for, with the analysis focusing on how market solutions evolve. To illustrate the arguments, specific solutions, questions of stability and uniqueness, and conflicts between capital owners and laborers and between local and national governments, we use a specific functional form model. The specific functional form model developed here is simpler than the one used in Chapters 1 and 2 but it allows for solutions to problems that would otherwise remain somewhat intractable.[1] Moreover, for the problems addressed in this chapter we can use this simpler model of the internal structure of cities to illustrate propositions about a system of cities without loss of generality. Although we retain spatial dimensions in the simpler model, it is also possible to use a spaceless model, as in Henderson (1974a).

First, the solution for a single type of city or a system of identical cities is presented. Then an economy with multiple types of cities is examined.

1.   ONE TYPE OF CITY

Before presenting the model used to solve for a system of cities, we need to examine the economic agents in the model and the nature of their behavior, so as to determine what elements must be incorporated into a model of cities.

The Economic Agents in the System

In the model there are two basic visible groups of people, laborers and capital owners, whose decisions help determine city size. Laborers choose a city to live in from among the existing and potential cities of the economy, and thus through their location decisions they help determine city sizes. In picking a city in which to live, laborers examine the income, commuting costs, and housing prices associated with different cities and pick the city that offers them the highest utility level. We generally assume that laborers are identical in skills, tastes, and factor ownerships. In stable-market solutions, these identical laborers must achieve equal utility, or else bidding for spatial locations within a city and population movements between cities will continue until a set of prices and locations is determined that yields equal utilities.

---

[1] The intractability comes when trying to compare equilibrium with optimal solutions in this chapter and the next. To do that, we have to remove all sources of inefficiency in the model. In particular, we must allow the CBD boundary u_0 to vary so that equation (2.4) is satisfied and the city must pay out (rather than retain) agricultural land rents (this is the basic algebraic problem).

Capital owners choose how much to invest in different cities and thus through their investment decisions they help determine city capital stocks and influence city populations. Capital owners need not live in the cities where their capital is employed; therefore, in making investment decisions they are not concerned with living conditions, such as rents and commuting costs, in those cities. In making investment decisions, capital owners are concerned only with maximizing the return on capital. Since capital is perfectly mobile, in equilibrium we expect the rental return on capital to be everywhere equal.

We initially assume that capital owners do not work in cities as laborers and hence that they do not need to live in cities at all. They live either in the countryside or on the edges of cities where in both cases they rent land at the opportunity cost (usually zero) in agriculture and incur no commuting costs. In the model we are not concerned with their location decisions since they neither affect city sizes nor are affected by city sizes. Later we will consider a situation where capital owners work as laborers in cities, commuting and paying urban costs of living; and then we will be concerned with their location decisions.

There are three other groups of people in the model who are basically invisible[2] but whose role is important in determining what city sizes evolve, given the location decisions of laborers and investment decisions of capital owners. First, there are entrepreneurs (who could be capital owners), who implicitly manage production activity and ensure that factors are efficiently employed within firms. Second, there may be city governments seeking to be elected. By competing to be elected and remain in office, governments attempt to enact policies concerning city size that maximize the perceived welfare of city residents. Although the behavior of this group of people is interesting in this chapter, its actions are not as critical as they are in Chapter 2.

The third group of people are developers (who could also be city governments), who set up cities and manage land bank companies. In each city, land is owned collectively by all city residents through shares in a land bank company that efficiently manages that city's land. Each resident owns an equal share in the company. The land bank company pays out dividends, which normally equal average per capita land rents paid out less some negligible (invisible) return paid to the developer. This full distribution of land rents through dividends offered is ensured in a model with identical

[2] The term invisible is used because in long-run equilibrium solutions payments to these groups of people are not usually explicitly considered. This can be defended on two grounds. Total payments to these groups and the size of these groups are negligible *relative* to the total population in the economy. Second, these groups may subsist on short-run profits made on innovations relative to other firms and cities. Their static equilibrium long-run return is zero.

cities by competition among developers of existing and potential cities for residents, where dividends offered are one element in attracting residents to cities. However, if one city is in some way more efficient than other cities, this full distribution may not occur, at least initially; and, the income of the developer may go up temporarily. The temporary increase in income to developers from setting up or designing more efficient cities is critical to arguments later in the chapter because it provides an incentive for developers to design efficient cities.

1.1 A Simplified Model of a City

The location decisions of laborers and investment decisions of capital owners depend on the market opportunities they face, in terms of utility levels and capital rentals. Therefore, to solve for city sizes, which are in part determined by these decisions, we develop a model of a city to show how capital rentals and utility levels vary in the economy as we vary city sizes.

In the simplified model of a city we make the following new assumptions relative to the model in Chapters 1 and 2. The CBD becomes a point, or all urban land is residential and land is not used in commercial production. The degree of scale economies ε is fixed for the discussion that follows. In the residential sector, housing services are produced solely with land; capital is not used in housing production. Lots are of fixed equal size throughout the city. Commuting costs are now specified to be all out of pocket, directly affecting the budget constraint. The time and leisure aspects of travel are not explicitly considered. Finally, it is assumed that rents at the city edge, or agricultural rents, are zero.

Residential Sector. Consumers maximize utility, or $V = x^a z^b l^c$ where lot size l is fixed equal to 1, subject to a budget constraint $y - p_l(u) - tu - p_x x - p_z z = 0$ where y is income, $p_l(u)$ is the rent per fixed lot size, and t is the cost of commuting (there and back) a unit distance. Maximizing utility with respect to x and z, we have $aV/x = \lambda p_x$ and $bV/z = \lambda p_z$. Combining to get $bp_x x = ap_z z$ and substituting in the budget constraint for first x and then z, we have demand equations $x = a/(a + b)(y - p_l(u) - tu)p_x^{-1}$ and $z = b/(a + b)(y - p_l(u) - tu)p_z^{-1}$. Substituting these into the utility function, we get the indirect utility function

$$V = A(y - p_l(u) - tu)^{a+b} \tag{3.1}$$

where

$$A = p_x^{-a} p_z^{-b}(a/(a + b))^a(b/(a + b))^b.$$

Spatial equilibrium for identical consumers requires that $\partial V/\partial u = 0$. From equation (3.1), this means that $\partial p_l(u)/\partial u = -t$ or increased transport costs with increased commuting distance are offset by reduced rents. Integrating the equation $\partial p_l(u)/\partial u = -t$, we get $p_l(u) = C_0 - tu$. To evaluate the constant of integration we note by assumption that $p_l(u_1) = 0$ or $p_l(u_1) = 0 = C_0 - tu_1$. Therefore, the rent gradient is

$$p_l(u) = t(u_1 - u). \tag{3.2}$$

Total land rents in the city are

$$\int_0^{u_1} (2\pi u)p_l(u)\,du = \int_0^{u_1} (2\pi u)t(u_1 - u)\,du = \tfrac{1}{3}t\pi u_1^3.$$

If these rents are divided up equally among residents, then per person rental income is $\tfrac{1}{3}t\pi u_1^3/N$. However, given that lot size is fixed at 1 where N is city population

$$N = \pi u_1^2. \tag{3.3}$$

Therefore per person rental income may be written as (where $u_1 = N^{1/2}\pi^{-1/2}$)

$$\text{per person rental income} = \tfrac{1}{3}tN^{1/2}\pi^{-1/2}. \tag{3.4}$$

We can now define the equilibrium utility level for a representative person in the city. We take the person at the city edge. His income is wages, p_n, plus per person rental income of $\tfrac{1}{3}tN^{1/2}\pi^{-1/2}$. Land rents $p_l(u_1)$ are zero and commuting costs are tu_1 where $tu_1 = tN^{1/2}\pi^{-1/2}$ from equation (3.3). Substituting these relationships into the indirect utility function in equation (3.1), we have

$$V(u_1) = A(p_n - \tfrac{2}{3}tN^{1/2}\pi^{-1/2})^{a+b}. \tag{3.5}$$

To determine wages in this equation we turn to the production sector of the economy. Analysis of the production sector also indicates how capital rentals vary with city size.

The Commercial Sector. The firm production function is $x = N^\varepsilon n^\alpha k^{1-\alpha}$ where n and k are, respectively, firm employment of labor and capital; N is city population; and N^ε is the scale economy shift factor. Given that all firms are identical in technology, total city production may be written as $X = N^\varepsilon N^\alpha K^{1-\alpha}$ where N is city labor force and K is city capital stock. The first-order conditions for firm profit maximization state that $p_n = p_x\alpha N^\varepsilon n^{\alpha-1}k^{1-\alpha}$ and $p_k = p_x(1-\alpha)N^\varepsilon n^\alpha k^{-\alpha}$. Normalizing so that $p_x = 1$, at the city level we have

$$p_n = \alpha(K/N)^{1-\alpha}N^\varepsilon, \tag{3.6}$$
$$p_k = (1-\alpha)(K/N)^{-\alpha}N^\varepsilon. \tag{3.7}$$

Aggregate Relationships in the City

Equation (3.7) describes p_k as a function of the K/N ratio and city population. For a given K/N, because of scale economies, p_k increases continuously as N rises. This relationship is pictured in Figure 3.1 by what is termed a capital rental, or p_k, path. From equation (3.7), if K/N rises [falls], at each N the capital rental path shifts down [up], a normal factor ratio effect. Note that if land is reintroduced as a factor of production, for reasons discussed in Chapter 2, the p_k path could eventually turn down as city size increases. Commercial land rents may escalate so quickly that to maintain a competitive output price, payments offered to all other factors must decline.

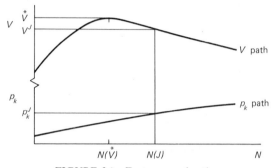

FIGURE 3.1   Factor reward paths.

Equation (3.6) shows how wages vary with city size. As is the case for capital rentals, wages increase continuously as city size increases for a given K/N ratio. The wage path shifts up [down] at each point if the K/N ratio increases [declines]. We substitute equation (3.6) back into the indirect utility function to get

$$V = A[\alpha(K/N)^{1-\alpha}N^{\varepsilon} - \tfrac{2}{3}tN^{1/2}\pi^{-1/2}]^{a+b}. \tag{3.8}$$

We limit parametric values to ensure that the expression in the brackets in equation (3.8) is positive (or $\alpha(K/N)^{1-\alpha}N^{\varepsilon} > \tfrac{2}{3}tN^{1/2}\pi^{-1/2}$).

Before turning to solutions to city sizes, we must determine how V varies with city size. Differentiating equation (3.8) with respect to N while holding K/N constant yields

$$\frac{dV}{V} = (a + b)A^{1/(a+b)}V^{-1/(a+b)}[\alpha\varepsilon(K/N)^{1-\alpha}N^{\varepsilon} - \left(\frac{t}{3}\right)N^{1/2}\pi^{-1/2}]\frac{dN}{N}. \tag{3.9}$$

This is a potentially unwieldy relationship to work with since for different parametric values $dV/V \gtreqless 0$ over some or all ranges of city sizes. To limit the number of solutions that we must consider, we assume that parametric values are such that as N increases from zero, dV/V is initially positive, then zero, then negative. (Since we have assumed that $\alpha(K/N)^{1-\alpha}N^{\varepsilon} > \frac{2}{3}tN^{1/2}\pi^{-1/2}$, for dV/V ever to have a negative value, ε must be less than $\frac{1}{2}$.) This relationship between V and N is graphed in Figure 3.1 by what is termed a utility path. If K/N increases [declines], this path shifts up [down] at all points due to the beneficial factor ratio effect on wages. The utility path in Figure 3.1 has a unique maximum when $dV = 0$; or, rearranging equation (3.9), at the maximum V city population is

$$N(\overset{*}{V}) = [3\alpha\varepsilon\pi^{1/2}t^{-1}(K/N)^{1-\alpha}]^{1/(\frac{1}{2}-\varepsilon)}. \tag{3.10}$$

For parametric values of $K/N = 1$, $\alpha = \frac{3}{4}$, $\varepsilon = \frac{1}{4}$, $t = \frac{1}{10}$, $N(\overset{*}{V}) = 9880$.

Having derived and defined utility and capital rental paths as pictured in Figure 3.1, we can now solve for city sizes.[3]

1.2 The Solution to City Sizes

To solve for city size we make use of the factor reward paths in Figure 3.1. In Figure 3.1 for city sizes smaller than the one that maximizes utility, which is $N(\overset{*}{V})$, both groups of people in the model experience increases in real factor income as city sizes increase. Thus we should suspect that city sizes smaller than $N(\overset{*}{V})$ are unstable, since up to at least $N(\overset{*}{V})$ any city larger than current cities will always be able to attract factors from the smaller cities, because it can pay them more. However, beyond $N(\overset{*}{V})$, whereas capital owners benefit from further increases in city sizes, laborers are made worse off. It is in this range beyond $N(\overset{*}{V})$ that equilibrium city sizes occur.

With one type of city in the economy, there is a unique stable equilibrium city size, such as depicted by $N(J)$ in Figure 3.1. We first define the properties of $N(J)$ and then demonstrate the uniqueness and stability of the solution.

Two conditions define $N(J)$. First, all cities are identical, which means all cities have the same K/N ratio, which equals the national ratio, and all cities are of equal size. Secondly $N(J)$ occurs when the marginal gains to capital owners from increasing city size beyond $N(\overset{*}{V})$, $K(dp_k/dN)$, just equal the marginal losses to laborers from increasing city size, which are $N(dV/dN)$ in utility units or which are $N(dV/dN)/(\partial V/\partial y))$ in monetary units. Therefore, market city size occurs when

$$N \frac{dV/dN}{\partial V/\partial y} + K \frac{dp_k}{dN} = 0. \tag{3.11}$$

---

[3] Similar paths can be derived using the model in Chapter 2. In differentiating equations of the model and solving, we now hold K/N, rather than p_k, fixed.

Substituting in equation (3.9) for dV/dN, from equation (3.1) for $\partial V/\partial y$, and from equation (3.9) for dp_k/dN, and rearranging terms, we find

$$N(J) = (3\varepsilon\pi^{1/2}t^{-1})^{1/(\frac{1}{2}-\varepsilon)}(K/N)^{(1-\alpha)/(\frac{1}{2}-\varepsilon)}. \qquad (3.12)$$

Note that $N(J)$ is a strictly monotonic function of the K/N ratio (given $\varepsilon < \frac{1}{2}, \alpha < 1$).

Before [after] $N(J)$, the gains to capital owners exceed [are less than] the losses to laborers. That is, at $N(J)$ the sum of real factor rewards evaluated in dollars is maximized. This is critical since it implies that at any other city size, the sum of factor returns could be increased by moving city size to $N(J)$. For the illustrative parametric values used earlier, where $K/N = 1$, $\alpha = \frac{3}{4}$, $\varepsilon = \frac{1}{4}$, and $t = \frac{1}{10}$, $N(J)$ is 31,200.

In stating that $N(J)$ is the solution we must assume that the economy is very large and there are many cities of size $N(J)$. This assumption must be made because there is a divisibility or lumpiness problem here, which can be illustrated as follows. Suppose there is currently economy population for two and a half cities of size $N(J)$. In Section 1.4, we will argue that the market solution will be to have two cities form with the remaining half city split evenly among the two cities, so they are each one and a quarter times $N(J)$. However as the number of cities increases, any remainder is split among more and more cities, and the part of the remainder going to any one city becomes very small. Then all cities may approach size $N(J)$. In this section we assume the economy is sufficiently large so that this condition is met and there are no problems with lumpiness. Once we have solved for city size $N(J)$ we divide $N(J)$ into the total economy population to get the total number of cities in the economy.

The attainment of the $N(J)$ solution depends on the behavior and nature of land developers. We assume land developers are competitive, each attempting to set up new cities by attracting investment and population and forming new land bank companies. We also assume for now that land developers are fully knowledgeable, the meaning and implication of which will become apparent later. Given these assumptions, we show that the $N(J)$ solution is the only globally stable solution. The proof is in two stages. First we show that *if* cities satisfy equation (3.11) and are sizes $N(J)$, they must be *identical*, or have both the same size $N(J)$ and the same K/N, in order for utility levels and capital rentals to be equalized across cities. We then show that stable city sizes must satisfy equation (3.11) or be sizes $N(J)$. We combine the latter stage of the proof with a demonstration of the dynamics of moving from a nonequilibrium solution to an equilibrium solution.

Suppose cities satisfy equation (3.11) or are of sizes $N(J)$. The question is whether cities in equilibrium could be nonidentical and have different K/N and hence different $N(J)$ but still pay the same factor rewards. The negative answer may be seen as follows. Substituting from equation (3.12) for $N(J)$ into equations (3.7) and (3.8), we find

$$V = C_1(K/N)^{\frac{1}{2}(1-\alpha)(a+b)/(\frac{1}{2}-\varepsilon)}, \qquad p_k = C_2(K/N)^{(\varepsilon-\alpha/2)/(\frac{1}{2}-\varepsilon)}.$$

Therefore, for city sizes $N(J)$, V is a strictly monotonic function of the K/N ratio (given $\varepsilon < \frac{1}{2}$). Hence, any two cities satisfying equation (3.11), such that utility levels are equalized between the cities, must have the same K/N ratio and hence, from equation (3.12), the same size or $N(J)$. The same statements apply to the p_k function (unless $\varepsilon = \alpha/2$). Therefore, if equation (3.11) is satisfied, cities must be identical.

It remains to show that cities must satisfy equation (3.11) and be sizes $N(J)$. Suppose cities are not size $N(J)$ but are some larger size, such as $N(A)$ in Figure 3.2. We start the analysis assuming cities are identical at $N(A)$ with a K/N equal to the national ratio. This is done only for expositional simplicity in describing the process by which we move to equilibrium solutions; we will show that any city with any K/N must satisfy equation (3.11). In the solution at $N(A)$, developers have dissipated profits through competition for factors, so that land rents are fully distributed. At $N(A)$ capital rentals are higher and utility levels lower than at $N(J)$. Suppose a land developer sets up one city of size $N(J)$ where producers borrow at the prevailing high capital rental rate. In this new city producers temporarily operate at a lower K/N ratio than in the rest of the economy, so that they can pay competitive capital rentals given reduced scale efficiencies in production. The effect of the temporarily lower K/N ratio is to shift the p_k path up in this one city and the V path down relative to other cities.

In this new city the land developer will be able to ensure that utility levels are competitive and, unlike developers in other cities, he will be able

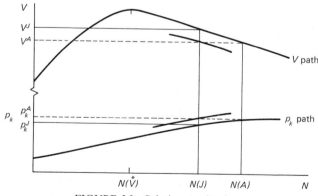

FIGURE 3.2   Solutions to city sizes.

to retain some land rental income as profits. This occurs for two reasons. Given the definition of $N(J)$ in equation (3.11), if the city were to operate with the national K/N ratio (which pertains in cities of size $N(A)$), the sum of factor rewards would be maximized at $N(J)$. At any other size the sum of factor rewards would be less. *Therefore, for the same K/N a city of size $N(J)$ will be able to pay factor rewards at $N(A)$ and have a surplus left over.* (This in itself is sufficient to show that any city with any K/N must satisfy equation (3.11), or else an entrepreneur could set up another city (with the same K/N) satisfying equation (3.11) and could both hire away the factors in the first city and make a profit.) The fact that when moving from $N(A)$ to $N(J)$ producers operate temporarily with a lower K/N only enhances this surplus, since the losing factor, capital, is used relatively less than the gaining factor, labor. (Alternatively viewed, producers operate at the temporarily efficient K/N ratio given the current opportunity cost of capital.)

The developer who manages the land bank company simply takes this surplus out by retaining some land rental income. He pays out sufficient dividends to ensure that, including wages, laborers are getting the same or higher utility levels than in the rest of the economy. The magnitude of this surplus may be illustrated using the example where $K/N = 1$, $\alpha = \frac{3}{4}$, $\varepsilon = \frac{1}{4}$, $a = b = \frac{1}{2}$, and $t = \frac{1}{10}$. If $N(A) = 40{,}000$, then from equations (3.7) and (3.8) initially $p_k = 3.535$ and $V = 1.542$. Suppose an entrepreneur sets up a city of size $N(J) = 31{,}200$ and borrows at the prevailing rate $p_k = 3.535$. For this rate, from equation (3.7), K/N in this one city will be 0.92. For $K/N = 0.92$ and $N = 31{,}200$, the city could offer utility levels from equation (3.8) of $V = 1.558$. If the entrepreneur skims off the surplus, his temporary profits are $31{,}200(1.558 - 1.542)$ utils, which are converted to monetary units by dividing by $\partial V/\partial y = \frac{1}{2}$. This equals \$1070. (If the city operated with the same K/N as nationally, profits would be less (\$845), since capital would be used inefficiently relative to the current price.)

This profit earned by the developer will induce other entrepreneurs to set up cities of smaller sizes, such as $N(J)$.[4] In the national factor markets, given the lower K/N initially associated with a smaller city size and factor prices at $N(A)$, this will reduce [increase] the aggregate demand for capital [labor]. This in turn will bid up utility levels and lower capital rentals relative to those at $N(A)$. In the process the entrepreneur will be forced to pay out more land rental income in order to attract residents. City sizes and factor prices will adjust and new cities will continue to spring up,

---

[4] We have implicitly assumed for expositional purposes that entrepreneurs can limit city sizes to $N(J)$. This is not essential. The setting up of any new city of size less than $N(A)$ will cause all cities to fall in size (as they lose population to the new city). As long as it is profitable to set up a city of size even slightly less than $N(A)$, an entrepreneur will set up a new city. Entrepreneurs will keep setting up new additional cities until all cities are forced to size $N(J)$.

attracting residents and investment as long as old cities are of inefficient sizes, or until equation (3.11) is satisfied and land developers' profits are dissipated through competition for laborers to form cities. A similar argument can be used to show that cities smaller than $N(J)$ are also unstable. In short, with identical cities, any city size other than $N(J)$ is globally unstable.[5]

A problem with the foregoing discussion is that it is not clear that we should be ascribing to entrepreneurs the actions depicted. For new cities to spring up if other cities are of inefficient size, we have assumed that there are entrepreneurs in the economy who have sufficient information on the properties of efficient cities and are willing to gamble that they can design a city that is of more efficient size than existing sizes. Suppose that no one knows about the properties of efficient cities nor is there any certain way of investing explicitly to discover this information. Therefore, there would be no basis for entrepreneurs to set up new, more efficient size cities. Then, to achieve efficient city sizes it would be necessary to specify a model of random entry or random attempts to set up cities. An entrepreneur, essentially by accident, sets up a city of more efficient size and hence attracts residents to that city. In doing so, the entrepreneur makes a temporary profit. Other entrepreneurs will observe this profit and adjust their city sizes accordingly. That is, over time, people will "learn" what more efficient city sizes are. This random-entry argument essentially proposes that any inefficient solution is *unstable* in the long run, since any random entrant would lead to the disintegration of an inefficient market solution.

There are a number of additional points that can be made about the solution. First, it is consistent with the partial equilibrium model in Chapter 2. In a partial equilibrium model, city sizes may be determined by city governments seeking to restrict city size so as to maximize utility levels, given the prevailing return on capital. This behavior on the part of city governments yields city sizes of $N(J)$. The proof of this is as follows.

In a partial equilibrium model, $\bar{p}_k$ is exogenous to the city and the city can only influence local utility levels. If $\bar{p}_k$ is exogenous, from equation (3.7) we may solve for K/N as a function of $\bar{p}_k$ and N. Substituting for K/N into equation (3.6) for wages, we find that $p_n = \alpha(1-\alpha)^{(1-\alpha)/\alpha}\bar{p}_k^{(\alpha-1)/\alpha}N^{\varepsilon/\alpha}$. Therefore, from equation (3.5) indirect utility may now be written as

$$V = A[\alpha(1-\alpha)^{(1-\alpha)/\alpha}\bar{p}_k^{(\alpha-1)/\alpha}N^{\varepsilon/\alpha} - \tfrac{2}{3}tN^{1/2}\pi^{-1/2}]^{a+b}.$$

[5] The question of local instability may be illustrated as follows. Suppose that with all cities at $N(A)$, an entrepreneur sets up one city that is *slightly* smaller. If he makes a profit, other entrepreneurs will set up (slightly) smaller cities and the $N(A)$ solution will be unstable. In general, local instability in the present context means that any movement (not just large movements) toward $N(J)$ from current city sizes yields profits for developers. This is true if the monetized sum of factor rewards declines strictly monotonically as we move away from $N(J)$.

From the point of view of the city government, efficient city size occurs when $\partial V/\partial N = 0$ for p_k fixed, or when

$$\alpha(1 - \alpha)^{(1-\alpha)/\alpha}\overline{p}_k^{(\alpha-1)/\alpha}(\varepsilon/\alpha)N^{\varepsilon/\alpha-\frac{1}{2}} = \tfrac{1}{3}t\pi^{-1/2}. \tag{3.13}$$

However, in equilibrium in national factor markets, where utility levels and capital rentals must be equalized across cities, cities must be identical.[6] This means from equation (3.7) $p_k = (1 - \alpha)(K/N)^{-\alpha}N^{\varepsilon}$ where $\overline{K/N}$ is the national K/N ratio. Substituting this expression for p_k into the optimality condition yields a city size defined by the expression for $N(J)$ in equation (3.12). Hence, the partial equilibrium and general equilibrium approaches are consistent.

Second, in the present context with only one type of city, we will show in the next chapter that $N(J)$ is the Pareto-efficient city size when incomes are determined on the basis of factor ownership and private marginal products. Since $N(J)$ is the point where total real factor rewards are maximized, or where the marginal gains to capital owners from increasing city size just equal the marginal losses to laborers, this is intuitively appealing. However, as we will discover later, for multiple types of cities market solutions may not always be efficient, due to scale externality problems.

These last two points about the general equilibrium solution being consistent with the partial equilibrium solution and Pareto efficiency should sound familiar. It is simply the normal idea of the discipline of the marketplace and the workings of atomistic competition where we are discussing cities instead of firms. The firm/city faces fixed output and input (capital) prices set at the industry/national level. For a firm/city to survive, it maximizes profits/utility levels, competes for its market share of sales/residents, and through competition achieves efficient size. This behavior results in a Pareto-efficient set of input and output prices and welfare levels. The existence of land developers seeking to maximize profits ensures that scale economy benefits of increasing city size versus commuting cost increases are traded off implicitly or explicitly to achieve optimal city size.

Finally, we note that there are dynamic problems in attaining efficient city sizes in a more complicated model of an economy. Given that capital is not particularly malleable (versus our assumption of perfect malleability and mobility) and given that there is continual technological progress in both transportation and industry that alters the efficient sizes of cities, it is

---

[6] This can be shown as follows. In any city $p_k = (1 - \alpha)(K/N)^{-\alpha}N^{\varepsilon}$. We substitute this into the equation for V and differentiate both the p_k and this V equation, allowing N and K/N to vary. N and K/N must vary such that $dV = dp_k = 0$, so factor rewards remain equalized. Given that, it is possible to show there is no nonzero variation in N and K/N that is consistent with equation (3.13) being satisfied. Therefore cities must be identical.

difficult to imagine cities and their capital stock either springing up or dissolving and it is very difficult to conceive that people at any given time have a reasonable idea of what optimal city size is. Thus in a dynamic world the notion of the working of the marketplace to achieve efficient city sizes is one of a long-run tendency, rather than a presumption that cities at any time are of efficient size.

Political Problems. $N(J)$ is not the city size that either capital owners or laborers would want to impose on all cities in the economy. If these groups knew the shape of the paths in Figure 3.2 and income was distributed according to marginal productivity, they would favor national legislation to alter sizes of all cities. Laborers would favor policies that tend to reduce equilibrium city size below $N(J)$. Capital owners would promote national policies that tend to increase equilibrium city size. However, it is not clear that either group could ever have an idea of what these paths look like, nor could they organize to promote their legislation over the opposing legislation of the other group. If both groups behave somewhat atomistically, they generally perceive that both the borrowing rate and the utility level are fixed in national markets by market forces; and they will perceive that they are individually maximizing their own welfare at city size $N(J)$.

However, to the extent that capital owners can and do collude, they could work to promote national policies encouraging the growth of individual city sizes. Moreover, in extreme situations, they could collectively deny investment funds for the development of new cities and encourage the growth of old cities.

1.3 National Constant Returns to Scale

We note that when city sizes approach efficient city size, or $N(J)$ in Figure 3.1, at the national or aggregative level there is a constant returns to scale world. Doubling factor endowments would double the number of cities, leaving utility levels and capital rentals unchanged. This fact will be useful in adapting the model to incorporate growth and international trade.

1.4 Extensions

Capital Owners as Laborers

So far, we have assumed that capital owners are a separate group of people who do not commute to the city center and who live at city edges or in the countryside. Hence, their travel costs and housing expenditures are independent of city size and exogenous to the problem. Suppose instead that capital owners also work as laborers, commute to the city center, and incur urban costs of living. How does this affect our analysis? We assume capital ownership is equally divided among all laborers in the economy. Capital rentals are now spent in cities. However, capital owners, given perfect mobility of capital, do not need to invest in the city where they live. They can invest in any city in the economy.

City sizes are now determined by the location decisions of capital owner–laborers and the investment decisions of these people. In investing, people seek to maximize the nominal return on capital. In locating they seek to maximize utility, given commuting and housing costs and income. The utility level of the capital owner–laborers is determined as follows.

In addition to land rental income, per person income now equals $p_n + p_k(K/N)$ where K/N is the national capital-to-labor ratio and hence the per person ownership of capital. From the marginal productivity conditions of the firm, $p_n + p_k(K/N) = \alpha N^\varepsilon (K/N)^{1-\alpha} + (1 - \alpha)N^\varepsilon (K/N)^{1-\alpha}$ if cities have the same K/N ratio as the national ratio. Therefore, from equation (3.5) the utility of a representative person is

$$V = A[N^\varepsilon (K/N)^{1-\alpha} - \tfrac{2}{3}tN^{1/2}\pi^{-1/2}]^{a+b}. \qquad (3.14)$$

In Figure 3.3 we plot V as a function of N under parametric restrictions that yield the curve pictured. We also plot the p_k path.

Equilibrium city size now occurs at $N(\overset{*}{V})$ when the utility path is maximized. If we maximize V in equation (3.14) with respect to N, $N(\overset{*}{V})$ is given by the expression for $N(J)$ in equation (3.12). This implies that market city size is the same in this model whether capital rentals are spent in cities by laborers or they go to capital owners. This result only occurs because lot size is fixed. In models where lot size is endogenous, city size is smaller if capital rentals are spent in cities. If income per person goes up in cities, more

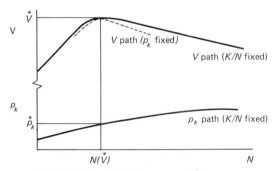

FIGURE 3.3   Capital owners as laborers.

housing and land will be demanded. More land demanded implies for the same population an increase in the spatial area of the city and hence in commuting costs. That is, for any given city size and scale economies, the marginal and total commuting costs rise if capital rentals are spent in cities. Hence, city sizes should be smaller.

To show that $N(\overset{*}{V})$ is the equilibrium city size we could repeat the stability arguments given earlier and show that developers maximize profits by moving city size to $N(\overset{*}{V})$. If one city size increases beyond $N(\overset{*}{V})$ in Figure 3.3, even though it can pay higher capital rentals to its own or other residents, the utility level it can offer residents declines, so that no one would want to live in that city. That is, at $N(\overset{*}{V})$ only, real factor income from all sources is maximized. We can also show that $N(\overset{*}{V})$ is consistent with partial equilibrium city size determination. The argument is as follows. City governments seek to maximize V in equation (3.4) where they view the borrowing rate on capital and capital income of city residents ($p_k K/N$) as fixed. Maximizing the perceived utility of city residents and setting $\partial V/\partial N = 0$ yields equation (3.13). Incorporating the constraint of a cleared national capital market by substituting $p_k = (1 - \alpha)N^\varepsilon(K/N)^{-\alpha}$ into equation (3.13), as we did earlier, we find that partial equilibrium city size turns out to be $N(\overset{*}{V})$.

Note that because the capital rental path rises beyond $N(\overset{*}{V})$, it is possible that laborers in their role as capital owners will lobby with the federal government for larger city sizes to raise their capital income. If cities other than the one in which an individual capital owner lives increase in size and the owner rents capital in these cities, his income rises and he is better off. Each capital owner thus has an incentive to increase other people's city sizes. If capital owners collectively succeed in increasing city size, then all capital owners/laborers will be worse off.[7]

City Size with Lumpiness

In the preceding sections we ignored the lumpiness problem by assuming that there were a sufficiently large number of cities to make the problem negligible. When lumpiness exists, cities in general will not be size $N(J)$. To limit the possible solutions, we are going to impose restrictions on city sizes through stability requirements. Throughout this section it is assumed that capital owners are a separate group of people who do not work as laborers.

In general, it is possible to show that when there are two or more cities, no city size can be less than that size where the utility path has a maximum.

---

[7] In Henderson (1974a) this was suggested to be the only market solution.

That is, all city sizes must lie at $N(V)$ or beyond. Smaller city sizes can be shown to be unstable.[8] This restriction is imposed on solutions below.

We demonstrate lumpiness solutions as follows. Suppose the economy is growing with a fixed K/N ratio. There is currently only one city in the economy, with utility and capital rental paths as pictured in Figure 3.5. As this city grows past size $N(J)$, at some point a second city will form when the losses to laborers from there being only one city just equal or start to exceed the gains to capital owners or when

$$N \frac{\Delta V/\Delta N}{\partial V/\partial y} + K \frac{\Delta p_K}{\Delta N} \geq 0 \qquad (3.15)$$

where Δ indicates a discrete change. Alternatively stated, the sum of the

---

[8] We assume that the shape of utility and capital rental paths are as in Figure 3.4. Cities of size less than $N(\overset{*}{V})$, when there is *more than one* city, are unstable. Suppose there are two cities of size $N(m)$. A random movement of a few units of capital and labor (say, maintaining the existing K/N ratio in each city) from one city to another would raise [lower] V and p_k in the gaining [losing] city. This would induce further factors movements between cities and hence the original solution is unstable. Alternatively, suppose a city were of size $N(m)$ and other cities of size $N(n)$ where the corresponding differences in utility and capital rental paths ensure equalization of both utility and capital rentals between cities. $V(m)$ shifts down and $p_k(m)$ shifts up relative to $V(n)$ and $p_k(n)$ through the m city having a lower K/N ratio relative to other cities. A random movement of a unit of capital and labor to the $N(m)$ city would raise utility and capital rents there relative to other cities and would result in further movements of factors to that city. Size $N(m)$ is unstable.

The only possible exception is if there are only a few cities, one of size $N(m)$ and perhaps only one of size $N(n)$. Then when there is a random factor movement to the smaller city, there is an appreciable effect on factor rewards in the larger city(s). With many cities this effect is dissipated among so many cities as to be negligible. For $N(m)$ to be unstable with only one city of size $N(n)$, the rising part of the V path may need to be steeper than the declining part of this path, so if factors move to $N(m)$, factor rewards rise faster there than they do in the losing $N(n)$ city.

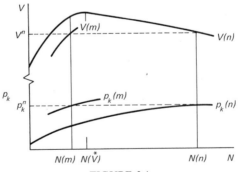

FIGURE 3.4

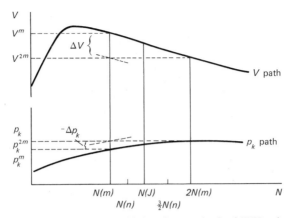

FIGURE 3.5   City size with lumpiness and a fixed K/N ratio.

monetary value of utility levels and capital rentals is increased by two cities forming. Such a point could be at $2N(m)$, where the city splits into two cities, each of size $N(m)$ (providing $N(m) \geq N(\overset{*}{V})$ for stability). As these two cities grow, when they each reach some point, such as $(3/2)N(n)$, a third city forms and all cities are size $N(n)$. As the economy grows, city size oscillates around $N(J)$ until at the limit the number of cities approaches infinity and city size approaches and remains at $N(J)$ with further growth (when a new city forms, each existing city's loss or contribution of factors becomes negligible). This is the no-lumpiness case discussed extensively earlier.

Achievement of these city sizes follows from the behavior and nature of land developers. Once equation (3.15) is satisfied, a developer can always attract residents and investment to a new city, since the total monetary value of utility plus capital rental levels has risen. For example, when there is just one city larger than size $2N(m)$, in a potential new city of size $N(m)$ an entrepreneur can match utility and capital rental levels in the initial city with some profit left over. By paying current market factor rewards he will temporarily operate with a lower K/N ratio than nationally (hence, the dashed shifts in the V and p_k paths). This will result in a reduced national demand for capital relative to labor and downward pressure in the existing city (whose K/N ratio is also being forced up) on capital rentals relative to utility levels. The result is that as the new city forms and the old city shrinks and we approach the new equilibrium city sizes $N(m)$, capital rentals [utility levels] will fall [rise] by discrete amounts, as pictured in Figure 3.5.

There are potential problems in achieving this solution. First, to set up a new city of size $N(m)$ requires starting or at least planning to start the city at this size, not anything smaller, or else the city will not be able to pay competitive factor rewards, given equation (3.15). For this to happen, the entrepreneur must recognize the problem as it is pictured in Figure 3.5, understanding what factor reward payments can be paid out at different city sizes. That is a major information requirement for an entrepreneur, where he must know the *nature* and *extent* of scale economies and commuting costs at different city sizes and their impact on both utility levels and capital rentals.

Second, if cities can limit entry, once the initial city reaches size $N(J)$, it will exclude all new people, forcing a second city of small inefficient size to form.[9] Our stability requirements rule this out, but given effective means of restricting city size, it is a possible solution. In particular, in a partial equilibrium model, a city government once city size reaches $N(J)$ could restrict further growth and force new people to form a small separate city. In this case there is a conflict between the partial equilibrium and general equilibrium solutions to city size. (However, the excluded people could bribe the initial city to admit them, with the newer people hence being paid less than the original residents.)

2. MULTIPLE TYPES OF CITIES

So far, we have discussed city size when there is only one type of city. Our results generalize directly to a situation in which there are two or more types of cities. Each type of city specializes in the production of a different traded good or bundle of goods. Specialization occurs if there are no production benefits or positive externalities from locating two different industries in the same place. If they are located together, because workers in both industries are living and commuting in the same city, this raises the spatial area of the city and average commuting costs for a given degree of scale economy exploitation in any one industry. Separating the industries into different cities allows for greater scale economy exploitation in each industry relative to a given level of commuting costs and city spatial area. The extent of specialization is limited by the costs of trade between different types of cities and production interrelations between industries. Industries that use each other's inputs, a common labor force, or a common public good or intermediate input, such as a transportation system, will tend to locate together.

Characterizing equilibrium in the economy when there are several types of cities is fairly straightforward, particularly if there are large numbers of

---

[9] Note that if the sum of the weighted (by K/N) capital rental path plus the monetized value of the utility path is convex over some range before or after its maximum value at $N(J)$, sometimes it may be most efficient to have nonidentical size cities when, because of lumpiness, all cities cannot be size $N(J)$. That is, relative to identical cities, having nonidentical cities with transfer payments among cities to equalize factor rewards may sometimes yield higher factor rewards.

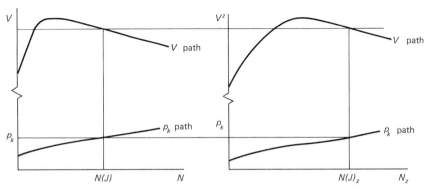

FIGURE 3.6 Multiple types of cities.

cities of each type. The size and number of each type of city are determined by the degree of scale economies in the production of that city's traded good, by the demand for the city's output as determined in national and/or international markets, and by the factor intensity of that good relative to the factor endowments of the economy. An equilibrium for two types of cities is pictured in Figure 3.6. City x produces x as a traded good and city z produces z for trade.

The figure indicates equilibrium size for a representative city of each type, where city sizes differ because type z cities have greater scale economies and hence reach a larger size before commuting cost effects overtake scale economy benefits. Given possible city sizes, the numbers of each type of city are determined by the relative demand for its product and the economy's size or total endowments. Utility levels and capital rentals are equalized between cities for factor market equilibrium. Equalization of utility levels implies that wages will vary between cities of different sizes, being higher in larger cities to offset increased commuting and housing rental costs. This equilization occurs through the K/N ratio for each type of city adjusting, consistent with the total numbers and employment of each type of city and the economy endowment of K and N. An increase in K/N shifts the V path up by increasing the marginal product of labor and shifts the p_k path down. Equalization of factor rewards can also be facilitated by relative traded good prices adjusting in national retail markets as the size, number, and production of each type of city changes.

Equilibrium city size is determined the same way as before. In each city, equilibrium city size satisfies the criterion that

$$N \frac{\Delta V/\Delta N}{\partial V/\partial y} + K \frac{\Delta p_k}{\Delta N} = 0.$$

The N and K refer to national endowments of these factors and the $\Delta V/\Delta N$ and $\Delta p_k/\Delta N$ refer to the changes in the type of city being considered. However, since V and p_k are equalized nationally, they must change or adjust throughout the economy in all cities. Again, stability arguments can be used to show that this solution is achieved. The solution is also consistent with partial equilibrium solutions.

An Example

The model of a system of two types of cities is fairly easy to outline. There are x cities and z cities where the production functions are, respectively, $x = n^\alpha k^{1-\alpha} N^\varepsilon$ and $z = n^\beta k^{1-\beta} N_z^{\varepsilon z}$. From marginal productivity conditions, wages and capital rentals in the z cities are $p_n = p_z \beta (K/N)_z^{1-\beta} N_z^{\varepsilon z}$ and $p_k = p_z(1-\beta)(K/N)_z^{-\beta} N_z^{\varepsilon z}$ where N_z is employment in z cities and p_z is the price of z in units of the normalized good x. In both cities consumers maximize the utility function $V = x^a z^b l^c$ where l is fixed at 1. The model can be solved by utilizing market equilibrium conditions.

First, given the demand equations associated with logarithmic linear utility functions, we know a fixed proportion of income is spent on each market good. Therefore, with output market equilibrium

$$bX = ap_z Z \tag{3.16}$$

where X and Z are total economy demands for these goods. Demand equals supply in national markets. The supplies of X and Z are given by their production functions and the resources devoted to these goods. Therefore,

$$X = mN^{\alpha+\varepsilon}K^{1-\alpha}, \tag{3.17}$$
$$Z = qN_z^{\beta+\varepsilon z}K_z^{1-\beta}, \tag{3.18}$$

where m and q are, respectively, the number of x- and z-type cities.

Input market equilibrium requires that utility levels be equalized between cities; or from equation (3.1) $y - tu - p_l(u)$ is equalized. Given expressions for wages, rental income, and commuting costs, for people at the city edges from equation (3.8) this equality reduces to

$$\alpha(K/N)^{1-\alpha}N^\varepsilon - \tfrac{2}{3}t\pi^{-1/2}N^{1/2} = p_z\beta(K/N)_z^{1-\beta}N_z^{\varepsilon z} - \tfrac{2}{3}t\pi^{-1/2}N_z^{1/2}. \tag{3.19}$$

Capital rentals must be equalized between cities, or

$$(1-\alpha)(K/N)^{-\alpha}N^\varepsilon = (1-\beta)(K/N)_z^{-\beta}N_z^{\varepsilon z}. \tag{3.20}$$

Finally, there must be full employment in the economy or

$$mN + qN_z = \bar{N}, \tag{3.21}$$
$$mK + qK_z = \bar{K}. \tag{3.22}$$

So far we have equations (3.16)–(3.22) or seven equations in nine unknowns or p_z, N, K, X, Z, m, q, N_z, and K_z. The final two equations are ones determining city size. If m and q are large such that the lumpiness problem disappears, we may simply use the two equilibrium equations defining city size given optimal entrepreneurial/government behavior. From equation (3.12) these are

$$N_z = (3\varepsilon_z \pi^{1/2} t^{-1} (K/N)_z^{1-\beta})^{1/(\frac{1}{2}-\varepsilon_z)}, \tag{3.23}$$

$$N = (3\varepsilon \pi^{1/2} t^{-1} (K/N)^{1-\alpha})^{1/(\frac{1}{2}-\varepsilon)} \tag{3.24}$$

3.   EXTENSIONS OF THE MODEL

3.1   International Trade and Growth

In the case where the numbers of each type of city are very large, as stated in Section 1.3, there is a constant returns to scale situation at the national level. In that case variants of the basic trade and growth theorems are directly applicable.

Trade.   Let us examine the Rybczynski and Stolper–Samuelson trade theorems. From the Rybczynski theorem, for an economy facing fixed prices set in international markets for its two manufactured and traded goods, an increase in the endowment of N will lead to an increase [decrease] in the production of the N- [K-] intensive good, say x [z], in that economy with unchanged factor proportions in either industry. In a system of cities these results are effected by an increase in x-type cities and a decrease in z-type cities with no resulting changes in K/N ratios for different cities, in utility levels, in wages in different types of cities, or in capital rentals.

Similarly, if we compared two countries, both producing the same goods with many cities of each type and trading these goods with no transport costs, we would expect cities of each type to be the same size between countries and to pay the same wages, utility levels, and capital rentals. The only additional constraint on this version of the Stolper–Samuelson theorem is that the countries must have the same commuting and intraurban transport cost technology, and people in the two countries must have identical preferences, at least for the nontraded good, space.

Growth.   In terms of growth theory, the basic theorems apply directly. In a steady-state equilibrium, capital and labor will grow at the same rate, to maintain the same laborer utility levels, the same return on capital, the same ratios of types of goods, and hence the same ratios of numbers of cities of each type. Clearly, to develop growth theorems from scratch incorporating the spatial dimensions of cities would be a very difficult task. However, if we specify the basic growth model, assuming constant returns to scale at the national level and subsuming the spatial characteristics of cities, then the properties of simple growth models will follow directly.

3.2   Natural Resources

The introduction of natural resources into the model opens up the situation to all the basic location theory results. Without natural resources, cities would presumably locate on the seacoast so as to trade internationally. With natural resources, we need mobile resources engaged in inland extraction and cities to carry out weight-reducing processing. We also need footloose industries or cities to produce services and retail goods to trade with the heavy-industry inland cities. These cities could just locate on the seacoast but they may also locate inland to avoid transport costs of trade with inland cities. Note that the term city refers here to a production center that has its own residential area and that is both residentially and commercially independent of adjoining cities (in particular, there is little cross commuting with adjoining cities). For example, the greater metropolitan area of Chicago may contain several "cities" or urban areas.

Natural resources in terms of fertile agricultural land necessitate the consideration of market areas of cities within which trade with agricultural producers occurs; it raises the possibility of city hierarchies (Beckmann, 1968). In incorporating an analysis of market areas into our model, we would start by making the price of city output an endogenous and decreasing function of the level of output traded (hence market area). The other comment of interest is that given competitive industries, in our model, any monopoly or monopolistic rents accruing from beneficial market area sizes would be reflected in higher wages and land rents through firms bidding for factors.

4

The Efficient Allocation of
Resources in a System of Cities

In this chapter, we examine the Pareto-efficient allocation of resources among and within cities in an economy, as solved for by an omniscient social planner. We then interpret the planner's solutions in a market economy and determine whether market solutions, such as presented in the previous chapter, correspond to the planner's solutions. Given the nature of the questions asked in this chapter, we can revert to the general functional form model used in Chapter 1 and derive results for a general monocentric model of a city.

In specifying the model we continue to assume that urban agglomeration occurs because of external economies of scale in production. Given the specification of these scale externalities, when a person migrates, he affects the level of scale efficiencies and the productivity of other factors in the cities he leaves and enters. In making his location decisions he does not account for these external effects; and, therefore, under certain conditions he may make socially inefficient location decisions.

We also consider the possibility of agglomeration occurring because of scale economies in consumption. For example, people may agglomerate in cities for the purpose of exploiting the publicness of pure public goods. By definition, the addition of another person in the city does not affect other people's consumption benefits from a given level of government expenditures on pure public goods. However, an additional person does reduce everyone else's tax cost, since there is now an additional person to share in taxes. For example, if the cost of a unit of public goods is $1 and tax shares are equal, the per person tax price of a unit of public goods is $1/N$, where N is city population. As population grows, the per person unit tax price declines, a benefit to all residents from adding population. This phenomenon is sometimes called a fiscal externality, since people do not account for the positive or negative effect they have on other people's tax costs in the cities they enter or leave. This may lead to situations where people's location decisions may not always be socially optimal.

The arguments in this chapter define important relationships, particularly those between land rents and the degree of scale economies, that must hold when cities are Pareto efficient in size. Second, in comparing market city sizes with Pareto-efficient city sizes, the analysis provides an efficiency basis for federal intervention into the affairs of cities or local governments. The arguments in this chapter for efficient federal intervention are based on the work of Flatters, Henderson, and Mieszkowski (1974), who develop their results in a regional Ricardian model rather than an urban model. Mirrlees (1972) has also worked on a similar problem. It is important to note that intervention on efficiency grounds should be distinguished from intervention based on equity considerations in a model with imperfect mobility of labor, where the federal government may want to transfer income from richer to poorer cities and regions. This type of intervention is discussed in Chapter 9.

To obtain criteria for the efficient allocation of resources in an economy, the usual welfare maximization problem facing a social planner is to maximize the utility of a representative individual subject to production and resource constraints, holding the utility level of all other individuals constant. We place two other additional constraints on the social planner, both of which are designed to make planning solutions directly comparable to market solutions. In general, these constraints are not binding and do not restrict us to second-best solutions. However, since they identify the only solutions we wish to consider, they always explicitly appear in the model.

First, people with the same utility functions and opportunity sets must have equal utility levels. This constraint ensures that planning solutions are consistent with stable-market solutions where with nondiscriminatory government intervention,[1] identical perfectly mobile people must achieve identical utility levels, given their respective spatial locations in a city or economy (see Chapters 1 and 3).

---

[1] Government intervention does not discriminate in outcomes among individuals in a group, although it may discriminate within certain limits among groups of individuals (e.g., progressive taxation). If factor supplies and effort are fixed, then most planning solutions can be realized in a market economy through taxation alone, *given* the equal utility constraint.

The second constraint imposed on the social planner is that cities that face identical production and consumption conditions and technology must be identical in size and other characteristics. In Chapter 3 we showed that stable-market solutions must generally adhere to this condition. Therefore, we impose it on planning solutions to make these solutions comparable to stable-market solutions.

In maximizing utilities, the planner is concerned with the welfare of two basic groups of people in the model, laborers and capital owners. For most of this chapter we assume that laborers are identical in skills, tastes, and factor ownership, so that they all achieve the same utility level. Given two differing groups of people, by definition, a planner's Pareto-efficient solution is one that either maximizes the utility of laborers while holding the welfare of capital owners fixed or maximizes the welfare of capital owners while holding the utility of laborers fixed.

In the planning solution, the utility of laborers is a function of their consumption of produced goods and urban amenities such as commuting time and hence leisure. On the other hand, capital owners need not live in the cities where their capital is employed. We assume capital owners live either in the countryside outside cities or on the edges of cities, where in both cases they rent land at the (usually zero) price in agriculture and incur no commuting costs. Therefore, the amenity consumption of capital owners is exogenous to the problem. For the planner the only variable affecting the welfare of capital owners is their consumption of market goods. Therefore, the planner's problem is to maximize the utility of laborers either for a fixed total consumption of capital owners or, equivalently, for a fixed real return per unit of capital (given a fixed capital stock).

We first present a solution for the situation where there is only one type of city in the economy and sufficient cities of that type so we may effectively ignore the lumpiness problem mentioned in Chapter 3. In this situation, the size that is individually efficient for one city will be efficient for all cities, given that all cities will be identical. We then turn to the more interesting case in which there are multiple types of cities and some lumpiness in the solutions.

1. ONE TYPE OF CITY

With only one type of city and no lumpiness problems, the planner's allocation problem is simple. Given that cities have identical production and consumption technology, they will all attain the same size and have the same characteristics. In particular, their capital-to-labor ratio K/N will equal the national ratio. Therefore, the only question is what is the optimal size of any representative city and hence of every city. The planner's problem can be formulated as follows.

As in Chapter 1, a consumer at distance u from the city center consumes the city's produced good $x(u)$, its import good $z(u)$, housing $h(u)$, and leisure $e(u) = T - tu$ where t is unit distance commuting time. The utility function of a resident at location u is $V = V(x(u), z(u), h(u), e(u))$. N is city population, and u_0 and u_1 are CBD and city radii. Therefore, for any city, the planner seeks to maximize the utility V^0 of a representative individual subject to constraints, or to

$$\max J = V^0(x(u), z(u), h(u), e(u)) \tag{4.1}$$

$$+ \int_{u_0}^{u_1} \lambda_1(u)(V(x(u), z(u), h(u), e(u)) - V^0)\, du \tag{4.1.1}$$

$$+ \lambda_2\left(N - \int_{u_0}^{u_1} N(u)\, du\right) \tag{4.1.2}$$

$$+ \lambda_3\left(N - \int_0^{u_0} n(u)\, du\right) \tag{4.1.3}$$

$$+ \lambda_4\left(K - \int_{u_0}^{u_1} k(u)N(u)\, du - \int_0^{u_0} k(u)\, du\right) \tag{4.1.4}$$

$$+ \int_{u_0}^{u_1} \lambda_5(u)(2\pi u - l(u)N(u))\, du \tag{4.1.5}$$

$$+ \int_0^{u_0} \lambda_6(u)(2\pi u - l(u))\, du \tag{4.1.6}$$

$$+ \int_{u_0}^{u_1} \lambda_7(u)(T - e(u) - tu)\, du \tag{4.1.7}$$

$$+ \int_{u_0}^{u_1} \lambda_8(u)(h(l(u), k(u)) - h(u))\, du \tag{4.1.8}$$

$$+ \lambda_9(\bar{C} - K/N) \tag{4.1.9}$$

$$+ \lambda_{10}\left(\int_0^{u_0} G(N)x(n(u), k(u), l(u))(1 - t_x u)\, du - \int_{u_0}^{u_1} x(u)N(u)\, du\right.$$

$$\left. - \int_{u_0}^{u_1} p_z z(u)N(u)\, du - p_k K\right). \tag{4.1.10}$$

The λ_i and $\lambda_i(u)$ are multipliers. Constraint (4.1.1) is the equal utility constraint for laborers who are the city residents. Where $N(u)$ and $n(u)$ are, respectively, population and employment at location u, constraints (4.1.2) and (4.1.3) state that city population equals the sum of all people living in the city and city population equals labor employment, or labor is fully employed in the city. Constraint (4.1.4) is a full employment of capital constraint where the sum of capital used in residential construction plus the sum of business capital equals the city's stock of capital. Constraints (4.1.5) and (4.1.6) state that land supplied ($2\pi u$) equals land used for residential or commercial purposes at each distance from the city center. Leisure and housing production at each distance are defined in (4.1.7) and (4.1.8). Constraint (4.1.9) requires that all cities face a fixed capital-to-labor ratio equal to the national ratio, or that there be full employment in the economy.

The final constraint is a production–consumption, or balance of trade, constraint, faced by the planner at the national and hence local level. The first term in (4.1.10) from equation (1.26) is total production in the city available (after paying transport costs) for distribution at the retailing–transport node at the city center. Where $x(u)$ is per person consumption at u, the second term is total city consumption of x, or per person consumption summed over all people and locations. The third term is the cost to the planner in units of x of importing z from other economies (or other cities, later in the chapter). The final term is the city's production of x allocated to capital owners. This is the number of units of capital multiplied by the fixed return p_k in units of x allocated by the planner to capital owners per unit of their capital stock. Note that it is assumed the city pays nothing for the land it is located on, or agricultural land rents are zero.

Problem (4.1) and the constraints (4.1.1)–(4.1.10) define the welfare maximization problem. If we maximize the Lagrangian with respect to the different variables, we get a set of first-order conditions that mostly relate to resource allocation within the city. They are the standard ones, namely, that the marginal products of mobile factors should be equalized in all uses within the city, that marginal rates of substitution in consumption should equal ratios of marginal costs or the marginal rates of transformation, and that the marginal products of land at the border of competing uses such as the CBD should be equalized. Since these conditions are standard, we do not present them specifically in the text.[2] Moreover, since we do not introduce any externalities into the internal structure of the city until the next chapter, market solutions discussed here will be consistent with efficient internal resource allocation. The basic concern in this chapter is with the allocation of resources among cities.

[2] Relevant first-order conditions are

$$\partial J/\partial K = \lambda_4 - \lambda_9/N - \lambda_{10}p_k = 0,$$
$$\partial J/\partial n(u) = -\lambda_3 + \lambda_{10}G(\partial x/\partial n)(1 - t_x u) = 0,$$
$$\partial J/\partial N(u) = -\lambda_2 - \lambda_4 k(u) - \lambda_5 l(u) - \lambda_{10}x(u) - \lambda_{10}p_z z(u) = 0,$$
$$\partial J/\partial k(u) = -\lambda_4 N(u) + \lambda_8(\partial h/\partial k) = -\lambda_4 + \lambda_{10}G(N)(\partial x/\partial k)(1 - t_x u) = 0,$$
$$\partial J/\partial l(u) = -\lambda_5 N(u) + \lambda_8(\partial h/\partial l) = -\lambda_6 + \lambda_{10}G(\partial x/\partial l)(1 - t_x u) = 0,$$
$$\partial J/\partial x(u) = \lambda_1(u)(\partial V/\partial x) - \lambda_{10}N(u) = 0,$$
$$\partial J/\partial h(u) = \lambda_1(u)(\partial V/\partial h) - \lambda_8 = 0,$$
$$\partial J/\partial z(u) = \lambda_1(u)(\partial V/\partial z) - \lambda_{10}p_z N(u) = 0.$$

To solve for Pareto-efficient city size, we maximize the Lagrangian in (4.1) with respect to N to get a first-order condition

$$\frac{\partial x}{\partial N} = \lambda_2 + \lambda_3 + \lambda_9\left(\frac{K}{N^2}\right) + \lambda_{10} \int_0^{u_0} \left(\frac{dG}{dN}\right) x(u)(1 - t_x u)\, du = 0. \quad (4.2)$$

To solve for λ_9 we maximize J with respect to K and then $k(u)$ and perform appropriate substitutions. To solve for λ_3 we maximize J with respect to $n(u)$. Finally, to solve for λ_2 we first maximize J with respect to $N(u)$ and then $k(u)$, $l(u)$, $h(u)$, and $x(u)$ to perform further necessary substitutions. All these first-order conditions used in substitution are listed in footnote 2. The result is

$$\frac{\partial V/\partial h}{\partial V/\partial x} h(u) + p_z z(u) + x(u)$$

$$= G(N)\frac{\partial x}{\partial n}(1 - t_x u) + \frac{\varepsilon X}{N} + \frac{K}{N}\left(G\frac{\partial x}{\partial k}(1 - t_x u) - p_k\right). \quad (4.3)$$

In writing equation (4.3) it is assumed that housing is produced with a linear homogeneous production function, so that $h = k\,\partial h/\partial k + l\,\partial h/\partial l$. ε is defined to be $(dG/dN)(N/G)$, which is the elasticity of scale effects with respect to the labor force. X is total net city output of x and it equals

$$\int_0^{u_0} G(N)x(u)(1 - t_x u)\, du.$$

The left-hand side of equation (4.3) is the social costs to the economy of adding an additional resident to the city. This is the value of the additional consumption of x, z, and h (in units of x) that a new resident takes from the total available, such that all residents have equal utility. Note that amenities or commuting costs borne by this resident are not a direct cost to the social planner, although any differential amenity or leisure loss borne by the resident must be compensated with produced goods to maintain equal utility with other residents.

The right-hand side of (4.3) is the social benefit to the planner of adding an additional resident to the city. The first term is the private marginal product of n. The second is the scale externality or the effect of an additional member of the labor force on efficiency as measured by increased output of all firms. Therefore, the first two terms are the social marginal product (SMP) of labor to city x. The third term is the net benefit to the city that results from employing the additional capital that comes along with the additional resident so as to maintain the fixed capital-to-labor ratio in the economy. (The net benefit (loss) to laborers from additional capital is proportional to the difference between the additional contribution to production of a unit of capital $(G(N)(\partial x/\partial k)(1 - t_x u))$ and unit payment for capital

(p_k). This difference is multiplied by the additional quantity of capital matching the new resident, or K/N, to get the full net benefit from this additional capital.)

Equation (4.3) states that optimum city size occurs when the marginal social benefits to city residents of increasing city size equal the marginal social costs given fixed consumption of capital owners.[3] The question is whether this condition is satisfied in a market economy. To find that out, we must first interpret equation (4.3) in a market context.

The Market Interpretation of One Pareto-Efficient Solution

The Pareto-efficient solution we examine in a market context is the one for a competitive economy where factors are paid the value of their marginal product by profit-maximizing firms and land rental income in a city is divided up equally among laborers by a city land bank company. In that case, since capital is paid the value of its marginal product, $p_k = G(N)(\partial x/\partial k)(1 - t_x u)$; and the capital effect term equals zero in equation (4.3).

In a market economy, as suggested earlier, given consumer and producer optimization behavior and perfect competition, the first-order conditions in footnote 2 with respect to consumption of x, z, and h and employment of k, n, and l will be met. Of relevance here are the marginal rate of substitution and marginal productivity conditions, which state that $(\partial V/\partial h)/(\partial V/\partial x) = p(u)$ where $p(u)$ is the unit price of housing in terms of x and that the wage rate $p_n = G(N)(\partial x/\partial n)(1 - t_x u)$. Substituting these conditions into equation (4.3), we get

$$p(u) + p_z z(u) + x(u) = p_n + \varepsilon X/N. \tag{4.4}$$

The left-hand side of (4.4) is the expenditures of a resident. This equals his income in a market economy where income is composed of wages plus a land rental share that equals average land rental income. Therefore, equation (4.4) reduces to

$$\text{land rent share} = \varepsilon X/N. \tag{4.5}$$

This equation defines a general relationship which must hold in a market economy, when any individual city is of efficient size. This condition has a simple intuitive explanation.

---

[3] Note that if there is more than one type of labor in the economy, this condition becomes more complicated. Cities still remain identical, and thus the ratios of the first type of labor to both capital and the second type of labor must remain fixed. If we add the necessary consumption, production, resource, and spatial constraints for this second type of laborer, and maximize J with respect to the first type of labor, equation (4.3) has a new term on its right-hand side. This term adds on the difference between the social marginal product of a second type of laborer and the consumption of that person, multiplied by the increase in type-two labor as type-one labor increases. Essentially, to the benefits of having an additional type-one laborer we add the net costs/benefits of the matching increase in type-two labor.

The benefit of an additional resident to other residents in the city is the increase in production available to them caused by increased production efficiency, or $\varepsilon X/N$. The cost to initial residents in the city is the additional land rent share (or share in old production not paid out in wages and capital costs) that must now be allocated to the new resident. Optimal city size occurs when the increases in new production to residents, $\varepsilon X/N$, equal the losses in old production, or an additional land rent share. Since per person land rents in a market economy start at a nominal level and then rise with city size (see Chapters 1 and 2) and marginal scale economies are positive and perhaps declining, initial net marginal benefits of additional residents are positive. These net marginal benefits then may start to decline as land rents rise and marginal scale economies decline. Optimal city size is reached when net marginal benefits decline to zero.[4]

Are Market Solutions Pareto-Efficient?

Under the assumption of only one type of city, equation (4.5) is generally satisfied in market solutions, indicating that market solutions are Pareto-efficient. For example, in the model in Chapter 3, which is a special case of the current model, average rental income from equation (3.4) is $\frac{1}{3}tN^{1/2}\pi^{-1/2}$. From the production function $\varepsilon X/N = \varepsilon(K/N)^{1-\alpha}N^{\varepsilon}$. Equating these terms to obtain the optimal city size criterion in equation (4.5) yields the result that for a Pareto-efficient city,

$$N = (3\varepsilon\pi^{1/2}t^{-1})^{1/(\frac{1}{2}-\varepsilon)}(K/N)^{(1-\alpha)/(\frac{1}{2}-\varepsilon)}.$$

From equation (3.12), this is identical to the condition defining $N(J)$, the market city size in Chapter 3.

This equivalency makes sense for two reasons. First, the statement of the planner's problem, which is to maximize laborers' utility for a given return to capital, is consistent with the way in which market solutions were defined in Chapters 2 and 3. In a partial equilibrium model, city governments limit city size so as to maximize laborers' utility given a fixed borrowing rate on capital.[5] In a general equilibrium model, equilibrium city size occurs

---

[4] Of course, there is no certainty that equation (4.5) is satisfied at a unique city size or even that it is satisfied at all. Given different assumptions about how marginal scale economies change with city size, optimal city size could be infinite or infinitesimal or there could be a number of local optima where equation (4.5) is satisfied.

[5] Equation (4.5) and the condition for efficient partial equilibrium city size are simply different ways of defining equivalent changes in real income. In a partial equilibrium model, we examine the changing utility level of a representative person at the expanding city edge, with an infinitesimal change in city population. We can show that the utility change in monetary terms equals his change in income minus the value of his increased leisure losses as the city edge shifts out. To maintain spatial equilibrium all peoples' rent payments throughout the city

when the sum of total capital rental income and monetized utility levels is maximized. This sum can only be maximized when, while holding one element constant, the other is maximized. Accordingly, under the current assumptions, the market determination of city size and the planning solution are simply different ways of stating and approaching the same maximization problem.

The equivalency also makes sense from an externality perspective. Laborers in a market economy move to equalize the private marginal benefits of moving among cities. From a social perspective, they should incorporate into their calculus any external effects from their location decisions and move to equalize the social marginal benefits of moving among cities. However, if all cities are identical, the magnitude of these external effects will be equal between all cities; and when laborers move to equalize private marginal benefits they will incidentally equalize social marginal benefits. Therefore, the fact that laborers do not account for migration externalities does not adversely affect the allocation of resources in this simple situation.

Public Goods

So far, we have assumed that external economies of scale are the basis for agglomeration. Suppose we assume instead that the basis is the existence of local pure public goods.

The planner's problem in solving for optimal city size is easily revised to incorporate public goods. We assume the city is still monocentric and people still commute to work in the CBD. The level of public services g enters each utility function and the cost of public goods in units of x enters the consumption–production constraint (4.1.10). We assume that the cost of g in units of x is 1. Resolving the maximization problem assuming there are no longer (marginal) economies of scale yields two important results. First, there is the Samuelson condition on public good consumption, or

$$\int_{u_0}^{u_1} N(u) \frac{\partial V/\partial g}{\partial V/\partial x(u)} \, du = 1.$$

---

must increase by an amount equal to the value of the additional lost leisure of the representative individual. So, the monetized utility change of this person equals his income change minus the increase in per person rent payments in the city. His income change equals the per person increase in production due to increased scale economies minus the per person reduction in share of initial land rents (due to additional sharers) plus the increase in per person land rental income (due to the general increase in land rents). This last term cancels out with the representative person's value of increased lost leisure in the monetized utility change calculation. If we multiply the resulting utility change expression by N and set it equal to zero, the result is equation (4.5)

Second, the new condition on optimal population is[6]

$$\frac{\partial V/\partial h}{\partial V/\partial x} h(u) + p_z z(u) + x(u) = \frac{\partial x}{\partial n}(1 - t_x u). \qquad (4.6)$$

The marginal benefit of adding a new resident is his marginal product. The marginal cost of adding a new resident is the additional consumption of goods that must be allocated to him such that he has equal utility with other residents, given prevailing commuting costs and the level of public goods.

In market variables the consumption of private goods equals income less taxes paid for the public good. Income equals land rent shares plus wages, which equal the marginal product of labor. Substituting these into (4.6) yields

$$\text{land rent share} = \text{per person taxes}. \qquad (4.7)$$

In market terms, to other residents the marginal cost of an additional resident is the land rent share he gets. The marginal benefit is the tax share he incurs, reducing everyone else's taxes. City size is optimal when these are equalized.

As explained in Flatters, Henderson, and Mieszkowski (1974), another implication of equation (4.7) is that total taxes and hence total expenditures on public goods should equal total land rents in the city. (This result does not depend on the way land rents are distributed.) This could be realized by taxing away all land rental income and using that revenue and only that revenue to provide public services. This is an equivalent policy to Henry George's proposal in 1879 of a single tax levied on land rental income to tax away all surplus land rent (above frontier rents, which are zero here) (see George, 1938). In some sense the foregoing analysis is a modern vindication of Henry George, although the intent and logic behind the proposals are somewhat different.

Similar to the scale externally situation, we expect equations (4.6) and (4.7) to be satisfied in a market economy given the competitive behavior of land developers in setting up cities. The Samuelson condition will be satisfied within cities, given competitive city governments seeking to be (re)elected by providing public services efficiently.

2. MULTIPLE TYPES OF CITIES

Suppose instead of there being just one type of city there are multiple types of cities, each type specializing in the production of a different traded good. Moreover, suppose that although there are a large number of cities in the economy, there is not a sufficient number of any one type to assume away lumpiness problems. Given these assumptions, we illustrate the

---

[6] This assumes capital is paid its marginal product.

planner's problem using an example with only two types of cities, each specializing in the production of a different good. The second type of city specializes in the production of z (see Chapter 3 on specialization arguments). We also show that the results generalize to situations with many types of cities.

The maximization problem in (4.1) can be adjusted fairly easily to account for two types of cities. Added on to the constraints of (4.1) are a second set of employment and spatial characteristics (equations (4.1.2)–(4.1.8)) for the type z city, a constraint equalizing utility levels between types of cities, full employment constraints for the economy (replacing (4.1.9)), and a production–consumption constraint for the z good.[7]

If we maximize the new Lagrangian with respect to N and N^z and combine the conditions to solve for a condition describing the optimal allocation between x- and z-type cities, the result after substitution of various other first-order conditions is

$$G(N)\frac{\partial x}{\partial n}(1 - t_x u) + \frac{\varepsilon X}{N} - \left(\frac{\partial V/\partial h}{\partial V/\partial x}h(u) + x(u) + \frac{\partial V/\partial z}{\partial V/\partial x}z(u)\right)$$

$$= \frac{\gamma_9}{\lambda_9}\left[F(N)\frac{\partial x}{\partial n}(1 - t_z u) + \frac{\varepsilon_z Z}{N} - \left(\frac{\partial V/\partial h}{\partial V/\partial z}h(u) + z(u) + \frac{\partial V/\partial x}{\partial V/\partial z}x(u)\right)\right]$$

(4.8)

[7] Where m and q are the numbers of the x- and z-type cities, $\bar{K}$ and $\bar{N}$ are economy endowments, γ_i are the multipliers for the z city, and z superscripts refer to variables for type z cities, the new maximization problem is to

$$\max J = V^0(x(u), h(u), z(u), e(u)) + \int_{u_0}^{u_1} \lambda_1(u)(V^0 - V(x(u), z(u), h(u), e(u)))\,du$$

$$+ \int_{u_0^z}^{u_1^z} \gamma_1(u)(V^0 - V(x(u), z(u), h(u), e(u)))\,du + \lambda_2\left(N - \int_{u_0}^{u_1} N(u)\,du\right)$$

$$+ \gamma_2\left(N^z - \int_{u_0^z}^{u_1^z} N(u)\,du\right) + \lambda_3\left(N - \int_0^{u_0} n(u)\,du\right) + \gamma_3\left(N^z - \int_0^{u_0^z} n(u)\,du\right)$$

$$+ \lambda_4\left(K - \int_{u_0}^{u_1} k(u)N(u)\,du - \int_0^{u_0} k(u)\,du\right) + \gamma_4\left(K^z - \int_{u_0^z}^{u_1^z} k(u)N(u)\,du\right.$$

$$\left. - \int_0^{u_0^z} k(u)\,du\right) + \int_{u_0}^{u_1} \lambda_5(u)(2\pi u - l(u)N(u))\,du + \int_{u_0^z}^{u_1^z} \gamma_5(u)(2\pi u - l(u)N(u))\,du$$

$$+ \int_0^{u_0} \lambda_6(u)(2\pi u - l(u))\,du + \int_0^{u_0^z} \gamma_6(u)(2\pi u - l(u))\,du$$

$$+ \lambda_7(h - h(l(u), k(u))\,du + \lambda_8(\bar{N} - mN - qN^z)$$

$$+ \gamma_8(\bar{K} - mK - qK^z) + \lambda_9\left[m\int_0^{u_0} G(N)x(1 - t_x u)\,du - m_u\int_{u_0}^{u_1} x(u)N(u)\,du\right.$$

$$\left. - q\int_{u_1^z}^{u_1^z} x(u)N(u)\,du - p_k mK\right] + \gamma_9\left[q\int_0^{u_0^z} F(N)z(1 - t_z u)\,du\right.$$

$$\left. - m\int_{u_0}^{u_1} z(u)N(u)\,du - q\int_{u_0^z}^{u_1^z} z(u)N(u)\,du - p_k^z qK^z\right].$$

where ε and ε_z are the scale effect elasticities with respect to population or, for example, $\varepsilon = dG(N)/dN \cdot N/G(N)$. X and Z are total outputs per city of x and z available for consumption at the retailing–transport node of each city.

In the first line, the first two terms represent the social marginal benefits in units of x of increasing population to city x, which from above equal the social marginal product (SMP) of labor to city x. The last three terms in parentheses are the social marginal cost of labor (SMC) to the city or the value (in x units) of the additional consumption of x, z, and h of a new resident such that all residents have equal utility.

The second part of equation (4.8) is the corresponding expression for city z. In the brackets everything is defined in z units, but $\gamma_9/\lambda_9 = (\partial V/\partial z)/(\partial V/\partial x)$ converts the second line to x units. The first two terms are the social marginal product of labor to city z (SMP_z) and the last three are the social marginal cost (SMC_z).

We may thus rewrite (4.8) more informally as

$$SMP - SMC = SMP_z - SMC_z. \tag{4.8a}$$

If there are more than two types of cities, (4.8a) reads $SMP - SMC = SMP_z - SMC_z = SMP_i - SMC_i$ for all i. Equation (4.8a) states that the gap between the SMP and SMC of labor should be equalized in all cities. If, for example, $SMP - SMC > SMP_z - SMC_z$, city x is underpopulated. Since the gap between per person productivity and consumption is greater in city x, we could move a person from city z to city x with utility levels unchanged and have a residual of goods left over.

The basic concern is under what conditions equation (4.8) will be satisfied in a free-market economy. The problem in attaining efficient city sizes given more than one type of city is due to the existence of different degrees of external economies of scale between cities. If economies of scale differ between cities, the external effect of labor migration decisions will differ among cities. Laborers will move to equalize the private marginal benefits of moving among cities; but given different marginal scale effects, the social marginal benefits will not be equalized. Given the way in which land rents are distributed in the model, there is also a problem of land rent shares varying among cities. Under alternative distribution schemes, such as rents going to a group of rentiers, the land rent share problem disappears but the scale economy problem does not.

To determine which cities are under- or overpopulated in a market economy, as in Section 1, we interpret equation (4.8) in a market economy where factors are paid the value of their marginal product. The SMP of labor in city x equals $p_n + \varepsilon(X/N)$. Given that price ratios equal marginal rates of substitution in a competitive economy, SMC of labor equals expenditures on market goods, which equals net income. Net income is wages plus the share in land rental income. Therefore, equation (4.8) becomes[8]

$$\varepsilon(X/N) - \text{land rental income share in city } x =$$
$$\varepsilon_z(Z/N) - \text{land rental income share in city } z. \qquad (4.9)$$

To see when equations (4.9) and (4.8) are likely to be satisfied without federal government intervention, we examine several possible situations in city x relative to city z. In any equilibrium, utility levels will be equalized between cities. If we define an indirect utility function for the person at the edge in each type of city, then in equilibrium

$$V = V(y^x, p_x, p_z, p(u_1), T - tu_1{}^x) = V(y^z, p_x, p_z, p(u_1), T - tu_1{}^z)$$

where y^i and $u_1{}^i$ are, respectively, the income and radius of city type i and it is assumed that land rents at the two city edges are equal. Thus commuting distance and income are the two variable arguments in the utility function. Suppose x cities are larger due to greater *total* or *intramarginal* scale economies and thus x cities pay greater wages and greater land rental income (average rents paid and hence rental income rises with city size, as in Chapter 2). However, relative to the smaller z cities with lower income, people in x cities are no better off because they have less leisure. An equilibrium holds.

Given this, because land rental income in x cities is greater than in z cities, if *marginal* scale effects are lower in x cities than in z, then from equation (4.9) x cities must be *overpopulated*. If marginal scale effects are greater in x cities than in z cities in this case, then either city may be overpopulated. If x [z] cities are overpopulated, some form of federal intervention is necessary to tax people living in x [z] cities and subsidize people living in z [x] cities to encourage population movements from x [z] to z [x] cities until equation (4.8) is satisfied. (The taxes would now be a part of equation (4.9), since they are now part of income. A tax-subsidy solution rather than just a subsidy solution or just a tax solution is suggested, since it should be possible to design a solution where total taxes equal total subsidies or the program is self-financing.)

Note that these statements and the general approach to the problem of population allocation in this chapter reject a partial equilibrium approach to the problem of determining whether cities are optimal in size. Under a partial equilibrium approach, viewing one city on its own when the social marginal benefit of labor exceeds the private marginal benefit of labor, it might seem desirable to subsidize immigration to that city. From a general equilibrium perspective, however, this is incorrect. Subsidizing labor to

---

[8] Note that if land rental income is paid out to rentiers, then equation (4.9) would read $\varepsilon(X/N) = \varepsilon_z(Z/N)$. Efficiency would only occur in the market solutions if marginal scale effects were equal, although this could have a disagreeable effect on income distribution.

migrate to one city would draw population away from other cities where the social marginal benefit of labor also exceeds the private marginal benefit. If these external effects are the same among cities, no subsidization is required.

In the foregoing discussion, the existence of external economies of scale is the basis for inefficiencies in population allocation among cities. One can introduce a variety of other externalities connected with population size, such as congestion on roads (see Mirrlees, 1972) or congestion in the provision of public services (see Flatters, Henderson, and Mieszkowski, 1974). These considerations result in other terms being added to equation (4.8). For example, for congestion, two new terms would enter, describing the increased travel costs for commuters in cities x and z from adding additional residents who then increase congestion levels. As always, the question whether a particular city is over- or underpopulated depends on the magnitude of its positive and negative externalities *relative* to other cities.

This analysis of externalities is concerned with optimal population allocation at the margin among cities. There is, however, another problem that is more global in nature. Cities individually would be best off satisfying equations (4.3)–(4.5) where the marginal benefits and costs of an additional resident are *equal*. However, the economy is usually best off when there is a *gap* between marginal benefits and costs that is equal between all cities. This is the problem mentioned in Chapter 3 that, with lumpiness, free-market equilibrium will result in cities that are not the most efficient size individually. This provides a basis for city governments to try to restrict their city sizes to the individually efficient level by excluding some residents, who would then be forced into very small inefficient cities.

However, if there are sufficient cities of both types, the lumpiness problem becomes negligible and both the global and marginal problems of allocating labor between cities will be solved. As the number of each type of city becomes very large, the gap between the SMP and SMC of population for each type of city in equation (4.8) approaches zero. At the limit both gaps are zero, so both equations (4.8) and (4.3) are satisfied. That is, with no lumpiness, all cities approach their individual efficient sizes and there is no longer a problem of population allocation at the margin. This is intuitively appealing.

When the number of cities becomes very large and they approach their most efficient size, we approach a constant returns to scale world. That is, doubling the economy's endowments would double the numbers of each type of city, leaving city size unchanged, and would double production, without affecting utility levels or capital rentals. In this de facto constant returns to scale world at the economy-wide level, the problem of misallocation of resources from external economies of scale vanishes.

Public Goods

If we reintroduce pure public goods as the basis for agglomeration, there is also a problem of population allocation if cities are of different sizes. Assume cities are of unequal size and x-type cities are larger because of greater *intra*marginal scale economies. However, we assume for simplicity that marginal scale economies ε and ε_z are currently zero. Maximizing the relevant Lagrangian (with public goods entering utility functions and production–consumption constraints) yields the population allocation condition that

$$\frac{\partial x}{\partial n}(1 - t_x u) - \left[\frac{\partial V/\partial h}{\partial V/\partial x}h(u) + \frac{\partial V/\partial z}{\partial V/\partial x}z(u) + x(u)\right]$$

$$= \frac{\partial V/\partial z}{\partial V/\partial x}\frac{\partial z}{\partial n}(1 - t_z u) - \left[\frac{\partial V/\partial h}{\partial V/\partial x}h(u) + \frac{\partial V/\partial z}{\partial V/\partial x}z(u) + x(u)\right]. \quad (4.10)$$

Interpreting equation (4.10) in a market economy, we see that the expressions in square brackets are expenditures on market goods. These expenditures equal income less taxes. Income comes from wages and land rent shares. Given these relationships, in a market context equation (4.10) becomes

land rent share in x − per person taxes in x

= land rent share in z − per person taxes in z. (4.11)

This condition is unlikely to be satisfied in a market economy. If city x is larger than city z by assumption, land rent shares in city x are larger than in city z. The relative magnitude of per person taxes can be shown to depend on the compensated price elasticity of demand for public goods, given the dependence on the unit tax price of people's demand for public goods (Flatters, Henderson, and Mieszkowski, 1974). The per person unit tax price of public goods in units of x is $1/N$ where N is city population and the cost of a unit of public goods in terms of x is 1. Since N is larger in the x city, the tax price of public goods is lower in the x city; but utility levels are equal. If the compensated elasticity of demand equals one, expenditures on public goods, and hence per person taxes, will always be equalized among regions, regardless of differences in unit tax prices. (We use the compensated elasticity since in comparing cities and tax prices, utility is held constant.) If the elasticity is greater [less] than one, expenditures will be greater in the low [high] tax price city or in the larger [smaller] city. Given that the x city is larger and has a larger land rent share, equation (4.11) can only be satisfied if tax shares are larger in city x. This could only occur if the compensated elasticity were greater than one; but for optimality it would have to be the precise magnitude such that tax costs satisfy equation (4.11), given land rents. Otherwise, federal intervention in the form of income taxation and subsidization will be needed to encourage optimal population movements.

For public goods, we can see from equation (4.11) that this problem of misallocation of resources can also be solved by distributing land rents and tax shares on a national basis, so that everyone in the economy pays the same taxes and gets the same land rent shares. The idea is that tax or land rent *shares* do not in themselves affect or represent production or consumption capabilities in the economy. Therefore if we equalize these shares nationally so that no one has an incentive to move to pay less taxes or to get more land rents, then the population will make correct location decisions, based on national marginal productivity and public good exploitation conditions. Note however this implies the national government must supply local public goods and satisfy the local Samuelson condition. In a voting model utilized to determine public services in a market economy, it is not clear that local preferences will be revealed to the national government so that they may satisfy the Samuelson condition or that the national government will be politically bound to provide local public goods efficiently.

3. CONCLUSIONS

In this chapter we showed that in general there is a problem of population allocation among cities. Given an economy with multiple types of cities and a few cities of each type, if there are external economies of scale in production or pure public goods in consumption, federal government intervention will be needed to ensure an efficient allocation of resources among regions. Such intervention will involve the subsidization of labor incomes in underpopulated cities and taxation of income in overpopulated cities.

5

Externalities in a Spatial Context

The analysis of externalities plays an important role in the understanding of cities and the proper design of urban public policy. As discussed in Chapter 1, people crowd into urban areas to exploit external economies of scale in production which arise because of spillover benefits among firms in terms of labor and other input market efficiences. But this phenomenon of people crowding into a limited spatial area so as to have access to common work sites or other facilities is itself the cause of many disamenities and externalities.

The close proximity of residents results in social externalities, such as noise pollution, and general neighborhood externalities, such as the external benefits to residents from their neighbors maintaining their houses and gardens. Neighborhood externalities are discussed in Chapter 6. Congestion externalities associated with roads, parks, and beaches result from concentrations of people attempting to use the same public facilities at the same time. Congestion is analyzed in Chapters 7 and 8.

In this chapter we examine pollution externalities. Air and water pollution result from concentrations of firms and residents dumping untreated wastes into a limited environmental area and overburdening the absorptive capacity of the environment (see Ayres and Kneese, 1969, and Kneese, 1971). For example, limited amounts of untreated domestic wastes in rivers and lakes can be broken down into plant nutrients, such as nitrogen and phosphorus, without discernible loss of water quality by bacteria using free

oxygen to feed on the wastes. However, as the quantity of wastes increases relative to the volume of water, the quantity of plant nutrients created increases, resulting in algae growth, and the free oxygen becomes used up, resulting in an oxygen "sag." Because of the oxygen sag, bacteria start to use bound oxygen to feed on wastes, releasing odorous gases such as hydrogen sulfide. This process of the environment absorbing wastes ineffectively and inefficiently relative to a situation where wastes are treated results in loss of fish life (due to the oxygen sag), decreased recreational benefits, and increased cost of treating the same water for domestic consumption.

The literature on externalities is voluminous and it would be impossible in this chapter to comprehensively survey the many types of externalities, models, and results (see, e.g., Baumol and Oates, 1975; Mishan, 1971; Mohring and Boyd, 1971; Schall, 1971; Worcester, 1969; Coase, 1960; and Meade, 1952). Any survey would necessarily be arbitrarily select and abrupt. Moreover, many of the situations analyzed in the mainstream literature are not directly applicable to the major externality problems in cities.

In this chapter we concentrate on just one externality situation, where industrial production results in airborne emissions that pollute residents. Most of the basic propositions in the literature concerning pollution situations where there are a large number of both offenders and victims will be illustrated. Moreover, in this chapter we analyze externalities in an explicit spatial setting, something that is rarely done. This extends the basic analysis of Pigouvian taxes contained in Baumol and Oates (1975) to a spatial world. We show that a comprehensive environmental policy consists not only of Pigouvian taxes but also of land use regulation policies and policies concerning the explicit or implicit redistribution of proceeds from Pigouvian taxes. Much of the material in this chapter is based on Henderson (1977).

After outlining the nature of the environmental problem, we turn in the first part of the chapter to the problem of pollution control and the allocation of resources within a city. In the second part of the chapter we examine the allocation of resources among cities in the economy.

A Model of Industrial Air Pollution

As in previous chapters the spatial setting is a monocentric model of a city. Firms in the CBD produce a marketable good x according to the production function $x(u) = G(N)x(n(u), k(u), l(u))$, or equation (1.26). Instead of labeling $k(u)$ capital in this chapter we are going to call it natural resources, or raw materials, that are used in production and imported by the city. As before, $G(N)$ is a Hicks neutral shift factor and $n(u)$ and $l(u)$ are inputs of labor and land. Since firm size remains indeterminate in this formulation, we identify firms by distance from the city center or by rings.

The second output of firms is airborne emissions that result in pollution or a decline in air quality and an increase in fallout of particulates. Pollution enters the utility function as a disamenity but does not affect production activity. Emissions result from the employment of the resource k and may be abated by employment in antipollution activity such as scrubbing, filtering, and two-stage combustion. Pollutants are emissions that have been dispersed by air currents and acted upon chemically by the sun's radiation and moisture in the air. As distance from an emitting source increases, the volume of pollutants per cube of air declines due to horizontal and vertical spatial diffusion of emissions and fallout or environmental absorption of pollutants.

Since we only identify pollution damages for residents, we are primarily concerned with firms' contributions to pollutants at the circular residential–CBD boundary and beyond. As before, this boundary is at distance u_0 from the city center. We will examine pollution dispersion in the residential sector beyond the boundary, but we focus first on the buildup of pollutants at the residential-CBD boundary and on how much each firm's emissions contribute to the buildup of pollutants at the boundary.

It is not obvious how a firm's total contribution to pollutants summed over all points on the residential–CBD boundary varies with its distance from the city center. As a firm moves away from the city center toward the CBD boundary, it would seem that its emissions would have less opportunity to disperse before reaching residents and would contribute more to pollution. But as it moves closer to the CBD boundary in one direction, it is simultaneously moving farther from points on the boundary on the opposite side of the CBD, allowing for greater dispersion of emissions in that direction. However, if emissions disperse rapidly with distance, then this movement farther away from points on the opposite side of the CBD will have little impact on pollution there, since the firm's emissions will have almost entirely dissipated anyway. Then the critical factor is the movement toward points on its side of the CBD. We assume pollution is a convex function of distance from the source of emissions and that as a firm moves closer to a residential boundary its contribution to pollution for a given level of emissions increases. This argument essentially implies that additional emissions of firms at the city center contribute relatively little to total pollution, whereas additional emissions of firms at or near the CBD edge contribute more to increased pollution.

There are two ways to model this situation without undue complexity. First, we could avoid the foregoing problems by assuming that all firms contribute to a cloud of pollutants according to the emission level at the source, or at their location. The general cloud of pollution (without reference to individual contributions) then diffuses and dissipates before reaching residences according to the general size of the CBD.

The second way to model the situation and the one we utilize here captures some of the spatial complexity. We identify all firms by distance from the city center or the ring they are in and aggregate at the ring level. This simplification is possible since all firms are assumed to have identical production processes (and are of indeterminate size), the city is perfectly symmetrical, and stochastic factors such as wind direction and speed are ignored. Then the contribution to *pollutants* at all points *on the CBD boundary* of firms in a ring at distance u is

$$f(k(u), n_a(u), u_0, u)$$

where $k(u)$ is employment of natural resources in the ring at distance u from the city center and $\partial f/\partial k(u) \geq 0$. $n_a(u)$ is employment in antipollution activity where $\partial f/\partial n_a(u) \leq 0$. We assume that $\partial f/\partial u_0 < 0$, or that as the CBD expands, the emissions of a firm at distance u are more dispersed before they reach residences. $\partial f/\partial u > 0$, or as we move nearer the CBD edge, a given level of emissions contributes more to pollution. Also, $\partial^2 f/(\partial k\, \partial u)$ should be positive, or as a firm moves toward the nearest residential point, the marginal effect on pollutants of employing an additional unit of k increases.

Total pollutants at all points on the CBD boundary are described as a simple sum of contributions by all CBD rings, or total pollutants are[1]

$$F(u_0) = \int_0^{u_0} f(k(u), n_a(u), u_0, u)\, du. \qquad (5.1)$$

These pollutants in a symmetrical circular city are evenly distributed over all points on the residential boundary.

Residential pollution is then a function of the pollution level at u_0, or $F(u_0)$, and distance from the CBD. As we move beyond u_0, pollutants continue to diffuse. For a person located at distance u, pollution or the disamenity in the preference function is $a(u)$ and

$$a(u) = a(F(u_0), u, u_0) \qquad (5.2)$$

where $F(u_0)$ is as defined in (5.1) $\partial a/\partial F(u_0) \geq 0$; $\partial a/\partial u_0 > 0$, or as the CBD boundary shifts toward residents, for the same $F(u_0)$, pollution at each u rises. $\partial a/\partial u \leq 0$ or pollutants disperse with distance. It seems reasonable to assume that $\partial^2 a/\partial u^2 > 0$ or pollution is a convex function of distance. The radius of the city is u_1 and it is assumed that $a(u_1) > 0$. Although

----

[1] To account for increasing returns to pollution creation or decreasing ability of the environment to absorb and disperse pollutants, we could write (5.1) as $F(u_0) = \int_0^{u_0} g(F(u_0))f(u)\, du$ where $\partial g/\partial F(u_0) \geq 0$. Then in the sections that follow we would have to tax firms according to their own contributions to pollutants plus the effect of their emissions on reduced dispersion of other firms' emissions.

$a(u_1) > 0$, we assume one city's pollution does not extend to other cities. If it did, we would have a spillover situation and, in general, some form of federal intervention would be required to set optimal pollution taxes.

1. THE ALLOCATION OF RESOURCES WITHIN CITIES

1.1 Controlling the Output of Pollution

Without environmental policies, in a market economy firms are paid for their x output but they freely dispose of their airborne wastes or emissions. Therefore, they have no incentive to engage in antipollution activity or to account for marginal pollution damages in their decisions to employ additional units of natural resources. To induce firms to employ resources in a Pareto-efficient manner, it is necessary to charge them for their contributions to pollution at a price or unit tax equal to marginal damages of pollution.

Using the same welfare maximization model as in Chapter 4, we can derive criteria for the Pareto-efficient allocation of resources in a city and the economy. With optimal pollution taxation policies we can show that firms will satisfy these criteria and employ resources efficiently. Since the welfare maximization model has already been presented (in Chapter 4), we do not repeat it here, but proceed directly with an intuitive development of the derivation of optimal pollution taxation policies. The maximization problem is footnoted at appropriate points.

To find optimal pollution taxation policies we must calculate the marginal damages to residents of pollution. To do this we examine the residential sector of the city. Consumers at distance u from the city center consume the city's produced good $x(u)$, its import good $z(u)$, land $l(u)$, disamenities $a(u)$ defined in equation (5.2), and leisure $e(u)$. Leisure is the fixed amount of nonworking time less the time it takes to commute to work in the CBD. Therefore, the utility function of a consumer at location u is defined for this chapter as $V = V(x(u), z(u), l(u), a(u), e(u))$ where V is decreasing in $a(u)$ and increasing in all other arguments.

The utility lost from an increase in disamenities is $\partial V/\partial a(u)$, which evaluated in units of x is $(\partial V/\partial a(u))/(\partial V/\partial x(u))$. From equation (5.2) the increase in disamenities at location u with an increase in pollutants at u_0 is $\partial a(u)/\partial F(u_0)$. In the ring at each distance u from the city center there are $N(u)$ people, so that the total marginal damages at location u from additional pollutants at u_0 are

$$-\frac{\partial V/\partial a(u)}{\partial V/\partial x(u)} N(u) \frac{\partial a(u)}{\partial F(u_0)}.$$

Summing over all residential locations gives us the total marginal damages in the city from additional pollutants at u_0. This is defined as τ where

$$\tau = -\int_{u_0}^{u_1} \frac{\partial V/\partial a(u)}{\partial V/\partial x(u)} N(u) \frac{\partial a(u)}{\partial F(u_0)} \, du. \tag{5.3}$$

This is the price or unit tax firms should be charged for their contributions to pollution at u_0.

Let us examine the behavior of a firm given that such a tax can be set. The profits of a firm facing optimal pollution taxes are

$$\pi(u) = G(N)x(k(u), n(u), l(u))(1 - t_x u) - p_k k(u)$$
$$- p_n(n(u) + n_a(u)) - p_l(u)l(u) - \tau f(k(u), n_a(u), u_0, u). \tag{5.4}$$

The first term is the value of the firm's output of x where the price of x is normalized at 1 and all other prices are defined in units of x. The second, third, and fourth terms are factor payments of the firm where p_n and $p_l(u)$ are, respectively, the wage rate and land rental at u. The last term is the firm's pollution charges. τ is unit tax rate, and $f(u)$ is the assessed contribution of firm emissions to pollution at u_0. The firm views τ as a fixed price or tax that it cannot influence.[2] Given that firms are identified with CBD rings, additional pollutants are symmetrically distributed in the residential sector. τ is the same for different rings in the CBD.[3] It is $f(u)$, the assessed level of pollutants, that varies for the same level of emissions with location throughout the CBD.

Maximizing profits with respect to various inputs, we have as the first-order conditions for profit maximization

$$p_n = G(N)(\partial x/\partial n(u))(1 - t_x u) = -\tau(\partial f/\partial n_a(u)), \tag{5.5}$$
$$p_l(u) = G(N)(\partial x/\partial l(u))(1 - t_x u), \tag{5.6}$$
$$p_k = G(N)(\partial x/\partial k(u))(1 - t_x u) - \tau(\partial f/\partial k(u)). \tag{5.7}$$

Equation (5.5) states that the marginal product of labor will be equalized (to the wage rate) in its two activities, producing x and reducing pollution. In order to reduce its tax bill, the firm employs labor in antipollution activity until its marginal cost p_n equals its marginal benefit. This benefit is the reduction in pollution taxes from employing one more laborer, or the pollution reduction multiplied by the unit tax price of pollution. If τ is correctly assessed, then equation (5.5) satisfies conditions for the Pareto-

---

[2] If the firm can influence τ by its behavior, then the first-order conditions for profit maximization derived later will not be applicable, and implementing an optimal solution will be more difficult.

[3] Suppose there are multiple firms in each ring. In general, for practical purposes, it will be necessary to disaggregate from rings to coordinates and sum vertically and horizontally over all coordinates to assess taxes. Unlike a ring, a firm's pollutants will not be symmetrically distributed in the residential sector and the damages it causes different residents at the same u will vary.

efficient allocation of resources, since the social marginal product of labor is equalized across locations and activities.[4]

Equation (5.7) states that a firm employs natural resources until the social marginal cost of k to the city, which is p_k, is equated with the social marginal product of k, which equals the private marginal product less the marginal damages of additional pollution. Alternatively stated, the marginal benefits, or $G(N)(\partial x/\partial k(u))(1 - t_x u)$, equal the marginal cost under taxation. This marginal cost is the price of k plus the firm's increase in taxes from employing additional k, or $\tau(\partial f/\partial k(u))$. Again, equation (5.7) satisfies the criterion describing the efficient use of k within the city as derived in footnote 4. From a conceptual point of view there are alternative taxation policies to taxing pollution per se. One alternative is a policy of a tax $(\tau(\partial f/\partial k))$ on employment of k combined with a subsidy $(-\tau(\partial f/\partial n_a))$ on employment of labor in antipollution activity.

[4] This can be seen by examining the welfare maximization model. The maximization problem is identical to that in Chapter 4 except for four considerations. First, we have some labor employed in antipollution activity, and second, we have an additional constraint defining consumer amenities. Third, rather than dealing with capital and capital ownership, we assume that the city imports a natural resource $k(u)$ at a fixed price p_k. Finally, rather than consuming housing produced with capital and land, residents just consume land as their housing good. The planner maximizes

$$J = V^0(x(u), z(u), l(u), a(u), e(u))$$

$$+ \int_{u_0}^{u_1} \lambda_1(u)(V(x(u), z(u), l(u), a(u), e(u)) - V^0)\, du$$

$$+ \lambda_2 \left[\int_0^{u_0} G(N)x(n(u), l(u), k(u))(1 - t_x u)\, du - \int_{u_0}^{u_1} x(u)N(u)\, du \right.$$

$$\left. - \int_{u_0}^{u_1} p_z z(u)N(u)\, du - p_k \int_0^{u_0} k(u)\, du \right]$$

$$+ \int_{u_0}^{u_1} \lambda_3(u)\left(a(u) - a\left(\int_0^{u_0} f(u)\, du, u, u_0\right)\right) du$$

$$+ \int_{u_0}^{u_1} \lambda_4(u)(T - e(u) - tu)\, du + \lambda_5\left(N - \int_0^{u_0} (n(u) + n_a(u))\, du\right)$$

$$+ \lambda_6\left(N - \int_{u_0}^{u_1} N(u)\, du\right) + \int_{u_0}^{u_1} \lambda_7(u)(2\pi u - l(u)N(u))\, du$$

$$+ \int_0^{u_0} \lambda_8(u)(2\pi u - l(u))\, du.$$

If we maximize J with respect to k and then substitute in equation (5.3) for τ and substitute in the expression for $\lambda_3(u)$ found by maximizing J with respect to $a(u)$ and $x(u)$, the result is

$$p_k = G(N)(\partial x/\partial k(u))(1 - t_x u) - \tau(\partial f/\partial k(u)).$$

Similarly, maximizing J with respect to n and n_a and performing the same substitutions, we get

$$\lambda_5 = G(N)(\partial x/\partial n(u))(1 - t_x u) = -\tau(\partial f/\partial n_a(u)).$$

These are criteria for the optimal use of $k(u)$, $n(u)$, and $n_a(u)$.

Note that as marginal pollution damages rise, for a given opportunity cost of k, k should be employed such that its private marginal product rises. The positive benefits from employing k should rise to offset the increased negative pollution effects. In general, as marginal pollution damages increase, this implies less k should be used relative to other factors in x production, so that its private marginal product rises. For example, for firms located nearer the CBD boundary, $\partial f/\partial k(u)$ may be higher given the assumptions about pollution dispersion. In that case, $\partial x/\partial k(u)$ may be higher, indicating with a homothetic production function less use of k relative to other factors in x production. This implies that although marginal damages are higher for firms located nearer the CBD boundary, their total damages may not differ as much compared with firms interior to them, since less k relative to other factors is used.

We must also be concerned with the firm's profit position after taxation, which has implications for the stability of the taxation equilibrium. Substituting (5.5)–(5.7) back into (5.4) yields

$$\pi(u) = \tau((\partial f/\partial k)k(u) + (\partial f/\partial n_a)n_a(u) - f(k(u), n_a(u), u_0, u)) \gtreqless 0. \quad (5.8)$$

In a competitive industry with free costless entry, a stability condition on entry is that $\pi \to 0$. For example, if $\pi < 0$, firms will exit from the industry until $\pi \to 0$, if that is possible. In (5.8) π may not equal zero, in which case there will be either exit or entry *with no opportunity for $\pi \to 0$* in the model, providing (5.5)–(5.7) are always satisfied. Only if f is linear homogeneous in k and n_a does $\pi = 0$. This, of course, is a version of the familiar adding-up problem. If $\pi \neq 0$, this implies firms should be lump-sum taxed or subsidized so as to ensure that $\pi \to 0$.

This adding-up problem may be neutralized if there is a *fixed immobile* factor of production such as land so that (5.6) is generally not satisfied.[5] In our situation if the number of firms is fixed and there is an immobile fixed factor such as land, then $\pi(u)$ in (5.8) simply augments the residual return to land without affecting factor allocations. In a dynamic real world with a horizon of 1–15(?) years in policymaking, in a commercial area in a city the number of firms and their land inputs may well be fixed.

---

[5] However, it is not so helpful to have the fixed factor be the traditional entrepreneur used to give a determinate firm size, since in that case there is an optimality condition that says that shadow marginal products of the mobile entrepreneurs should be equalized across firms. If production functions are linear homogeneous and all other factors are paid the value of their marginal products, the residual return to mobile entrepreneurs should be equalized (to their shadow marginal product) across firms. However, with pollution entrepreneurs earn their shadow private marginal product plus/minus the residual in (5.13). With $\pi(u) \neq 0$ differing by location and with entry or exit, the return to entrepreneurs will exceed or fall short of their shadow private marginal product by varying amounts in these firms, indicating a suboptimal allocation of entrepreneurs within the city and economy (see Meade, 1952).

1.2 Problems in Policymaking

A major problem facing governments wanting to implement pollution policies is to acquire sufficient information to design optimal policies. If the policy is to tax pollution, then the information needed is the optimal tax rate τ, which is the same for all firms and the contribution to pollution of firms or $f(u)$. Knowledge of $f(u)$ requires monitoring firm emissions and determining how they disperse with distance. However, it does not require knowledge of individual firms' technologies or how much firms individually should pollute in the optimal solution. That is, given the optimal τ, firms are left on their own to adjust their technologies and determine their level of emissions (which, of course, will be optimal if τ is optimally set).

Comparing different potentially *optimal* pollution policies, pollution taxation requires less information than other policies. All optimal pollution policies require knowing the optimal marginal damages (and hence implicitly τ) and how pollution disperses with distance. However, policies other than pollution taxation generally require more information. For example, the policy mentioned in the previous section of taxing natural resources and subsidizing employment in antipollution activity requires knowing individual firms' technologies or the various $\partial f(u)/\partial k(u)$'s and $\partial f(u)/\partial n_a(u)$'s. A policy of direct controls where firms are allotted binding levels of $f(u)$'s requires knowing what the optimal $f(u)$'s are for each firm (where these $f(u)$'s are those that would result with optimal taxation). Given that firms' technologies, production conditions, and spatial locations vary, this again requires knowing individual firms' technologies (and all the information that entrepreneurs need in order to make their decisions) so as to ascribe to each firm what its equilibrium output levels and factor proportions should be.

If a policy of pollution taxation is chosen, the task of setting optimal pollution taxes is still formidable. The problems have been discussed in detail in the literature and we review them here. First, there is the general problem of empirically evaluating marginal damages to different consumers $(\partial V/\partial a(u))/(\partial V/\partial x(u))$. The empirical literature on this subject is not helpful since the direct estimates of pollution costs are most speculative and for indirect estimates of perceived pollution costs (land value studies utilizing how land values vary spatially with pollution) the results are sometimes perverse. Moreover, it is not clear that consumers understand or properly evaluate the health damages of pollution. Second, there is the problem of assessing or solving for the final *optimal* tax and *optimal* marginal damages as opposed to the initial pretax equilibrium values of these variables. People have suggested an iterative procedure of initially setting taxes equal to current marginal damages and then successively lowering the tax and marginal damages to their optimal level. This still requires knowing when the optimum is reached. Finally, there is the problem that pollution is determined on a day-to-day basis by the stochastic influences of wind and weather conditions and hence fluctuates from day to day for a given level of emissions. A basic question is whether policymakers should be concerned about average annual or monthly pollution levels or about maximal pollution levels during these time intervals.

We have noted further problems in pollution control. First, there is the problem of evaluating the quantity of pollution according to the location of the firm. The same quantity of particulates emitted by firms located at different distances from a residential area results in different disamenities for residents. Second, it is necessary to know how pollution disperses within the residential area. It may be possible to estimate these technological relationships and just monitor emissions at their source.

Given the foregoing types of considerations, Baumol and Oates (1975) argue persuasively in a nonspatial context that the information required for policymakers prohibits achieving optimal pollution levels. They suggest a standards approach where desired community levels of air quality are set, presumably with the idea that the optimal level of pollution is considerably less than it currently is. As they make clear, the actual choice of standards is somewhat arbitrary. Unit pollution charges are then imposed and adjusted until, given firms' reactions, community air quality approaches the standards. Since all firms face the same pollution charges but are allowed to adjust to whatever pollution is efficient (profit maximizing) for them, when the target air quality level is reached, the allocation of resources among firms will be efficient. The marginal costs of reducing pollution will be equalized (to the unit pollution charge) across firms, which minimizes the cost of achieving a given set of standards.

This community standards policy contrasts to a situation where individual firms face standards specific to them. Such a policy generally does not allow the industry to adjust internally in an efficient manner. For example, a policy that forces all firms to reduce pollution by 50% is probably only efficient if firms have identical technologies and production costs. In contrast, a 50% reduction in community pollution levels achieved by unit pollution charges would probably induce the heaviest polluters to reduce pollution by more than 50% and light polluters by less than 50%.

In a spatial context, the argument (Tietenberg, 1974) is to divide up industrial areas into some type of grid or other geographic demarcation and assign a specific set of standards to each of the squares according to proximity to residential areas and possibilities for dispersion of emissions.

In the model in this chapter, efficiency in achieving a given air quality standard means the marginal product of labor in antipollution activity, or $-\tau(\partial f/\partial n_a(u))$, will be equalized (to p_n) across firms and the marginal product of capital, or $G(N)(\partial x/\partial k(u))(1 - t_x u) - \tau(\partial f/\partial k)$, will be equalized across firms. Note that τ is no longer defined by equation (5.3), but is set simply to achieve a given air quality standard. Equalization of marginal products of mobile factors is a prerequisite for efficiency. If marginal products of, say, labor in antipollution activity are unequal, the same standards can be achieved with less labor devoted to antipollution activity by shifting labor from firms where its marginal product is low to firms where its marginal product is high.

1.3 The Allocation of Land between Businesses and Residences

The normal market interpretation of conditions describing the optimal allocation of land between competing uses in situations where there are *no* externalities is that unit land rents should be equalized at the border of competing uses. In a free-market situation with or without externalities, this condition is satisfied in long-run stable equilibrium in the land market. However, when externalities are present, in general, it is not optimal for land rents to be equalized at the border of competing uses, especially where one competing use is imposing externalities on the other (see Stull, 1974). In a monocentric model of a city, we are concerned with the optimal allocation of land between businesses and residences. This is essentially a question of determining the optimal relative size of the CBD, or the location of the border of the CBD, u_0.

If one obtains the general criterion defining the optimal location of u_0 and interprets it in a market setting, the result is[6]

$$\text{business rents at } u_0 + \tau \left(-\int_0^{u_0} \frac{\partial f(u)}{\partial u_0} \, du \right)$$

$$= \text{residential rents at } u_0 + \int_{u_0}^{u_1} \left(-\frac{\partial V/\partial a(u)}{\partial V/\partial x(u)} \right) N(u) \left(\frac{\partial a(u)}{\partial u_0} \right) du. \quad (5.9)$$

[6] To find the optimal location of the CBD boundary u_0, we maximize J in footnote 4 with respect to u_0 and then $n(u)$, $n_a(u)$, $a(u)$, $x(u)$, $N(u)$, $l(u)$, and $k(u)$ to solve out the multipliers. The result is

$$G(N)(1 - t_x u_0) \left(x(u_0) - \frac{\partial x}{\partial n(u_0)} n(u_0) - \frac{\partial x}{\partial k(u_0)} k(u_0) \right)$$

$$+ \int_{u_0}^{u_1} \frac{\partial V/\partial a(u)}{\partial V/\partial x(u)} N(u) \frac{\partial a(u)}{\partial F(u_0)} \left[f(u_0) - \frac{\partial f}{\partial k(u_0)} k(u_0) - \frac{\partial f}{\partial n_a(u_0)} n_a(u_0) \right] du$$

$$+ \int_{u_0}^{u_1} \frac{\partial V/\partial a(u)}{\partial V/\partial x(u)} N(u) \left[\frac{\partial a(u)}{\partial F(u_0)} \int_0^{u_0} \frac{\partial f(u)}{\partial u_0} du + \frac{\partial a(u)}{\partial u_0} \right] du$$

$$= \frac{\partial V/\partial l}{\partial V/\partial x} l(u_0) N(u_0).$$

This criterion has a straightforward explanation. The first line of (5.9) is the marginal benefits of extending the business district one more unit, which includes two factors. First, there is the productivity of land in production of x as represented by rents businesses are willing to pay at location u_0. Second, there is the effect of extending the area of the CBD on increased dispersion of the firms' emissions. This increased dispersion or reduction in pollution is measured as $\int_0^{u_0}(-\partial f(u)/\partial u_0)\,du > 0$ and the value throughout the city of this reduction is τ.

The marginal cost of extending the CBD boundary one unit includes two factors. First, there is the lost value of land in consumption as measured by rents residents are willing to pay for this land. Second, there is increased residential pollution $(\partial a(u)/\partial u_0)$ caused by moving the CBD boundary closer to residents and hence raising the level of pollution throughout the residential sector of the city.[7]

An efficient division of land occurs when the marginal benefits of increasing commercial land use equal the marginal cost. In the literature that deals with similar situations (e.g., Stull, 1974), the effect on pollution dispersion of increasing the CBD edge either is not relevant in the model or is ignored. If that were the case here, the only externality would be that when firms expand into the residential area they do not account for the effect of their expansion on moving pollution sources closer to residents. Equation (5.9) then states that business land rents should equal residential rents plus a positive term, or that in a market situation business land rents should *exceed* residential land rents at the border of their competing uses. However, given the second externality or the effect of increasing u_0 on pollution dispersion within the CBD, it is no longer clear that business rents should exceed residential rents at the border.

The market interpretation of this equation is straightforward, assuming all other pollution policies are optimally set. Using equation (5.8) for profits π, the definition of τ, and equations (5.5)–(5.7) for the marginal productivity of n, n_a, $l(u)$, and k, the first two lines of this equation reduce to $\pi(u_0) + p_l(u_0)l(u_0)$. From (5.8), we know $\pi(u_0) = 0$ if f is linear homogeneous in k and n_a. Alternatively, $\pi = 0$ if the government follows a policy of optimal lump-sum taxes or subsidies when f is not linear homogeneous. In either case the first two lines of the equation above reduce to business land rents actually paid out at the edge of the CBD. The right-hand side of the equation from the first-order conditions of the consumer maximization problem equals residential land rents at the interior edge of the residential area. Given these relationships, this equation reduces to equation (5.9).

[7] Even if u_0 changes by a discrete amount, this has a negligible effect on u_1, the radius of the city, since the circumference at u_0 is a fraction of the circumference at u_1. Therefore, if u_0 increases discretely, that increase will result in a discrete increase in general residential pollution levels caused by moving firms nearer to all residences (even if u_1 expands and some residents move slightly farther away).

These comments imply that the rent gradient in the city should, in general, be discontinuous at u_0. In Figure 5.1, we illustrate a possible rent gradient. The initial rising part of the residential rent gradient as we move away from u_0 is possible because, in addition to the negative effect of declining leisure on rents, there is now a positive effect of declining pollution as we move farther from the CBD. From the analysis of Chapter 1, the slope of the residential rent gradient can be shown to be

$$\frac{\partial p_l(u)}{\partial u} = l(u)^{-1}\left(-\frac{\partial V/\partial e}{\partial V/\partial x}t + \frac{\partial V/\partial a}{\partial V/\partial x}\frac{\partial a}{\partial u}\right) \lesseqgtr 0. \tag{5.10}$$

Given $\partial V/\partial a, \partial a/\partial u < 0$, the second term of (5.10) is positive. Thus the whole expression may take a positive value, especially when $\partial a/\partial u$ is large near the CBD.

To maintain a discontinuity in the rent gradient at u_0 it will be necessary to increase or decrease the size of the business area relative to the free-market equilibrium where land rents are equalized at u_0. This requires zoning land use and changing the area of the business district so equation (5.9) is satisfied and land rents are no longer equalized at the border of competing uses.

Evaluating equation (5.9) accurately has basically the same information requirements as setting optimal pollution taxes. Moreover, equation (5.9) is dependent on there being only optimal pollution policies, such as optimal pollution taxation and lump-sum taxes/subsidies if needed. If a standards policy or no policy is followed because of information constraints, then the form of equation (5.9) would change given the new pricing constraints and

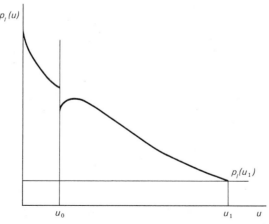

FIGURE 5.1   Rent gradient with pollution.

efficiency conditions. Since it is theoretically unclear whether unzoned free-market commercial areas are too big or too small and since the information required to evaluate equation (5.9) is difficult or impossible to obtain, it is uncertain whether a policymaker should intervene on this basis in the urban land market. Only if it seems clear that unzoned commercial areas are, say, too large might a policymaker intervene to restrictively zone commercial areas, even though the precise magnitude of the variables in equation (5.9) is unknown.

Commercial areas could also be restricted in size relative to a free-market situation by discriminatorily taxing potential business land use relative to residential use, exterior to the optimal u_0. In some ways this is a more attractive policy than zoning. In a dynamic situation with changing land use it is more flexible. With zoning, businesses cannot expand beyond the zoned u_0 until regulations are revised. With taxation businesses can expand if they are willing to pay the (outdated) optimal tax.

Note that these problems in the allocation of land apply in any spatial setting where polluters and their victims are separated spatially by a border. The free-market determination of the border will not account for the effect of the border location on pollution dispersion and the damages suffered by victims. As such, in general, land rents should not be equalized at the border of competing uses, when one set of users pollutes the other.

2. THE ALLOCATION OF RESOURCES AMONG CITIES

In Section 1 we examined the internal allocation of resources in a city and derived optimal environmental policies. Given the nature of the maximization problem, these policies must make everyone in the city (potentially) better off relative to a situation with no policies. This is an important consideration in the decision to implement such policies for a local environmental authority seeking reappointment or reelection. However, if we consider the city in the context of an economy in which labor is mobile among cities, with the implementation of pollution policies, a city may experience a reduction in population. Also, for the economy as a whole it may not be efficient for a city to retain all of its pollution tax proceeds.

Given the political structure of the economy where pollution taxation may be a local matter, local authorities may be unwilling to enact optimal pollution policies if they involve a loss of population or weak control over tax proceeds distribution. A full explanation of the reasons for this is beyond our scope but it involves the impact upon political decision making and elections of considerations such as short-run unemployment and a loss of population caused by pollution policies, as well as voter uncertainty as to the costs and benefits of pollution control. These considerations relate to the distribution of tax proceeds, since the magnitude of net benefits to local residents from pollution taxation will obviously be affected by whether local pollution taxes are redistributed to local residents as opposed to being withdrawn from the local community. Since political considerations are very relevant in determining the possibilities of implementing an optimal pollution policy, it is useful for us to examine the optimal allocation of pollution tax proceeds and to determine which cities should retain tax proceeds. We will also speculate on what happens to city size with the implementation of pollution taxation, although we do not actually do any comparative statics.

As suggested in Baumol and Oates (1975), pollution does not directly distort consumer choices of goods by creating divergences between marginal rates of substitution and ratios of marginal costs of market goods.[8] Thus there is no basis because of pollution to use pollution tax proceeds to subsidize consumers to consume more or less of any particular good,[9] and it may appear that there is no pure efficiency basis for redistributing pollution tax proceeds in a particular manner among the population. However this is not the case.

The distribution of tax proceeds will affect the allocation of population. Whether a local government is allowed to redistribute its tax proceeds to its residents or whether the federal government intervenes to take some or all of the proceeds and distribute them nationally will affect the fiscal attractiveness of that city relative to the rest of the nation. Hence, this will affect movements of population to this city from the rest of the economy. Since there is an optimal allocation of population in the economy, the distribution of tax proceeds will affect whether such an allocation is realized.

In the following discussion, we assume that whatever tax proceeds the local government retains are distributed equally to all residents of the city. Entering residents get a share, whereas exiting residents lose their share. The distribution of proceeds can be done explicitly or implicitly (by the money entering the local treasury and reducing local taxes and/or raising local expenditures).

To determine the optimal distribution of pollution tax proceeds, we must go back to the theory of optimal population allocation presented in Chapter 4. As in Chapter 4, a second type of city is introduced that produces z and now also produces pollution. If we derive the condition for optimal

---

[8] Of course, taxation affects the relative price of the polluting good; but the resulting price effect on consumption is optimal since with taxation all goods are then priced at social marginal cost.

[9] For a discussion of externalities that affect other firms' production functions and the need for taxation or subsidization of these victims see Meade (1952), and Kraus and Mohring (1975) (for reciprocal externalities) as well as Baumol and Oates (1975).

population allocation, we get the same result as in Chapter 4. For an x- and z-type city the optimality condition or equation (4.9) is

$$
G(N) \frac{\partial x}{\partial n} (1 - t_x u) + \varepsilon \frac{X}{N} - \left(\frac{\partial V/\partial l}{\partial V/\partial x} l(u) + x(u) + \frac{\partial V/\partial z}{\partial V/\partial x} z(u) \right)
$$

$$
= \frac{\partial V/\partial z}{\partial V/\partial x} \left[F(N) \frac{\partial z}{\partial n} (1 - t_z u) + \varepsilon_z \frac{Z}{N} - \left(\frac{\partial V/\partial l}{\partial V/\partial z} l(u) \right. \right.
$$

$$
\left. \left. + z(u) + \frac{\partial V/\partial x}{\partial V/\partial z} x(u) \right) \right].
\tag{5.11}
$$

As before, the interpretation of this equation is that we want to equalize the net social benefits of moving people between cities. The net social benefit of an additional resident in a city is his social marginal product minus his consumption of *market* goods. As is the case for leisure, disamenities do not explicitly enter equation (5.11). They are implicitly accounted for in that increased disamenities in one city relative to another city means that residents in the first city must consume more market goods to compensate them for the increased disamenities and thus maintain equal utility levels between cities.

   In a situation where pollution tax proceeds are distributed locally (in the city of origin), the market interpretation of equation (5.11) is straightforward. Workers are paid their marginal product and their market expenditures exactly equal their income. Income now consists of wages, land rent share, and proceeds from pollution taxes. Accordingly, equation (5.11) may be interpreted in a market setting as

$$
\varepsilon \frac{X}{N} - \text{land rent share in } x - \text{pollution tax share in } x
$$

$$
= \varepsilon_z \frac{Z}{N} - \text{land rent share in } z - \text{pollution tax share in } z.
\tag{5.12}
$$

   To isolate the problem of distributing pollution tax proceeds, assume for now that marginal scale effects equal zero and land rents go out of the system or are redistributed to a class of absentee rentiers (alternatively we could assume that total land rents in the economy are divided equally among all citizens). Then equation (5.12) reduces to

$$
\text{pollution tax share in } x = \text{pollution tax share in } z.
\tag{5.12a}
$$

Optimality in equation (5.12a) will be guaranteed if per person pollution tax proceeds are the same in all cities. Since pollution levels and per person proceeds are likely to vary among cities, in general, equality of per person pollution income could only occur if the federal government intervened to redistribute proceeds among cities. One possibility would be for the federal government to collect all pollution tax payments and distribute the money equally to all residents of the nation. Obviously in cities where pollution levels and pollution tax proceeds are high this would involve a loss in potential income, and perhaps less enthusiasm on the part of local residents for pollution control policies.

The specific nature of this equal per person pollution income result in part follows from the equal utility constraint imposed on all laborers in the nation. The point of the result is to ensure that the distribution of pollution tax proceeds does not affect consumer location and migration decisions. Since income from pollution tax proceeds is everywhere the same, that effect is realized. If we remove the equal utility constraint, we could achieve the same effect of not inducing population movements by distributing proceeds randomly or all to one person.

Alternatively, without the equal utility constraint, tax proceeds could be distributed to the initial residents of the city of origin such that emigrants retained their share in proceeds and immigrants did not receive a share. Then the distribution of proceeds would not affect location decisions. Moreover, since initial city residents get the benefits of the proceeds, they might find the implementation of pollution taxes more politically palatable.

If we reintroduce marginal scale economies and land rents, the evaluation of when equation (5.12) will be satisfied in a market economy is more complex and is similar to the analyses in Chapter 4. The collection of tax proceeds means the federal government could use the distribution of pollution taxes to encourage optimal population movements. For example, if city x is both overpopulated and heavily polluted, the federal government might be able to effect an optimal allocation of population by simply paying more per person pollution tax income in city z than in x. If local governments distribute tax proceeds where the per person proceeds are higher in city x, that only aggravates the problem of overpopulation in city x.

The Effect of an Optimal Environmental Policy on City Size

Suppose in our economy, prior to enacting an environmental policy, the production of x results in heavy pollution, whereas the production of z involves little or no pollution. The usual analysis of externalities states that by taxing the emissions associated with x production the private cost of production and hence price of x will rise, lowering the demand for x relative to z. This in turn will lower the absolute demand for labor used in x relative to z production and will lead to a decline in population in the x city. While this outcome may result in the model in this chapter, the opposite may also occur.

The standard proposition overlooks the basic fact that costs of producing x and z should be viewed at the city rather than firm level. As we saw earlier, the social costs of employing labor in x production in x-type cities are the consumer goods implicitly or explicitly allocated to these laborers such that they have equal utility with residents in other cities, given relative leisure consumption and pollution disamenities. By enacting optimal environmental policies, the cost of employing labor in x production and cities and the relative price of x may decline. For example, suppose that with the enactment of an optimal environmental policy, a very small amount of employment in antipollution activity is needed to reduce pollution in the x city from its initial high levels to almost zero. The cost of employing labor in the x city should decline substantially, since the wages needed to compensate labor for living in a polluted city would now decline substantially. This decline in wages could offset the effects on production costs of pollution taxes and employment in antipollution activity, leading to increased production of x and employment in x-type cities.

The basic idea is that firms by imposing disamenities on residents raise the cost of employing labor in the city, a relationship not perceived at the firm level. Enactment of an optimal environmental policy could cause the actual costs of production for firms to decline, given the same prepolicy population, the same utility levels of residents, and lower wages. In that case we could have a final equilibrium with a larger x city, more x production, and higher utility levels in the economy, but lower wages in the x city and a lower relative price of x.

Therefore, even if the city does not get to retain all of its tax proceeds, the implementation of optimal environmental policies in a heavily polluted city may lead to an increase in city size as well as an increase in the welfare of its residents. Obviously this makes the imposition of optimal environmental policies more attractive to local political officials.

3. CONCLUSIONS

In this chapter we demonstrated that in a spatial setting optimal environmental policies consist of three parts.

(a) Pigouvian taxes must be levied on firm pollutants to induce firms to substitute away from polluting inputs in production and to employ resources in antipollution activity.

(b) Land usage may need to be zoned to ensure an optimal allocation of land between polluting (commercial) and nonpolluting (residential) activities. For example, efficiency may require commercial land rents to exceed residential land rents at the border of commercial–residential areas. Zoning will be needed to prohibit the commercial area from expanding into the residential area and bringing polluting activities closer to residents.

(c) In general, the proceeds from Pigouvian taxes should be redistributed so as to not induce in themselves any population movements. That is, by moving, people should not be able to increase their income from the distribution of pollution tax proceeds. To implement this policy in certain situations may require taking some of the tax proceeds of heavily taxed and polluted communities and redistributing them to less taxed and polluted communities.

6

Housing

In this chapter we restructure the model of housing services and the housing market presented in Chapter 1, so as to be able to consider some of the more complex problems and situations encountered in the housing market. Given that housing is a capital good, the main adjustment is to consider provision of housing services in a dynamic context where housing is subject to depreciation, maintenance, and rebuilding. In Section 1, two simple models of the housing market are outlined and within the context of these models the investment and maintenance decisions of an individual landowner are analyzed rigorously. Building upon the concepts developed, topics such as filtering down, rent control, and the tenure decisions of housing occupants are investigated.

The models and problems outlined in Section 1 have been developed and studied extensively in the literature. Although we survey some of the models and theorems in the literature, the basic goal here is to provide a common underlying framework within which to interpret, question, and read the literature. In particular, using a model of firm investment, we focus on the investment decisions of landowners and their impact on the housing market. As we develop the framework we summarize and try to give intuitive explanations of the results found in the literature.

In Section 2, we examine two types of neighborhood externalities and associated policies such as zoning, building codes, home improvement subsidies, and the use of eminent domain in land assemblage. At the end of Section 2 we turn to the possible causes of housing segregation.

1. SIMPLE HOUSING MODELS

In the literature there are two simple ways to model the housing market, both of which are sketched out here. Both models treat housing as a capital good subject to depreciation, maintenance, and replacement. However, the first assumes the housing services offered by a housing unit are a perfectly divisible good, whereas the second assumes nondivisibility in consumption where the services of a housing unit can only be consumed by one individual. In either case the consumption good, housing services, is essentially a hypothetical good that is meant to measure the combined quality and quantity of services from housing components such as floor space, fireplaces, bathrooms, garages, and exterior quality.[1]

1.1   Model 1

Consumers living in the jth neighborhood of a city consume housing services, a homogeneous divisible good sold in the housing market at a uniform price per unit *within* the neighborhood. A consumer buys as many or as few units as he wants at the going market price. Each of the n neighborhoods in the city has a particular vector of amenities, A_j, associated with it. Amenities include commuting time from the neighborhood to the city center, pollution levels, parks, income level and composition of the neighborhood, crime rates, etc. Each consumer lives in only one neighborhood and chooses his optimal neighborhood after scanning the n city neighborhoods, the amenities in each neighborhood, and the housing prices p_j associated with each neighborhood.

To solve for the equilibrium set of neighborhood housing prices and housing patterns in any period, one would utilize a model similar to that in Chapter 1. Each consumer has a bid rent function (equation (1.7)) where $p_j^0 = p(V, y, p_x, p_z, A_j)$. From the analysis in Chapter 1 we known that p_j^0 varies as A_j (equation (1.3)) varies, and p_j^0 varies as income y varies (equation (1.9)). Given how much different types of consumers are willing to bid for different types of amenities and neighborhoods, consumers would be allocated to different neighborhoods. At the equilibrium set of prices, each

---

[1] There is a literature on measuring hedonic price indexes for housing where the marginal evaluation as well as the demand by consumers for these components is measured. For example, see King (1974).

consumer would be in his utility-maximizing location and each housing owner would be renting to the higher bidder. Because A_j is a vector where the elements may vary noncontinuously among neighborhoods, and because neighborhood sizes may not correspond to the group sizes of the different types of consumers, the precise calculation of equilibrium is not as straightforward as in Chapter 1.

However, two points can be made. First, neighborhoods should be fairly homogeneous, containing people with similar demands for amenities, just as people in Chapter 1 were ordered spatially by demand for leisure. Second, we can depict equilibrium within a neighborhood in a demand and supply curve framework. In Figure 6.1 the supply curve in any period is upward sloping because there is a fixed amount of land in each neighborhood and diminishing returns to the variable factor capital applied to land in producing housing services. Equilibrium is at H_j and p_j.

Demand in any period is an increasing function of the number of residents, income per resident, own amenities, and prices in other neighborhoods. It is a decreasing function of amenities in other neighborhoods and own price. An increase in own amenities will shift up the demand curve due to increased demand to live in the neighborhood and due to a possible increase in neighborhood income level. The rise in price will reduce per resident housing consumption at each income level or more people may crowd into the neighborhood so as to consume the increased amenities.

This sketches out the demand side of the housing market. On the supply side, we must look at the underlying individual producer decisions.

An individual landowner in the neighborhood buys a lot in time 0, builds housing on it, and sells divisible housing services at the going market rental, such as p_j in Figure 6.1. Housing services $h(t)$ in any period are a function of fixed lot size $L(0)$ and total capital stock $K(t)$. Therefore,

$$h(t) = h(L(0), K(t)) \tag{6.1}$$

where $\partial h(t)/\partial K(t) > 0$, $\partial^2 h(t)/\partial K(t)^2 < 0$. Given a fixed lot size, housing

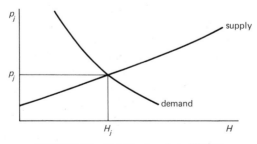

FIGURE 6.1   Neighborhood equilibrium.

services are a strictly monotonic increasing function of capital stock, but there are diminishing marginal returns to capital in producing housing services. Thus for a given $L(0)$, since $\partial^2 h(t)/\partial K(t)^2 < 0$, the marginal productivity of capital, $\partial h(t)/\partial K(t)$, is a strictly monotonic decreasing function of housing services. Accordingly, each value of $\partial h(t)/\partial K(t)$ is associated with a unique level of housing services $h(t)$.

Capital stock is the sum of depreciated previous capital inputs $k(t)$ where $K(0) = k(0)$ is the initial structure and $k(t)$ for $t \geq 1$ is maintenance or investment in each period. If $\delta(t)$ is the rate of depreciation in time t of *all* capital (regardless of age) invested in the landowner's housing, then in any period s,

$$K(s) = \int_0^s k(t)e^{-\int_t^s \delta(v)\,dv}\,dt.$$

Differentiating, we get the change in capital stock in any period or

$$\partial K(t)/\partial t \equiv \dot{K}(t) = k(t) - \delta(t)K(t). \tag{6.2}$$

The change in capital stock in each period is gross investment in that period minus depreciation of the existing capital. The specification of a depreciation rate that is a function of time from initial construction of the house is meant to capture the possibility of housing aging over time. If $\delta(t)$ increases over time, this means that new additions and the existing capital stock will wear out more quickly as housing gets older.

The landlord maximizes the present value of future profits, or maximizes

$$\pi = \int_0^T (p_j h(t) - p_k k(t))e^{-rt}\,dt - s(0) + s(T)e^{-rT} \tag{6.3}$$

where p_j is the unit price of housing services in neighborhood j and p_k is the purchase price of capital. We assume these prices are viewed as being time invariant. r is the discount rate and T is the time the house is torn down. $s(0)$ is the purchase price of land and $s(T)$ is the selling price of the housing and land in time T. $s(T)$ includes the price of land in time T, the proceeds from the sale of the remaining capital stock $p_k K(T)$, and the costs of demolition or restoration of the land to a preconstruction condition. With perfect competition and knowledge in the marketplace, $\pi \to 0$. Then the price of land $s(0)$ will equal the present value of future profits and the return on housing investment will equal the discount rate. The landowner may sell the building before time T but with perfect market information his selling price will be the present value of future profits. Therefore, his objective function is the same whether he intends to hold the building to time T or not.

To describe the properties of the optimal planned maintenance path that maximizes perceived profits in equation (6.3), from equation (6.2) we substitute in $\dot{K}(t) + \delta(t)K(t)$ for $k(t)$. The necessary condition for optimization is the Euler equation. Rearranging terms, we know that on the optimal maintenance path[2]

$$p_j(\partial h(t)/\partial K(t)) = (r + \delta(t))p_k. \tag{6.4}$$

This states that the marginal benefits of investing an additional unit of capital in any period, which are $p_j(\partial h(t)/\partial K(t))$, should equal the opportunity cost of holding capital for one period. This cost is foregone interest plus losses in the capital stock through depreciation. The period in which housing is torn down if it is finite is determined by the terminal condition (see footnote 2)

$$p_j h(T) = p_k \delta(T)K(T) - \dot{s}(T) + rs(T). \tag{6.5}$$

Equation (6.5) states that in the period in which housing is torn down the marginal benefits of holding housing one more period, or the rental revenue $p_j h(T)$, should equal or be less than the marginal costs. The marginal costs of holding housing one more period are (i) further losses from depreciation of the capital stock, (ii) less any capital gains on the house, (iii) plus foregone interest on the sales value.

Given equation (6.4), we can examine the characteristics of the optimal maintenance path. Suppose $\delta(t)$ is constant over time, which is the normal assumption in capital theory. Then the right-hand side of equation (6.4) is constant and to maintain equality in (6.4) the left-hand side must be constant. Given that p_j is viewed as time invariant, this implies that $\partial h(t)/\partial K(t)$ is the same in each period. From equation (6.1) this in turn implies $h(t)$ and $K(t)$ are the same in each period. If the capital stock is the same over time, then maintenance planned for each period must exactly equal depreciation, or $\dot{K} = 0$ and $k(t) = \delta K(t)$. As long as p_j/p_k is constant, the housing situation for a landowner in neighborhood j is static. Given the same prices and technical conditions for all landowners in the neighborhood, the neighborhood situation must also be static.

The only way in which neighborhood housing services will change will be if p_j/p_k changes. p_j will change through an exogenous shift in the demand curve in Figure 6.1 due to city-wide population changes or changes in relative amenity levels among neighborhoods. If for example the demand curve shifts back and p_j falls, to maintain equality in equation (6.4), $\partial h/\partial K$ will rise and the optimal stationary values of $K(t)$ will decline. This decline in housing services reflects the reduced return to investing in housing for individuals and results in a reduced level of neighborhood housing in Figure 6.1.

These changes in housing services are all because of changes on the demand side. This is the antithesis of filtering-down models in which housing deterioration is endogenous to the supply side. If the depreciation rate $\delta(t)$ is constant over time or housing does not age in housing models, any

---

[2] If $I = (p_j h(t) - p_k(\dot{K} + \delta K(t))e^{-rt}$, the Euler equation is $\partial I/\partial K - d(\partial I/\partial \dot{K})/dt = 0$ and the transversality condition is that $I - \dot{K}(\partial I/\partial \dot{K}) + \partial(s(T)e^{-rT})/\partial T = 0$.

observed filtering down in the housing market is not a "natural" or technical phenomenon but is induced by demand shifts in the market place. For example, the decay of the housing stock in many core cities could be a result of population and income movements out of the core city caused by external factors such as suburbanization for fiscal reasons (see Chapter 10), rather than the opposite causal relationship of the decay leading to out-migration. I personally favor models where $\delta(t)$ is fixed and explanations of filtering down are found on the demand side (see, e.g., Chapter 10) because in some North American cities there has not been comprehensive filtering down (e.g., Toronto and Vancouver). However, the literature has many supply-induced filtering-down models and we now proceed to analyze this phenomenon.

The way in which we start to get the rudiments of filtering down in a housing model due to supply or technical conditions is to assume that housing ages, or $\delta(t)$ increases over time. For example, we could assume $\delta(t) = \delta e^{\gamma t}$ where $\dot{\delta} = \gamma\delta$. Instead of assuming that $\delta(t)$ increases over time, we could equivalently assume that the cost of maintaining housing at a given level of services increases over time. Our formulation of the assumption is consistent with the traditional firm investment literature.

If $\delta(t)$ increases continuously in equation (6.4), the right-hand side increases continuously. For a given p_j, for the left-hand side to increase, $\partial h(t)/\partial K(t)$ must increase and planned $K(t)$ and $h(t)$ must decline. Then in the sense that the landowner offers less and less housing services in each succeeding period, housing filters down. However, in the sense that this depreciated housing passes to lower and lower demanders of housing or, presumably, lower- and lower-income people, we do not necessarily have filtering down. Given that housing services are homogeneous and divisible, lower levels of housing services could be bought by fewer of the initial-income (or even higher-income) people as well as by lower-income people. To ensure that housing filters down through different income groups, we need a model where not only is $\delta(t)$ increasing, but housing services from a housing unit are indivisible on the consumption side. We turn to such a model in the next section.

Note that if housing investment for individual landowners is declining and all housing in the neighborhood was built at the same time, then neighborhood housing must be declining. In that case the supply curve in Figure 6.1 must be shifting back, and either price must be rising or the demand curve must also be shifting back (so as to maintain price). In general, as the supply of neighborhood housing falls, one would expect the demand curve to shift back as people moved to other newer and lower-priced neighborhoods. On the other hand, if the age distribution of housing in a neighborhood in the stationary state is uniform, then p_j may remain fixed, with new housing just replacing demolished housing in each period. In that case on a neighborhood basis it is not clear that there is filtering down in any sense of the term.

Finally we note that the lot size of a landowner is fixed in the foregoing analysis. When a whole block deteriorates and the buildings are all torn down, given suitable transactions among landowners, lot size can obviously be redesigned and becomes an endogenous variable. However, given the assumptions of constant returns to scale and perfect divisibility and homogeneity of housing services, lot size is not determinate in the model. To get a determinate lot size it is necessary to relax one or more of these assumptions. For example, we could assume nonhomogeneity, where certain types of housing services and buildings require different minimum lot sizes (single-family homes versus apartments) and hence lot size will depend to some extent on which type of housing can be most profitably built on the vacant land.

Before proceeding to the second model, we comment on the process of net housing disinvestment or net depreciation that occurs when either market housing prices decline or housing ages (or both). There are two possibilities for net depreciation and downward adjustment in the housing stock such that equation (6.4) is satisfied. The first is that gross investment $k(t)$ remains positive but depreciation $\delta(t)K(t)$ exceeds gross investment, so net additions to capital $\dot{K}$ ($=k(t) - \delta(t)K(t)$) are negative. The alternative is that gross investment itself is negative. In our model when this occurs, we have assumed complete reversibility of investment where the landowner can sell off unwanted capital (doors, closets, stairways, fireplaces, etc.) at the full market price (p_k) at any time.[3] This is a strong assumption.[4] If instead we assume investment is irreversible and impose a nonnegativity constraint on $k(t)$, for the maximization problem in equation (6.3), equation (6.4) is generally only valid if the $k(t)$ that satisfies (6.4) is nonnegative for all t (i.e., the nonnegativity constraint imposes no costs).[5] Although the issue of

---

[3] We have already assumed reversibility in the last period, or that $K(T)$ can be sold off at full market value. Note that without demolition costs if $\delta(t)$ increases with the age of the house, it would be efficient to tear housing down in each period and completely replace it so $\delta(t)$ is always at its initial low value. Demolition costs prevent this from happening.

[4] To illustrate the problem, assume price is expected to rise above its normal level p_j for one instant only and then return to the normal level. If $k(t)$ can be positive or negative, housing producers will plan to expand their housing for one period to satisfy equation (6.4) at the cost $(r + \delta)p_k$ and then sell off the surplus $k(t)$ at a price p_k in the next period. On the other hand, if $k(t) \geq 0$ is constrained to be nonnegative, there will probably be only a negligible change in their investment pattern.

[5] If investment is irreversible, the general optimality condition is that in any period s we invest until

$$p_k = \int_s^T p_j \, \partial h(t)/\partial K(t) e^{-rt - \int_s^t \delta(v)\,dv}\,dt$$

or until the marginal cost of investment p_k equals the discounted sum of future marginal benefits. These benefits are the value of marginal product of a unit of capital discounted by the extent of depreciation of capital invested in s. See Arrow (1968) and Gould (1968) on this.

reversibility versus irreversibility is important, we avoid an extended discussion of it by assuming either that investment is reversible or that equation (6.4) is satisfied with desired $k(t) \geq 0$ for all t for the situations we consider. Note that by introducing adjustment costs in terms of selling off unwanted capital, we can model a situation that lies somewhat between complete reversibility and complete irreversibility. However, these adjustment cost formulations usually only refer to the high costs associated with carrying out large positive or negative adjustments in any one period and suggest that adjustments should be spread over time. They do not really deal with the asymmetry involved here where additions may be made at constant unit cost but gross disinvestment may be almost impossible whether it occurs in one period or is spread over time.

1.2 Model 2

A city is divided into n neighborhoods within which there are m_j housing units where j denotes the jth neighborhood. A housing unit is a house or apartment and each family in the city rents only one unit. The level of housing services per unit may vary. Total families in the city are $\sum_{j=1}^{n} m_j$. Using linear programming techniques, it can be shown that there exists a set of prices for each rental unit such that (a) all units are rented to the highest bidder, (b) each resident is at his optimal location given the set of prices, and (c) all units are rented at nonnegative prices (see Herbert and Stevens, 1960; Davis and Winston, 1964; Wheaton, 1974).

Our concern is with the decisions of individual tenants and owners and what their decisions must imply for the housing market over time. The ith housing unit in the jth neighborhood offers h_{ij} housing services. To find the rental schedule facing the landowner offering h_{ij} services, we examine Figure 6.2. In Figure 6.2 using the curves $W(A)$, $W(B)$, and $W(C)$, we show what consumers A, B, and C are willing to bid in total for different h_{ij}, given their alternative utility levels obtained by renting at their best alternative

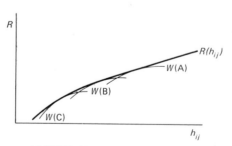

FIGURE 6.2   Rental opportunities.

locations in the city.[6] The concavity of the willingness-to-pay curves follows from the convexity of indifferences curves, reflecting diminishing marginal rates of substitution in consumption. (The concavity may be seen by twice differentiating $V(y - W, h)$ for y and V fixed or by plotting W, h_{ij} in Figure 6.2 from indifference curve space for housing and all other goods given a fixed V and y.) We assume willingness-to-pay or the marginal evaluation of housing increases with income. Given the set of willingness-to-pay curves for all consumers, in an atomistic housing market, the owner of the housing unit ij faces a set of realizable rents $R(h_{ij})$. $R(h_{ij})$ *is the locus of the highest willingness-to-pay curves facing the owner.* As long as willingness-to-pay and income increase smoothly from curve to curve the rent opportunities facing the owner are described by a concave relationship where

$$R = R(h_{ij}), \qquad \partial R/\partial h > 0, \qquad \partial^2 R/\partial h^2 < 0. \tag{6.6}$$

For the moment we assume $R(h_{ij})$ facing the landowner in one period is the same in all periods. What this implies in the housing market and when this could be true is discussed later. For notational convenience we drop the ij subscript in the following discussion.

Given an $R(h)$ facing a landowner, we can now examine his maintenance and investment decisions. Each housing unit is built on a lot of fixed size. As before, the landowner has a production function for housing services described by equation (6.1) and a capital adjustment equation (6.2). He maximizes the present value of profits as in equation (6.3) except that the revenue expression $p_j h(t)$ is now simply $R(h(t))$. The new Euler equation is

$$(\partial R/\partial h(t))(\partial h(t)/\partial K(t)) = (\delta(t) + r)p_k. \tag{6.7}$$

As before, if $\delta(t)$ is constant over time, planned R, h, and K will be the same in each period unless there are demand-induced changes in R. If housing ages and $\delta(t)$ increases over time, then the right-hand side of (6.7), and hence the left-hand side, must increase. This happens by planned $K(t)$ declining over time (although $k(t)$ may be positive, as illustrated later). As $K(t)$ declines, from equation (6.1) $\partial h/\partial K$ rises and h falls. As h falls, from equation (6.6) R falls but $\partial R/\partial h$ rises. Therefore, in equation (6.7) both $\partial R/\partial h$ and $\partial h/\partial K$ rise [decline] as $K(t)$ falls [rises].

As $K(t)$ and $h(t)$ decline, the owner is moving along $R(h)$ in Figure 6.2b. This implies that in each succeeding period he plans to rent to lower and lower housing demanders and probably lower- and lower-income people. This is filtering down, in the sense of both housing decay and the passage over time of a house to lower- and lower-income people. The landowner

---

[6] See Sweeney (1974a) for a similar discussion.

plans to demolish the deteriorating house when the terminal condition, equation (6.4), is satisfied.[7]

Rather than having the owner change tenants from period to period, one could incorporate moving costs into the model and optimize to show that tenants may stay longer than one period. They will also pay the owner to "overmaintain" his units relative to the housing provided along $R(h)$ if housing changed hands each period. The tenants have some desired housing $\overset{*}{h}$ given incomes and market opportunities. They will move in when $h > \overset{*}{h}$ and move out when $h < \overset{*}{h}$ and pay the owner to "overmaintain" housing

---

[7] It is fairly easy to illustrate this filtering process for one housing unit. Assume a time-invariant revenue function $R = h^\eta$ where $\eta < 1$. Housing services $h(t) = AL(0)^\alpha K(t)^\beta$ where $L(0)$ is fixed and $\alpha, \beta < 1$. The aging process is described by $\delta(t) = \delta e^{\gamma t}$, so that $k(t) = \dot{K}(t) + \delta e^{\gamma t} K(t)$. Therefore, the present value of profits is

$$\pi = \int_0^T [A^\eta L(0)^{\alpha \eta} K^{\beta \eta} - p_k(\dot{K} + \delta e^{\gamma t} K(t))]e^{-rt}\, dt - s(0) + s(T)e^{-rT}.$$

The Euler equation reduces to $A^\eta \beta \eta L^{\alpha \eta} K^{\beta \eta - 1} = p_k(r + \delta e^{\gamma t})$; or rearranging, the optimal value of capital stock in any period is

$$K(t) = [p_k(r + \delta e^{\gamma t})A^{-\eta}\beta^{-1}\eta^{-1}L^{-\alpha \eta}]^{1/(\beta \eta - 1)}.$$

Given $\beta, \eta < 1$, $K(t)$ decreases over time or net investment declines continuously. If we differentiate the Euler equation with respect to time and substitute in the expressions for $\dot{K}$ and $K(t)$, we find

$$k(t) = [p_k(r + \delta e^{\gamma t})\beta^{-1}\eta^{-1}A^{-\eta}L^{-\alpha \eta}]^{1/(\beta \eta - 1)} \delta e^{\gamma t}\left[1 - \frac{\gamma}{(r + \delta e^{\gamma t})(1 - \beta \eta)}\right].$$

Despite the decline in net capital stock, gross investment $k(t)$ is always positive if $\gamma < (r + \delta e^{\gamma t})(1 - \beta \eta)$ or if the aging parameter γ is small relative to the discount or depreciation rate δ.

To solve for the length of life of a building, we assume perfect competition, or that $s(0)$ is such that $\pi = 0$. We decompose $s(T)$ into demolition costs $D(T)$, scrap value $p_k K(T)$, and land price in T. We assume the selling price of land in T is the same as in 0, or the opportunities for investment are static. Therefore, with $\pi = 0$ for our example the profit equation may be re-written as

$$s(0)(1 - e^{-rT}) = \int_0^T [A^\eta L^{\alpha \eta} K(t)^{\beta \eta} - p_k k(t)]e^{-rt}\, dt + e^{-rT}(p_k K(T) - D(T)).$$

If we substitute in for $k(t)$ and $K(t)$ and integrate, we get an equation containing parameters and the variables T and $s(0)$. ($s(0)$ is a dependent variable since it must be consistent with the arbitrary revenue and production functions.) To solve for $s(0)$ and T, we need a second equation containing these variables. This is the terminal condition equation (6.5), where now

$$A^\eta L^{\alpha \eta} K(T)^{\beta \eta} = p_k K(T)(r + \delta e^{\gamma T}) + r(s(0) - D(T)).$$

Substituting in for $K(T)$, we have an expression in parameters and unknowns T and $s(0)$. Given these two equations we can solve for T and $s(0)$ in terms of our parameters. For example, for $L(0) = p_k = A = 5, \beta = \frac{2}{3}, \eta = \frac{3}{4}, r = 0.05, \delta = 0.05, \gamma = 0.025, D(T) = \$343$, rough calculations indicate $T = 25$ and $s(0) = \$732$.

to keep it near $\overset{*}{h}$ during their tenure so they may consume almost their desired housing without moving. Sweeney (1974a) presents an extended analysis of a similar situation.[8]

Filtering Down and Market Equilibrium

For an individual landowner facing a time-invariant $R(h)$ we have derived optimal maintenance and length of building life policies. It remains to examine filtering down as a market process. In examining the market process, we are concerned with the implications that profit-maximizing behavior has for filtering down in the market as a whole and vice versa. For example, one question is whether, given filtering down in the market as a whole, the $R(h)$ schedule facing an individual landowner can be time invariant, even in a city with static population and income.

Consider a housing market with a spectrum of consumers demanding different levels of housing based on their differing incomes. Corresponding to the spectrum of consumers, in equilibrium there will be a spectrum of housing units providing varying levels of housing services. Housing tends to be built at higher housing levels, although not necessarily only at those levels; it then filters down through lower and lower levels. At housing levels where there is construction, the price of all housing units at that level is determined by construction costs; whereas at levels where there is no construction, prices are determined by demand conditions given the number of units supplied at that level. The length of time that a house provides approximately the same level of services, which is related to the speed at which housing filters, is determined by general supply and demand conditions around that level of housing services. On the supply side, to maintain housing services at approximately the same level requires increasing quantities of maintenance over time as $\delta(t)$ increases in magnitude. However, if around that level of services there are many demanders relative to units, so that price is high, then housing may filter quite slowly around that level.

If city population, production conditions, income distribution, and technology are constant, we should have a stationary solution in the housing market. In each period the same quantity of housing services is provided at each level, the same quantity of construction and demolition occurs, and

---

[8] Sweeney compares the optimal maintenance policies of owner-occupied housing (where desired tenure is long) with rental housing, where he implicitly assumes renters move every period (perhaps for exogenous reasons). In our situation we could compare maintenance policies in buildings with a high turnover rate (due to external mobility decisions of the type of tenants in those buildings) with policies in buildings with a low turnover rate (the elderly). One would expect the relative amount of maintenance in the low turnover buildings to exceed that in high turnover buildings for the reasons discussed in the text.

individuals consume the same quantity of housing. In a stationary solution, over time there can be no profits to be made from changing the quantity (and price) of housing supplied to any individual. Also the $R(h)$ facing an individual owner will remain constant over time if the aggregate market opportunities are stationary. All this implies that the age distribution of housing remains constant even though there is continuous filtering. This age distribution will be structured through the price mechanism (the $R(h)$'s facing different landowners) so as to provide the same quantity of housing demanded by each income group in each period.

In terms of housing construction and filtering, if the income distribution has a tail, with a few high-income people spread over a wide income range, a few new housing starts will probably occur at the highest levels, with these houses filtering through the high-income range. However, most new housing starts will probably occur at the first (high) income levels where there is a substantial number of people. As indicated earlier, the speed at which housing filters varies over the life of the house. It probably moves most slowly through that modal part of the income distribution, so as to ensure in aggregate, sufficient housing supply through filtering at that income level. Housing will be demolished at varying low-income levels over the low-income tail of the income distribution. Housing constructed at the highest levels may or may not filter all the way through the income distribution, depending on the cost of, say, converting large houses into apartments as opposed to the profits from tearing the house down early and reconstructing a high-quality house. Sweeney (1974b) has a complete and rigorous analysis of this process.

When neighborhood externalities are introduced (see next section) where the quality of the houses adjacent to a resident affects his well-being, one would expect market equilibrium to be characterized by housing being age homogeneous within neighborhoods. All the housing within neighborhoods would be built at the same time and would filter down together so as to minimize problems with these externalities. The reasoning behind these statements will become apparent later.

Rent Controls: An Application of Housing Models

We consider rent control in a particular situation where only part of the housing market is rent controlled, such as has been the case in New York over the last two decades (see Kristoff, 1968). Rent control is often interpreted as control over the price of a unit of housing services. However, rent control administrators (as well as economists) have not yet solved the problem of quantifying units of the abstract good called housing services and hence have yet to define the price of a unit of housing services. Accordingly, we choose here to interpret rent control as control over the total rent that can be charged for a given housing unit, independent of the services provided with that unit. (Of course, if housing services decline over time with rent control, the authorities may lower the allowable rent so as to effectively maintain approximately a fixed unit price of housing services.)

In Figure 6.3 $R(h)$ is the schedule of housing rents facing a landowner prior to rent control. Currently, h_A of housing services are being provided to person A at a rent R_A. The city government decides to impose rent control on a portion of the housing units in the city. The number of rent-controlled units is sufficiently limited so that for our purposes we may assume $R(h)$ and $W(A)$, which reflect the free-market opportunities of the owner and tenant, are virtually unchanged (at least initially). Rent control lowers the allowable rent on this unit to $\bar{R}_C$.

Assuming some type of irreversibility, so that the landowner cannot immediately sell off his now excess capital and go directly to point c, the owner ceases maintenance temporarily and net disinvestment takes place. Initially as h declines, the original tenant A stays in the unit, since his willingness to pay $W(A)$ exceeds the allowable payment $\bar{R}_C$ until point b. In the free-market filtering process, of course, the tenant would move out when housing filtered below h_A; but here the reduced rent increases his length of tenure because he is locked in by the rent savings from controls. Beyond point b tenant A leaves. The owner continues this (accelerated) disinvestment until point c is reached. At point c if δ is constant, net disinvestment ceases. If $\delta(t)$ increases with housing age, then filtering down continues along $R(h)$ since $\bar{R}_C$ is no longer effective.

This process has implications for the market as a whole. If rent control is initially imposed on the same proportion of housing at all ages and consumption levels, then, after the first stages of rent control, controlled housing will be in a decayed state and consumed disproportionately by lower income people relative to noncontrolled housing. This occurs, of course, because of the accelerated depreciation described in the preceding paragraph. After the initial tenants no longer wish to stay in the unit, it passes to lower

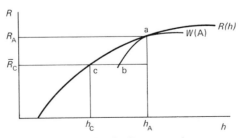

FIGURE 6.3   Rent control.

demanders or lower-income tenants. In aggregate this implies that after the initial stages of rent control, due to the accelerated depreciation of controlled housing, there is a reduction in the aggregate supply of high-income housing. There is also a corresponding temporary or permanent rise in the price of that housing in the noncontrolled market as higher-income people move out of controlled units and the demand to live in noncontrolled areas increases.

Finally, if once a rent-controlled building is demolished the owner is no longer subject to rent control (as is somewhat the situation in New York), this will advance the date of demolition and the rate of decay, since the opportunity value of the land is higher than in its current use. These points indicate that evaluations of the social welfare losses caused by rent control must be done carefully. The usual way of measuring social losses is to take the profits lost by owners and deduct the net gains to tenants (from reduced rent) in any period. This loss will vary from period to period and one really should calculate the present value of all losses. However, there may also be further social losses caused by possible price increases in the noncontrolled market; and the usual measures of welfare losses may not adequately measure losses due to the accelerated decay of the housing stock and the advanced date of demolition of controlled units.

2.   NEIGHBORHOOD EXTERNALITIES

The theoretical basis or reason for many housing and land use policies in an urban area is the hypothesized existence of neighborhood externalities. There are two related types of neighborhood externalities, each with a different set of public policies. We examine them separately.

2.1   Social Externalities

Social externalities arise because a resident's neighbors or their characteristics enter his utility function as separate arguments. The presence of different types of neighbors and their characteristics may increase, decrease, or leave neutral one's level of satisfaction. For example, one may have preferences defined over whether one's neighbors are noisy, friendly, generous, secretive, religious, white or black, childless, young or old, rich or poor, etc. In a city of N people, each person has preferences with respect to having everyone else as neighbors, so that whoever moves in next door to a person affects his utility and vice versa. Since these social preferences or externalities are unpriced in the market, we only expect a Pareto-efficient assignment of people if there exists a bribing mechanism that allows the possibility of any person bribing any other person or *set* of persons in the city to live or not live next to him or others and the tâtonnement process is costless. (This latter condition in part is necessary so that people can costlessly adjust locations after "trying" people as neighbors in potential solutions and "learning" their characteristics.)

Since in our economy explicit bribing among residents is not an acceptable social custom, a person will only alter his residential situation by moving himself. He will not bribe a person to live next to him or to switch places with others. Consequently, these preferences or neighborhood amenities are not priced and the equilibrium spatial arrangement will in general be nonoptimal. Davis and Winston (1964) demonstrate this in the context of a housing assignment problem. A simple (rigged) example can also illustrate the point.

Suppose we have three people bidding in an auction for contiguous locations numbered 1, 2, 3 along a straight line. The locations are owned by different landowners who behave atomistically and passively, in the sense that they are willing to simply accept the highest nonnegative bid offered to them during the auction process. The opportunity rent on the locations is zero. Table 6.1 is a matrix of preferences defining how much our three antisocial people are willing to pay not to have others as neighbors. The three are constrained, however, to live side by side along a line. The only stable configuration is the arrangement A, B, C (or C, B, A). An equilibrium set of prices for this arrangement is 3, 0, 3. The base price, 0, prices the middle spot. C pays $3 for location 3 because he is willing to pay $3 not to live at location 2 and have A as his neighbor, and because he must pay $3 or B will bid away location 3 to avoid living next to A. A pays $3 for location 1 so that C does not bid it away. The price of spot 1 must always equal the price of spot 3 in any stable equilibrium, since they both offer the same neighbor. The social loss from this arrangement is $1 for A, $4 for B, and $8 for C—a total of $13. The spatial arrangement B, A, C (or C, A, B) has a smaller social loss of $10. Without bribing, however, this spatial arrangement is not sustainable because starting from this arrangement A will always outbid B for

TABLE 6.1

Preferences for Neighbors

		Possible Neighbors		
		A	B	C
Loss from having various neighbors	A	0	−1	−3
	B	−3	0	−1
	C	−3	−8	0

spot 1. The assignment is only stable if C is willing to do one of the following—bribe B to bid more for spot 1, bribe A to locate in spot 2 or bribe the landowner of spot 1 to rent it to B. Although with only three people along a line it may seem naïve to rule out explicit bribes of this type, once the problem is expanded to n people arranged in a spatial area, the number of bribes required to reach an optimal arrangement becomes prohibitive. Moreover, the government certainly does not have this information about residents' preferences and thus cannot implement an optimal solution.

Although the market cannot solve this generalized problem, it may be able to solve gross problems of this sort. In particular, people's preferences about neighbors might be primarily determined by one or two characteristics, such as race, income, or land use. For example, suppose there are two land use groups in a city, retail and residential. (Or we could have two racial, income, or ethnic groups.) These groups generally prefer to locate next to others with similar land uses. (Retail users want to utilize common parking and mall facilities and attract each other's customers. Residents prefer not to locate next to commercial activity because of noise pollution and other disamenities.) Therefore, people within each group are always willing to bid more for a spot next to a similar type land user. As a result, the tâtonnement process should lead to a solution where renters in each group are clustered together. However, even with this type of situation where large groups of users prefer to separate themselves from others, the configuration of groups and division of land may still be suboptimal for several reasons.

Problems may arise if one group of people wants to live next to a second group, who would prefer to live separate from the first. A common example is the gas station owner who wants to locate in a residential neighborhood. The residents surrounding the gas station suffer from noise and odor pollution (although other nonimmediate but nearby residents may benefit in net from the proximity of a gas station). While the suffering of any individual resident is not sufficient to induce him to individually buy the gas station or bribe the owner to move, the total loss to all immediate residents is such that they could get together to bribe the owner to move. However, the social and monetary costs and the free-rider problems involved in forming a group prevent these residents from operating as a group to bribe the owner to move. Therefore, land use zoning is often recommended as a form of protection that ensures residents that a gas station will not locate next to them. (Of course, it is possible that although residents immediate to the gas station suffer from its presence, other nonimmediate residents may benefit more than the immediate residents lose.)

Another problem in land use allocation arises simply because people in different groups are willing to pay different amounts to live next to or separate from each other. We illustrate the situation using retailers and residents as our groups. The example is similar to the land use problem in Chapter 5 and was originally noted by Bailey (1957).

The urban area consists of a fixed amount of land to be divided among retailers and residents. Suppose retailers in net are neutral about locating next to residents, given the advantages of retailers clustering together weighed against the benefits of close proximity to residents. Because of pollution considerations, in net residents do not want to live next to retailers. The market operates to separate the two groups. In Figure 6.4a we illustrate one division of the urban area where land prices (and marginal products) are equalized between the interiors of the two areas, as should be optimal. At the border in the residential area, land prices are less by the amount needed to induce (and compensate) border residents to live next to retailers, as opposed to other residents. The configuration in Figure 6.4a, however, is not stable. Retailers will buy up the cheap border residential land and continue to encroach on the residential area until prices in the retail area equal prices on the border of the residential area. A stable solution is illustrated in Figure 6.4b. Prices in the interior of the residential area exceed prices in the retail area and on the residential border by the amount border residents are compensated relative to interior residents for living next to retailers. To prevent this, as was suggested in the similar pollution situation in Chapter 5, we would need land use zoning that would prevent the retail area from expanding in Figure 6.4a.

Note, however, that if there are a few residents who do not mind living next to retailers, the problem disappears and no zoning is necessary. The people who do not mind living next to retailers would occupy the border area in Figure 6.4a, for some negligible inducement in terms of a negligible reduction in price. Then the situation in Figure 6.4a will be stable.

Finally, we note that a problem occurs when there are more than two groups of people. Suppose there are three groups, retailers, residents, and

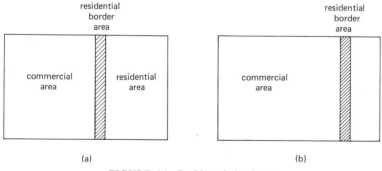

FIGURE 6.4 Problems in land use.

manufacturers. Even if the groups separate in an efficient manner and there is zoning to prevent nonoptimal encroachment of one group on the land of another, the spatial arrangements of the groups may not be optimal. For example, in a city retailers may border on residents, residents on retailers and manufacturers, and manufacturers on residents. (In Table 6.1, substitute retailers, residents, and manufacturers for A, B, and C.) Some other spatial arrangement, such as manufacturers bordering on retailers, retailers on manufacturers and residents, and residents on retailers, may minimize losses (or maximize the gains) to people on the borders who must live next to other land use groups. As was the case for individuals, atomistic bidding in the marketplace may not be enough to ensure that the groups will rearrange themselves optimally. Land use zoning could give us the optimal configuration. One could extend this example to the spatial arrangement of different clustered land uses such as retail, manufacturing, service sector, single-family, apartment, and high- and low-income residential land uses.

2.2   Housing Upkeep Externalities

The second type of neighborhood externality concerns the maintenance decisions of people's neighbors, rather than the characteristics of their neighbors per se. The externality involved is that the outside quality of a neighbor's house affects a resident's locational satisfaction by affecting his view and the pleasure and pride he takes in inviting friends to his house and hence neighborhood. Second, a neighbor's maintenance policies affect a resident's safety and the safety of his children, in terms of lighting at night; repairs of stairways, railings, and roofs; shoveling of snow; and garbage disposal. For a landowner (who may be the occupant), in the profit maximization expressions in equations (6.3) and (6.8) only the private benefits of maintenance are captured. In addition to the private benefits there are these external social benefits or neighborhood externalities from upkeep. Since the landowner is not compensated for these externalities, he does not account for them in his maintenance decisions and hence the level of upkeep is too low. If residents could bribe other landowners or residents according to these externalities, the maintenance on their house would go up. ·

There are three possible types of solutions to this problem. First, it should be noted that the externality is reciprocal where, while a resident's upkeep affects his neighbors' well-being, their upkeep affects his well-being. If people with similar tastes for housing are grouped together, the magnitude of the total and marginal external benefits will be approximately the same. Then the neighbors involved would all be willing to voluntarily agree to increase maintenance and housing services to the optimal level without bribing taking place. Essentially each resident would "bribe" his neighbors to increase their upkeep by increasing his own upkeep. (In a rental market, the tenants would be willing to pay the owner for higher upkeep or services.) Such a solution may be realized in many stable neighborhoods where people know each other. Various forms of social pressure can be applied to induce neighbors to maintain their houses and implicitly agree to internalize this externality. Of course, in transient neighborhoods where neighbors may not know each other, such solutions are less likely.

A second possible solution is through zoning ordinances and building codes that require landowners to light outdoor entrances, have adequate garbage disposal, and repair external structures. However, such ordinances are unlikely to deal with problems of gardening, landscaping, and painting. Of course, the residents may not be so concerned with these items, but may be mostly concerned with upkeep of items that involve safety considerations.

Finally, the government can subsidize home improvement loans as a general policy designed to induce all homeowners to increase maintenance on their housing.

Neighborhood externalities are also in part at the theoretical root of policies such as urban renewal and the use of eminent domain in land assemblage in urban areas. It is because of neighborhood externalities that redevelopment or reconstruction of housing must be done on a large scale and requires a large package of land. A developer is unlikely to build one or two new houses on a block of old and decaying houses because the externalities imposed by the decaying structures would lower the selling price of the new buildings relative to a situation where the whole block is redeveloped. If the whole block is redeveloped, then initially these externalities are internalized and the problem of having decaying buildings on the block is eradicated. However, redeveloping the whole block requires assembling a large quantity of land and buying up *all* the existing structures. This introduces the traditional holdout problem, where the last seller(s) of old structures on the block holds out for a tremendous price. At the limit the developer would have to pay all his potential profits from the redevelopment to the holdout and this discourages potential developers from undertaking the project. This then requires public intervention in the form of eminent domain where the initial residents are forced to sell (for the public "good") at "fair" market prices (which may be contested) to the developer (perhaps through the city government).

However, urban renewal and the use of eminent domain may in practice be dubious policies. The misuse of these policies to transfer land, housing, and probably wealth from the urban poor to the not so poor is well documented (see articles by Anderson, Groberg, Smith, and Gans in Wilson, 1966). Problems in urban renewal projects result because usually low income housing is demolished and replaced with much higher income housing. This decrease [increase] in the supply of low [high] income housing raises [lowers] the price of housing to that group. Not only have lower income people been inadequately compensated for their losses, but probably such a shift in the supply of housing is unwarranted. Moreover, at a theoretical level it is not clear that the holdout problem is generally a serious one, but only a problem when developers have inadequate purchase strategies, are inadequate bargainers, or the proverbial little old lady (or man) who holds out indefinitely really does exist on a particular block. It seems likely that if the buying is done carefully and secretively, most if not all houses and buildings on a block can be bought up by a single party before other owners find out. This seems most likely to be the case if the buildings are initially owned by a variety of absentee landowners who have little or no contact with each other. Even if holdouts arise, there should be some bargaining room in terms of potential profits to deal with holdouts, although this obviously raises the cost of land and discourages redevelopment. However, the cost of this discouragement in terms of reduced redevelopment may well be less than the cost of misused applications of eminent domain in urban renewal. There are few (if any) examples in the literature of urban renewal projects that were socially justified (ex post) (see Rothenberg's (1967) careful appraisal of urban renewal projects in Chicago).

2.3 Zoning

In the previous sections, zoning is suggested as one method of effecting optimal land use patterns. In Chapter 5 zoning is suggested as a method of prohibiting polluting commercial areas from nonoptimally encroaching on residential land. In Chapter 10 zoning also appears as a possible policy instrument. However, much like the use of eminent domain, zoning ordinances must be recognized as a potentially dangerous public policy instrument, because of opportunities for misuse as well as the inflexibility of the instrument. The basic problem is that zoning administrators and zoning boards may not be well controlled in the political process by voters (due in part to inadequate voter information on zoning policies and their effects); and they may be unduly influenced by special interest groups in the community.

For example, in dividing land between residential and manufacturing use, if manufacturers unduly influence zoning boards (and they are renters), there is a financial incentive for them to advocate restricting the spatial areas allocated to, say, residents and increasing it to manufacturers. This increase in supply to manufacturers would lower land rentals to them and make them better off. Alternatively, landowners may unduly influence zoning boards and advocate zoning which maximizes their profits (see Mieszkowski, 1974). Suppose manufacturers and residents have different price elasticities of demand for land, $\eta_M > 1$ for manufacturers and $\eta_R < 1$ for residents. There is a fixed supply of land to be allocated among manufacturers and residents. Rather than having equalized land rents and marginal products, the landowners would make more money in total if the residential area was restricted and the manufacturing area increased. (One can easily show that total profits are maximized when the ratio of residential to manufacturing prices equals $(1 + 1/\eta_M)/(1 + 1/\eta_R)$.)

Also, in a dynamic world with optimal land use changing over time, zoning boards, which may represent special interests in the community and which have limited information available to them may respond slowly and inadequately to market pressures.

There are alternatives to zoning as a means of effecting optimal land use. Siegan (1970) suggests that in Houston, where contractual arrangements rather than zoning govern land use, land use changes in response to market pressures are swifter than in zoned cities and spatial configurations and land use patterns are more flexible. The contractual arrangements are sales contracts that prohibit the resale of land for various nonconforming uses. The contracts may be broken through neighborhood consent or through lapses in enforcement. Although the contracts are more flexible than zoning, they provide the same types of guarantees against unwarranted and unexpected changes in land use.

Second, in almost all the situations where zoning is suggested as a policy instrument, there is a taxation policy that could accomplish the same objective as zoning. In general, the taxation policies require taxing one type of land use discriminatively compared to another type. For example, the solution in Figure 6.4a could be maintained by taxing retailers if they locate on residential land.

2.4   Residential Separation and Segregation

In this section we briefly review the various explanations for residential separation and/or segregation of blacks from whites. For our purposes separation is a free-market, or voluntary, phenomenon, whereas segregation involves market discrimination, or is separation that is involuntary and perhaps forced by collusive actions of various economic agents. The basic facts in the United States that researchers attempt to explain are that (a) blacks live separate from whites, (b) blacks pay higher rents than whites for comparable units in comparable neighborhoods (see King and Mieszkowski, 1973), and (c) within income groups blacks have a lower incidence of homeownership than whites,[9] which reflects reduced opportunities and increased costs of ownership. There is usually a presumption, which I will accept, that whites arrived first in the urban area and blacks came later and faced limited opportunities in terms of locational choice. In essence, blacks are restricted to a limited area of the city, or ghettoized, and as a result pay higher housing prices. Why does this situation persit today?

That blacks live separate from whites can be explained by simple preference models. If large groups of people, such as whites, have negative preferences about living next to other large groups of people, such as blacks, the market will work to allocate land such that these groups live separate. Suppose, for example, that blacks are indifferent about living next to whites but whites do not want to live next to blacks. Then the market will work to allocate land so as to separate the two groups. In this case, this is voluntary separation in that not only does neither party object to the arrangement but the solution can be achieved in an atomistic competition framework. This is the same situation as we discussed in Section 2.1 with retailers and residents.

However, these voluntary separation models fail to explain the differences in housing prices paid by blacks and whites. In fact, following the analysis in Section 2.1 and Figure 6.4, in the situation in the preceding paragraph, we would expect blacks to pay lower housing prices than whites. This pattern of housing prices is not consistent with the observed pattern. In this type of model the only hypothesis that is consistent with blacks paying higher prices is that blacks have a greater aversion to living next to whites than whites to blacks. This explanation for housing prices is never cited in the literature and is probably unacceptable to most people. Therefore, we must turn to other explanations of residential patterns and prices.

Collusion Models

The collusion models are based on the premise that it is profitable to discriminate against blacks so that they are spatially separated from whites into an area of restricted size such that they pay higher rents than whites. How does this ghettoization come about?

The first explanation is that real estate agents conspire *implicitly* or *explicitly* to ghettoize blacks. In evaluating this explanation it should be noted that real estate brokerage is a highly competitive industry whose firms are loosely connected. Even in smaller urban areas there are hundreds of real estate agents (even excluding those people whose private transactions

[9] However, the probability of holding a mortgage for all blacks versus whites within different income groups is about the same. That is, within the class of homeowners, blacks have a higher incidence of mortgages and a lower incidence of homeownership. See 1970 Census of Housing.

do not go through a broker). Therefore, this discrimination must occur either because of the personal prejudices of agents or because it is *individually* profit maximizing for these agents to discriminate and ghettoize blacks.

The latter explanation seems implausible. The commission-based income of real estate sales agents is an increasing function of volume, or the turnover of housing units, and of the level of sales prices. If blacks in the ghetto are paying higher housing prices than whites, a real estate agent could sell a black a home in the white area at a higher price than to whites and thus increase his profits (as blockbusters have done in many areas). Only if he perceives (which is unlikely in an atomistic competition situation) that his own actions will later lower market prices in the urban area and hence possibly income from future sales *might* this selling policy not maximize the present value of his commission-based income. That perception is inconsistent with the evidence on both perceptions (see Laurenti, 1960) and prices.

Therefore, those who allege the implicit collusion of real estate agents would seem to find their strength in arguing that because brokers are individually prejudiced, the search costs of finding homes and unprejudiced agents and owners is raised for blacks relative to whites. This increase in search costs lowers the rate of black homeownership and raises the prices paid by blacks.

A second possible conspiratorial group are mortgage lenders. Again, even in small urban areas there are dozens of mortgage lenders, including banks, savings and loan institutions, and private individuals. However, if a neighborhood bank or group of banks decides not to make mortgages to blacks in a white area, that in itself may be sufficient to reduce the supply and raise the cost of mortgage funds to blacks and discourage most attempts at integration. However, the case that it is unprofitable for a bank to lend to blacks, especially if they are willing to pay more for housing, rests on special presumptions (apart from considerations of differential perceived risk between blacks and whites, which in itself may or may not constitute prejudice). Only if the bank fears an ensuing mass exodus of whites might it refuse to make mortgages to blacks. Any expected decline in housing prices due to this exodus is in itself not a problem for the bank, since the value of already held white mortgages is essentially unchanged[10] and the black mortgages would offer additional opportunities for profitable investments. The problem concerns deposits, where the bank may fear that incoming blacks may have lower wealth and savings than whites. This would reduce the local supply of funds to the bank and the volume of bank business as whites withdraw their deposits, causing a capital loss.

---

[10] If whites have paid off much of their mortgage debt, they are unlikely to default on the remaining amount.

Another Explanation.   The simplest explanation for segregation is that because of their preferences many (or even just a few) whites are prepared to resist blacks moving into white areas. Such resistance takes the form of burning crosses, stones through windows, arson, physical violence, harassment of children, and social ostracism. These actions are by themselves without the aid of conspiratorial economic agents sufficient to explain racial segregation.

3.   CONCLUSIONS

In Section 1 of this chapter we examined two models of the housing market, focusing on an analysis of the investment and maintenance decisions of landowners. We explored the conditions under which filtering down occurs due to phenomena on the supply (as opposed to demand) side of the housing market. The general conclusion was that filtering down in the sense of a housing unit passing to lower- and lower-income people over time only occurs "naturally" or due to the technical nature of housing if housing ages and there are indivisibilities in housing consumption. By aging, it is meant that the rate of depreciation on any investment in a housing unit increases with the length of life of the unit.

In Section 2, social and neighborhood externalities were discussed. Remedies for these externalities, such as zoning and urban renewal, were examined. It was suggested that there are very basic problems with these remedies given the political institutions in the economy. Both zoning and urban renewal can easily be misused by special interest groups to improve their well-being at the expense of that of the general populace. Finally, the issue of housing segregation was examined and the simple collusion and Bailey-type separation models of housing segregation were critically evaluated.

7

Transportation and Modal Choice

In the next two chapters we analyze pricing and investment policies in urban transportation. Since most trips in urban areas are made by automobiles, we will tend to focus on policies affecting road travel. Travel patterns on roads are characterized by peak periods of heavy use when people are going to or returning from work and by nonpeak periods of lighter use when people are going to or returning from shopping and recreation.[1] During peak periods, roads are very congested and travel speeds are slow, resulting in large losses in potential leisure time for travelers. The choice of pricing and investment policies for congested roads may radically affect these congestion costs and travel patterns during the day. These policies will also affect the consumer's choice of travel modes and the use and potential of alternatives to road travel in peak periods, such as rapid transit or buses. Finally, we note that since commuting costs are a major determinant of city spatial characteristics, as demonstrated in Chapters 1 and 2, transportation policies will have a strong impact on city sizes and characteristics.

As a starting point in this chapter we examine the nature of road travel and congestion and analyze optimal investment and pricing policies for a

[1] Approximately 40–45% of all trips in North American cities are between home and work sites or business-connected activities; 15–25% are between home and social and recreation sites, and 10–20% are between home and shopping sites. In addition, probably well over 80% of all trips are made in automobiles. References on this include Wingo (1961, pp. 32, 33), Meyer *et al.* (1965, pp. 90, 91), and Fitch *et al.* (1964, p. 35).

congested system such as a road or for a system such as rapid transit. Using the concepts and model developed, we turn to situations where there are constraints prohibiting the implementation of optimal policies. For example, in general, it may not be feasible to impose congestion tolls on road users or there may be a nonoptimal budgetary limit on public financing of capital facilities. Of particular interest in this chapter are policies concerning the operation and use of alternative modes, such as roads and rapid transit, in circumstances where pricing and investment options for road travel are constrained. Finally, we review the question how much land should be devoted to roads at various distances from the CBD in a monocentric model of a city.

In the next chapter we examine the nature of peak-period travel, such as the morning or evening rush hours. Topics analyzed are the commuter's decision when to travel on a particular facility and the effect of congestion tolls on this decision, the cost of travel, the optimal provision of transportation facilities, and the peak-period regulation of traffic.

1. CONGESTED SYSTEMS

To understand the nature of congested systems such as roads and the nature of the congestion externality, it is helpful to specify fully the various ways of modeling the situation. Congestion occurs when the users of a system interfere with each other as they use the system, resulting in losses to all users. On a congested road, over normal ranges of road usage, the vehicular speed of travel is a decreasing function of density, or the number of cars per unit road length, and an increasing function of road capacity or width. The more tightly packed together cars are, the more they interfere with and impede each other, reducing the travel speed of all users. An increase in capacity relieves this packing together and mutual interference, increasing the travel speed of users.

We consider a congested road system where all vehicles enter the system at one point, travel through the system, and then exit at another point. For a flow of cars entering the road in a given time interval their speed of travel is initially just a function of the number of entrants, or how tightly packed together the entering cars are. Once in the system, the density of traffic for initial entrants changes as the initial entrants draw apart, overtake traffic already in the system, or are overtaken by later entrants. For cars traveling through the system, this process of changing densities, and hence speeds, and the general ebb and flow of traffic is very complex and difficult to model.

Three ways to model congested systems are discussed here, all involving different naïve assumptions but all useful for analyzing different aspects of the economics of transportation.

(a) *Current Demand Dependent on Past and Future Travel Conditions.*
In the next chapter we consider a situation where demand to travel at time
t is a function of speed and travel costs at times before and after t, as well
as at t. Analyzing this type of situation provides a basis for understanding
how consumers substitute on the demand side among alternative times of
travel and for understanding the nature of peak-period travel patterns and
problems. To carry out the analysis, however, we must assume on the supply
side that current travel conditions are not influenced by past or future travel
conditions. This means that for a given road capacity, the speed of travel
of an entrant is solely a function of the number or flow of cars entering the
road at the same time as he does. This speed of travel remains constant
throughout the journey, implying that entering groups do not draw apart
and are not overtaken by or do not overtake later or earlier entrants. At
different points on the road people will be traveling at different speeds,
according to the number of people who entered the system at the same time
they did. This simplification on the technical side of specifying speed–flow
relationships allows us to work with the sophisticated demand specification.

(b) *Current Travel Speeds Dependent on Past and Future Conditions.*
The second way to model a congested system is entirely different and treats
the system as a black box problem (Agnew, 1973). Although the model
probably best depicts computer operations it is helpful in analyzing road
travel. At any instant travel conditions and speeds are the same for all users
in the system regardless of where they are in the system or when they entered.
Speed of travel is a function of road capacity and system load or the total
number of cars on the road at a point in time. The load on the road changes
according to the difference between entrants and exits in any time period
and speed adjusts throughout the road uniformly and instantaneously to
the new load. This model is useful for illustrating how the speed of travel
for an entrant will be influenced by the number of later and earlier entrants.
It yields interesting steady-state solutions when load is constant or entrants
equal exits. It also provides for an understanding of movements to and away
from steady-state solutions and the role that congestion tolls play in such
movements (see Agnew, 1973). However, the model is too complex for us to
have the demand to travel at time t be a function of travel times and costs
at times before and after t, with consumers substituting among travel times.
Therefore, it is assumed that demand to travel at time t is only a function
of the travel cost associated with that time.

(c) *The Traditional Model.* The traditional way to model congested
systems is a "static" version of the first and second ways. Traffic flows and
density are assumed to be uniform in the single period of analysis, without
regard to how these densities and flows start up or dissipate at the beginning
and end of the single period or without regard to why consumer demand

should be uniform throughout the period. Essentially, the traditional model examines possible steady-state solutions, without considering the movement to the steady-state (as from the startup point of zero flows) and without considering how to move and how to price movements between different steady-state solutions with different densities and flows. Thus this model cannot adequately analyze peak-period and varying traffic patterns. However, it is quite adequate for analyzing modal choice and the steady-state allocation of traffic between different roads or between roads and transit in a given time period.

Having summarized various ways of modeling traffic situations, we are now ready to examine steady-state travel relationships and the externality nature of congestion. We denote D as density, or cars per mile on the road; S as speed, or miles per hour; and R as a measure of road capacity. Then in the steady-state where density is uniform throughout the system, speed is a nonincreasing function of density, or

$$S = S(D, R), \qquad \partial S/\partial D \leq 0, \qquad \partial S/\partial R \geq 0. \tag{7.1}$$

The steady-state uniform flow of cars per hour entering, exiting, and/or passing any given point in the road is F. F measures the rate at which cars are passing through the system; hence, F equals cars per mile multiplied by miles per hour, or

$$F = S \cdot D. \tag{7.2}$$

Comparing different steady states, as density on the road increases, flow will initially increase, but eventually may start to decline, or

$$\frac{\partial F}{\partial D} = S(1 - \varepsilon), \qquad \varepsilon = -\frac{\partial S}{\partial D} \cdot \frac{D}{S} \geq 0. \tag{7.3}$$

When density is very low and speed is correspondingly high, $\varepsilon < 1$ or $\partial F/\partial D > 0$. However, as density increases, because of the tighter packing of cars on the road, or increased congestion, speeds start to decline radically and eventually $\varepsilon > 1$ and $\partial F/\partial D < 0$.

These relationships are graphed in Figure 7.1. Each steady-state flow of cars is associated with two different possible steady-state densities, starting from an infinitesimal density where $F \to 0$ and going to the case where there are so many cars packed on the road that $S \to 0$ and $F \to 0$. A system operating beyond the point of maximal flow is clearly inefficient, since any flow beyond the maximal flow could be achieved with a lower density or less cars on the road, higher speeds, and hence with lower travel times and costs.

The congestion externality arises because, when an additional car enters the road and causes cars to be slightly more tightly packed together, that

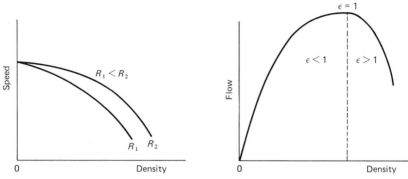

FIGURE 7.1   Speed–density–flow relationships.

additional car lowers the speed and raises the travel times of all other cars traveling at that time. The additional traveler does not account for the costs that he imposes on other users when making his decision to travel on this road as opposed to other roads or modes or when making his decision to travel at this time as opposed to other times. Because he does not account for the full social costs of his trip on this road at this time, his choice of this road and this time as opposed to other roads, times, or goods may be socially inefficient. It is this problem that we examine in much of the material to follow.

   Finally, we note that often when discussing single-period situations, it is assumed ε in equation (7.3) is always less than 1; hence, we are never operating on the back-bending part of the flow curve in Figure 7.1b. Since there is then a strictly monotonic relationship between flow and density, as well as between density and speed for a given R, there is a strictly monotonic relationship between flow and speed. Given this, it is convenient to describe speed as directly being a decreasing function of flow and to relate the congestion externality to traffic flows. Moreover, given that we are examining only a single period, flow equals total trips in each period; hence, the term trips rather than flows is commonly used. Speed is then a decreasing function of total trips. Although Agnew (1973) points out that this specification leads to problems and errors in analysis in some dynamic contexts, for expositional simplicity, we adopt this convenience in the next section.

2. MODAL CHOICE

   In this section we first examine optimal pricing and investment policies for congested systems such as roads, using the traditional single-period model. We allow there to be two modes of travel, such as roads and rapid transit, between which consumers can substitute, so as to highlight problems in consumer choice of different transport modes. Then pricing and investment policies in situations where road travel cannot be optimally priced or there are constraints on the financing of road or transit capacity are examined. In order to examine optimal and second-best pricing and investment policies we use a simple welfare maximization model, adapted from Mohring's (1970) peak-load model.

Consumers maximize utility, which is a function of a composite good g and two different transportation services, x and z. Different types of services might be travel on different roads by car or travel by car versus transit. Given the different types of services or amenities these goods offer and the different costs of the goods, the consumer has to decide how much of each to buy. Although for a particular trip, the consumer usually buys either x or z but not both, over the period of a week or year the individual or his family buys some of both services.

The I consumers in a city maximize $V(x, z, g)$ subject to a budget constraint $p_x x + p_z z + p_g g = y^i - h^i$. y^i is income measured in dollars of fixed resources available to consumer i; and h^i is the head tax imposed on consumer i where head taxes [subsidies] are designed to cover deficits [surpluses] in the government financing of transportation facilities. We use head taxes, rather than other more realistic types of taxes, to avoid discussion of problems associated with the welfare costs of more realistic types of taxes.

The per unit cost of producing g is a constant and, given perfect competition in the private sector, equals price p_g. The per unit variable costs of supplying x and z are $C(X, K_x)$ and $C'(Z, K_z)$, where $X = \sum_i x^i$ or total trips of all users, $Z = \sum_i z^i$, and K_x and K_z are expenditures on transportation facilities. Unit variable costs are a decreasing function of capacity, or $\partial C / \partial K_x < 0$; and they are an increasing function of total trips X, or $\partial C / \partial X > 0$. These variable costs may be interpreted as the time costs of travel and/or the physical (out-of-pocket) costs of operating cars, both of which utilize resources available to the consumer and society. Total variable costs for X are $X C(X, K_x)$ and hence the marginal cost of X is $C(X, K_x) + X(\partial C(X, K_x)/\partial X)$. The marginal cost consists of the average variable cost of producing the additional trip, $C(X, K_x)$, plus the amount by which the variable costs of all other trips are increased, $X(\partial C(X, K_x)/\partial X)$. This second term is the congestion factor.

Society's resources are spent on G, X, Z, K_x, and K_z where G is provided in the private sector and K_x and K_z are measured in dollars of resources spent on transport facilities. To find conditions for any Pareto-optimal solution we maximize the utility of one individual, holding utility levels of all others fixed. Maximization is carried out with respect to policy variables which are head taxes, prices of transportation services p_x and p_z, and capital expenditures on transportation K_x and K_z. Policymakers are constrained by the social resource constraint

$$\sum_{i=1}^{I} y_i \equiv Y = X \cdot C(K, K_x) + Z \cdot C'(Z, K_z) + p_g G + K_x + K_z.$$

Y is the total resources available to the society, which is simply the sum of individual resources. The other side of the equation is the cost of producing all goods in the system.

2.1 A First-Best World: No Institutional Constraints or Costs

Suppose policymakers face no pricing or financing constraints and the costs of implementing congestion tolls are zero. Then we may achieve an optimal solution by maximizing one person's utility level while holding other utility levels fixed at $\bar{V}^i$ subject to the resource constraint. We first examine optimal investment policies by maximizing

$$L = V^1 + \sum_{i=2}^{I} \alpha_i(V^i - \bar{V}^i) + \lambda[Y - C(X, K_x) \cdot X$$

$$- C'(Z, K_z) \cdot Z - K_x - K_z - p_g G] \tag{7.4}$$

with respect to K_x and K_z. Doing this and rearranging the first-order conditions, we get

$$-\frac{\partial C(X, K_x)}{\partial K_x} X = 1, \qquad -\frac{\partial C'(Z, K_z)}{\partial K_z} Z = 1. \tag{7.5}$$

Equation (7.5) says that capital facilities should be expanded until the last dollar spent on facilities brings forth one dollar in marginal benefits, or reduction in variable travel costs. This reduction in variable travel costs equals the reduction in unit costs or $\partial C(X, K_x)/\partial K_x$ multiplied by the units produced, or total trips on each facility.

To get the optimal pricing policy we differentiate (7.4) with respect to head taxes, p_x, and p_z. After various substitutions of well-known demand relationships, the result is[2]

$$\begin{bmatrix} S_{xx} & S_{zx} \\ S_{xz} & S_{zz} \end{bmatrix} \begin{bmatrix} p_x - SMC_x \\ p_z - SMC_z \end{bmatrix} = \begin{bmatrix} 0 \\ 0 \end{bmatrix}. \tag{7.6}$$

[2] This may be shown as follows. In the maximization problem we use indirect utility functions, define ϕ^i as the marginal utility of income for individual i, and recall from Roy's identity that $x^i = -(\partial V^i/\partial p_x)/\phi^i$ and $z^i = -(\partial V^i/\partial p_z)/\phi^i$. Then, maximizing V^1 with respect to p_x, p_z, and h^i, we get (after substitutions into the first term of these equations where $\alpha^1 = 1$)

$$-\sum_i \alpha^i \phi^i x^i - \lambda(SMC_x(\partial X/\partial p_x) + SMC_z(\partial Z/\partial p_x) + p_g(\partial G/\partial p_x)) = 0, \tag{a}$$

SMC_x and SMC_z equal the social marginal costs of an additional unit of x and y. They are defined to be

$$C(X, K_x) + \frac{\partial C(X, K_x)}{\partial X} X \quad \text{and} \quad C'(Z, K_z) + \frac{\partial C'(Z, K_z)}{\partial Z} Z.$$

Then for example, $C(X, K_x)$ is the average or private travel cost incurred on each trip; and $(\partial C(X, K_x)/\partial X)X$ is the increase in travel costs for all other travelers caused by the additional trip and the resulting increase in congestion.

The S_{ij} terms are pure Hicks–Slutsky substitution terms where, for example, for the ith individual

$$S^i_{xz} = \left.\frac{\partial x^i}{\partial p_z}\right|_{\bar{V}^i} = \frac{\partial x^i}{\partial p_z} - z^i \frac{\partial x^i}{\partial h^i}$$

where $\partial x^i/\partial h^i$ is usually negative since h^i is a tax, or negative income. S_{xz} then is simply $\sum_i S^i_{xz}$. The pure substitution effects with a change in p_x or p_z occur because when p_x and p_z are increased, more revenue is received

---

$$-\sum_i \alpha^i \phi^i z^i - \lambda(SMC_x(\partial X/\partial p_z) + SMC_z(\partial Z/\partial p_z) + p_g(\partial G/\partial p_z)) = 0, \tag{b}$$

$$-\alpha^i \phi^i - (SMC_x(\partial x^i/\partial h^i) + SMC_z(\partial z^i/\partial h^i) + p_g(\partial g^i/\partial h^i)) = 0,$$
$$\text{for } i = 1, 2, \ldots, I. \tag{c}$$

By differentiating the budget constraint of an individual with respect to p_x, p_z, and h^i, we know that

$$-x^i - p_x(\partial x^i/\partial p_x) - p_z(\partial z^i/\partial p_x) - p_g(\partial g^i/\partial p_x) = 0,$$
$$-z^i - p_x(\partial x^i/\partial p_z) - p_z(\partial z^i/\partial p_z) - p_g(\partial g^i/\partial p_z) = 0,$$
$$1 + p_x(\partial x^i/\partial h^i) + p_z(\partial z^i/\partial h^i) + p_g(\partial g^i/\partial h^i) = 0.$$

Aggregating the first two of these relationships over all individuals, we know $X + p_x(\partial X/\partial p_x) + p_z(\partial Z/\partial p_x) + p_g(\partial G/\partial p_x) = 0$ and $Z + p_z(\partial Z/\partial p_z) + p_x(\partial X/\partial p_z) + p_g(\partial G/\partial p_z) = 0$. From these relationships we substitute into equations (a)–(c) for $p_g(\partial G/\partial p_x)$, $p_g(\partial G/\partial p_z)$ and $p_g(\partial g^i/\partial h^i)$, where for example, equation (a) becomes

$$-\sum_i \alpha^i \phi^i x^i + \lambda(X + (p_x - SMC_x)(\partial X/\partial p_x) + (p_z - SMC_z)(\partial Z/\partial p_x)) = 0.$$

The new (a) and (b) equations we call equations (a') and (b'). In the new equations (c) we multiply each equation by x^i and sum over all individuals and repeat the process for z^i. Thus we end up with new two equations, one for X, or equation (c^x), and one for z, or equation (c^z), where for example, equation (c^x) is

$$-\sum \alpha^i \phi^i x^i + \lambda(X + (p_x - SMC_x)\sum_i (\partial x^i/\partial h^i x^i) + (p_z - SMC_z)\sum_i (\partial z^i/\partial h^i x^i)) = 0.$$

We then subtract equation (c^x) from equation (a') and (c^z) from (b') to get equation (7.6), given our definition of S_{ij}.

from the higher prices and individuals are compensated with lowered head taxes, since less revenue is needed from head taxes to pay for capital facilities.

In solving (7.6), from linear algebra we know that if the matrix is non-singular or its determinant $|S|$ is nonzero, then $p_x - SMC_x$ and $p_z - SMC_z$ must equal zero. The second-order conditions of utility maximization require that $|S| = S_{xx}S_{zz} - S_{xz}S_{zx} > 0$. Therefore, the solution to (7.6) is $p_x = SMC_x$ and $p_z = SMC_z$, or price equals social marginal cost. For transportation where $SMC_x = C(X, K_x) + (\partial C(X, K_x)/\partial X)X$, the individual incurs $C(X, K_x)$ privately when he travels but needs to be charged a congestion toll equal to the external costs imposed on other travelers, or $(\partial C(X, K_x)/\partial X)X$. If there is no congestion, $SMC_x = C(X, K_x)$ and no toll is needed for price to equal social marginal cost.

One final point in this first-best world is that tolls collected cover capital costs of facilities if there are constant returns to scale. The conceptual point is rather simple. If we apply a variable factor X to a fixed factor K_x and charge marginal cost, after we pay X the value of its marginal product, rents are left over. Under constant returns to scale, these rents exactly equal the value of the marginal product and the opportunity cost of the fixed factor.

In our model, the point may be made as follows. With constant returns to scale if all inputs, X and K_x, increase by the same percentage unit costs, or $C(X, K_x)$, remain unchanged by definition. That is, doubling capacity and doubling traffic flows will leave speed and travel costs unchanged. The change in unit costs with a change in inputs is $dC = (\partial C/\partial K_x)\, dK_x + (\partial C/\partial X)\, dX$ or, rearranging terms, $dC = K_x(\partial C/\partial K_x)(dK_x/K_x) + X(\partial C/\partial X)(dX/X)$. $dC = 0$ by definition when $dK_x/K_x = dX/X$ or factors increase by the same percentage. Therefore, with constant returns to scale the following relationship must hold.

$$dC = K_x \frac{\partial C(X, K_x)}{\partial K_x} + X \frac{\partial C(X, K_x)}{\partial X} = 0.$$

Multiplying through by X we get

$$-K_x\left(\frac{\partial C(X, K_x)}{\partial K_x}X\right) = X\left(\frac{\partial C(X, K_x)}{\partial X}X\right).$$

The term on the right-hand side equals tolls paid, or the individual toll $(\partial C(X, K_x)/\partial X)X$ multiplied by the number of units on which it is paid. In the expression on the left-hand side, from the optimal investment rule in equation (7.5) we know that $(\partial C(X, K_x)/\partial K_x)X = -1$. Therefore, the left-hand side reduces to K_x or capital expenditures. Thus capital expenditures equal tolls paid under constant returns and optimal pricing and investment. If there are increasing [decreasing] returns to scale, $dC < 0$ $[dC > 0]$ when inputs increase by the same percentage. Then tolls fall short of [exceed] capital costs and a head tax [subsidy] is needed to cover capital costs.

The foregoing analysis is an abstract description of a first-best world where all the basic results of welfare economics apply. Marginal benefits equal marginal costs in investment, price equals social marginal costs, and optimal rents on a capital facility cover its cost if there are constant returns to scale.

The framework developed can be applied directly to the issue of public subsidization of capital facilities and the question when revenues from marginal cost pricing are likely to cover total costs of providing a good. The framework can also be adapted to incorporate institutional constraints and phenomena faced in urban provision of transportation. Such constraints are the use of gasoline taxes for financing road capacity, budgetary limits on deficit financing of capital facilities, and the politicized issue of subsidization of transit fares.

We choose to apply the framework to examining the provision of rapid transit and the issue of whether rapid transit should be subsidized from general revenues. There are two interrelated subsidization issues. One is whether capital expenditures need be subsidized when transit fares are set equal to marginal costs of transporting passengers. The other is whether transit fares themselves should be subsidized so that private transit travel costs fall short of marginal costs.

2.2   The Case of Rapid Transit

Subsidization of Capital Expenditures

In the foregoing discussion of a first-best world we showed that if there are increasing returns or declining average costs to providing a service, then revenue from marginal cost pricing will not cover total costs. Subsidies from public tax revenues will in general be needed to make up the difference. In deciding if capital facilities for rapid transit should be subsidized we must determine whether rapid transit fits this description of declining average costs. At the same time we must also analyze under what conditions it is desirable to provide rapid transit at all, let alone subsidize it.

Rapid transit involves the provision of heavy initial fixed levels of capital expenditures in the form of basic track and stations, which are somewhat independent of traffic volume. Over low ranges of passenger volume, marginal operating costs in terms of trains, maintenance, safety measures, conductors, time costs of travel, and policing are assumed to be low and perhaps a declining function of volume. Therefore, at least for low to medium traffic volumes, average total costs are declining and subsidization of capital facilities to cover deficits, given marginal cost pricing, is justified. However, when passenger volume becomes high and facilities become very congested, marginal operating costs start to rise or at least level off, as breakdowns, theft, accidents, and crowding become more prominent and time costs of travel increase (e.g., the length of stops increases). Then average total costs may level out or even start to rise, eradicating the need for a subsidy.

Before providing any subsidy, it is necessary for a policymaker to decide if the provision of rapid transit at all is justified. That is, in general equilibrium terms, is social welfare raised by the existence of rapid transit, given its resource costs? This question is usually examined in a partial equilibrium diagram where the criterion for providing transit is that the consumers' surplus from the existence of rapid transit should exceed the deficit incurred, under marginal cost pricing.

It should be noted that public subsidies are never really necessary, even with declining average costs. The transit authority could adopt a two-part pricing scheme. To ride the trains at all, each year consumers would be required to pay an annual fee or purchase a card that permits them to buy transit tokens or fares (essentially, this would be a private head tax). Each trip or token would then be priced at marginal operating costs. The annual fee would be set to capture sufficient consumers' surplus so as to cover the deficit but it would not interfere with the consumers' decisions to purchase marginal trips.

Subsidization of Transit Fares

So far the discussion in this chapter has dealt with a first-best world, in which it is optimal to price goods according to marginal cost. However, in a second-best world the marginal cost pricing prescription and the optimal investment criterion may not hold, given the particular constraints that impose a second-best, as opposed to first-best, world on us. We illustrate a second-best situation in which it is efficient to subsidize rapid transit fares as well as capital expenditures.

In our welfare maximization model there are two transport goods, x and z, which we now designate as being, respectively, road trips and transit trips. We assume roads and transit are reasonably close substitutes for consumers, a *critical* assumption to the case for subsidizing transit fares. Unlike a first-best world, congestion on roads is unpriced. We assume the basic reasons congestion is unpriced are political and institutional constraints. Vickrey (1963) argues that the actual costs of pricing are very small, involving an inexpensive signaling device attached to a car that identifies the car as it passes through the congested system and a sensory system in the road picking up the signals. On this computerized system each person would be charged the appropriate congestion toll at that time and billed monthly. Over a period of time the commuter would become familiar with the cost of traveling at various times on various facilities and hence would be making choices in the face of known prices. The system is probably not inherently any more expensive than other monitoring and metering systems, such as for electricity, water, or telephones. Therefore, we view the congestion pricing constraint as basically a political or social constraint.

If congestion on roads is unpriced, this means automobile travel is priced at less than marginal cost. If other goods are priced at marginal cost, this implies that automobile travel is implicitly subsidized relative to other goods and thus is overconsumed relative to other goods. There are two optimal ways to solve this problem of distortions in relative prices and consumer choices. One is to impose congestion tolls, a solution we have ruled out. The other is to subsidize all other goods by the same relative amount as road travel, so that consumers are no longer encouraged to use roads relative to other goods. This proposition follows from the general literature on optimal taxation (Baumol and Bradford, 1970). The basic idea is that Pareto efficiency requires marginal rates of substitution in consumption (which will equal price ratios in a market economy) to equal *ratios* of social marginal costs of production for any two goods. With unpriced congestion this condition will not be satisfied, since consumer price ratios will not equal ratios of social marginal costs, but by subsidizing and lowering the price of all other goods we can bring consumer price ratios into equality with ratios of social marginal costs.

Clearly, in our complex world an urban policymaker cannot subsidize all goods in the economy because of unpriced congestion. However, he may do the next best thing, which is to subsidize close substitutes for automobile travel, such as rapid transit. To the extent that subsidization induces travelers to switch from roads to transit, road congestion will be alleviated and all travelers will be made better off.

This proposition is illustrated in Figure 7.2. Equilibrium without congestion pricing and without transit subsidies is at points *e*, where road travel is relatively underpriced and overconsumed. The effect of a subsidy *S* to transit is to shift down the supply curve in the transit sector, inducing greater use of transit. At the same time, in response to lower transit fares, the demand for road travel declines. This is represented by a shift back in the demand curve in that sector, as people shift to traveling by transit. As the size of the subsidy is increased, this shift from road to transit travel should be more pronounced.

Given the possibility of subsidization, the basic questions are, What is the magnitude of the optimal subsidy? How much of a shift from road to transit travel is desirable? Are optimal investment criteria changed because

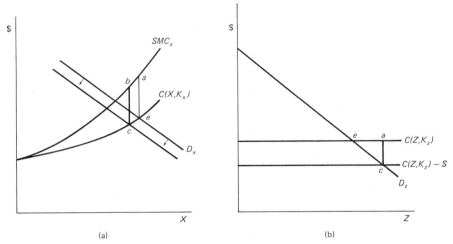

FIGURE 7.2   Subsidizing transit fares.

of the pricing constraint? To rigorously answer these questions we turn to our welfare maximization model.[3]

Each consumer maximizes $V(x, z, g)$ where x, z, and g are, respectively, the household consumption of auto trips, transit trips, and all other goods. The budget constraint is $y^i - h^i = C(X, K_x)x + p_z z + p_g g$ where for roads the individual simply pays the average variable cost of travel or there is no

[3] A common approximation of the criterion for the optimal subsidy is pictured in Figure 7.2. Suppose the subsidy is currently S in Figure 7.2b and equilibrium is at point c in both sectors. In Figure 7.2b at point c the welfare cost from having lowered price below social marginal cost is approximated by the area eac. In Figure 7.2a the welfare gain from having reduced road congestion is approximated by the area $eabc$. The optimal subsidy is attained when the increase in social costs from lowering transit price one more unit, which is the slice ac in Figure 7.2b, just equals the corresponding increase in social benefits as the demand curve for road travel shifts back, which is the slice bc in Figure 7.2a. (Note that there is no corresponding welfare change in the g sector of the economy.) In algebraic terms the area of the marginal welfare cost slice ac equals $-S(\Delta Z / \Delta p_z)$. The area of the marginal social benefit slice bc is $(X(\partial C / \partial X)(\Delta X / \Delta p_z)$. Therefore by this graphical derivation the optimal subsidy is

$$p_z - SMC_z \equiv S = -\frac{\Delta X / \Delta p_z}{\Delta Z / \Delta p_z} \left(X \frac{\partial C}{\partial X} \right).$$

As $\Delta p_z \to 0$, the expressions $\Delta Z / \Delta p_z$ and $\Delta X / \Delta p_z$ reduce to S_{zz} and S_{xz}. Therefore this expression is the same as equation (7.8), except for the term $(\partial C / \partial K)X$, which from equation (7.7) is a number somewhat greater than 1. Therefore the subsidy derived from a diagrammatic analysis that ignores the question of a changing optimal investment criterion is somewhat larger than the optimal subsidy.

toll. Since the government no longer controls p_x, or $p_x = C(x, K_x)$, it seeks to maximize utility with respect to K_x, K_z, p_z and the h^i. The Lagrangian function that is maximized with respect to K_x, K_z, p_z and the h^i is the one in equation (7.4), except that an additional term $\theta(C(X, K_x) - p_x)$ is added stating the pricing constraint.

Maximizing with respect to K_x, we see that the optimal investment criterion for roads changes to

$$-\frac{\partial C}{\partial K_x} X = 1 - \frac{\theta}{\lambda} \frac{\partial C}{\partial K_x}. \qquad (7.7)$$

Since $\partial C/\partial K_x < 0$, the right-hand side of (7.7) is greater than 1. This suggests that investment in roads should be restricted so that the marginal benefits of investment $((-\partial C/\partial K_x)X)$ exceed the marginal resource costs of investment (\$1). By "underinvesting" in road capacity, the transport authority raises the marginal private costs of travel (nearer its shadow cost), discouraging use of roads relative to transit and encouraging a more efficient allocation of resources in consumption. In Figure 7.2a, underinvestment shifts up the average and marginal cost curves, reducing the consumption of X. The optimal investment criterion for transit is the same as in equation (7.5).

Maximizing the new Lagrangian with respect to p_z and the h^i and performing appropriate substitutions, (we find the pricing criterion for transit.[4]) This criterion defines the magnitude of the optimal subsidy where

$$SMC_z - p_z \equiv S = \frac{S_{xz} (\partial C/\partial X)X}{S_{zz} (\partial C/\partial K_x)X} > 0. \qquad (7.8)$$

Because roads and transit travel are substitutes, $S_{xz} > 0$. The magnitude of the subsidy S is (a) an increasing function of the degree of road congestion as measured by $X(\partial C/\partial X)$; (b) an increasing function of consumer willingness to switch from roads to transit, thus relieving road congestion as measured by S_{xz}; (c) a decreasing function of the general switch to z consumption (from, say, g consumption) in response to lower z prices; and

---

[4] In footnote 2 only equations (b) and (c) are relevant. To the left-hand side of these equations we add the terms $+\theta(\partial C/\partial X)(\partial X/\partial p_z)$ and $+\theta(\partial C/\partial X)(\partial x^i/\partial h^i)$, respectively. Performing the manipulations in footnote 2, we obtain

$$p_z - SMC_z = -\frac{S_{xz}}{S_{zz}}\left[p_x - SMC_x + \frac{\theta}{\lambda}\frac{\partial C}{\partial X}\right].$$

Substituting in $p_x = C$ and for θ/λ from equation (7.7), we find that this equation reduces to equation (7.8).

(d) a decreasing function of the response of travel costs to changing capacity investment. These results are intuitively appealing. Subsidization is an attractive policy when the degree of road congestion is high and consumers can be induced through transit subsidization to switch away from road travel. It is also an attractive policy when underinvestment in roads is ineffective in raising travel costs and hence inducing people to travel by transit.

The size of the fare subsidy to rapid transit can be expressed in measurable variables. Rearranging (7.8), we obtain

$$SMC - p_z \equiv S = \frac{X(\partial C/\partial X) \, X \, \eta^s_{xz}}{X(\partial C/\partial K_x) \, Z \, \eta^s_{zz}} \tag{7.9}$$

where η^s_{ij} (are real income held constant price elasticities.) X and Y are observable and the actual form of the congestion relation, or $C(X, K_x)$, is well known. In applying equation (7.9) to the real world we would be particularly concerned with peak-period travel when road congestion is heaviest. The estimates of η^s_{ij} would need to be applicable to peak-period situations. The major objection to implementing or maintaining such policies concerns the size of η^s_{xz}. Many economists believe η^s_{xz} is very small or road users cannot be induced into transit cars within the range of feasible subsidies. (We rule out $p_z < 0$, since people could then earn their living from riding transit cars!)

Finally, we note that if demand for the combined transport goods is perfectly inelastic, so that underpricing roads distorts not the choice between roads and other goods but only the choice between roads and transit, the optimal policy is to subsidize transit such that both transportation goods receive the same percentage, implicit or explicit, subsidy. Under this assumption, there is no welfare loss from not being able to price road congestion explicitly. The only distortion created by not being able to price road congestion is between the consumption of transit and roads, and this can be fully corrected by subsidizing transit. However, given the possibilities for car pooling; for transforming single-purpose into multipurpose trips; for spatial rearrangement of job, retailing, and home sites; and for foregoing marginal trips, it seems unlikely that the demand for transportation trips is very inelastic.

The foregoing analysis could be applied to a situation where x and z are two competing roads but where only congestion on the z road can be priced. For example, z could be a tollway and x a freeway. The optimal congestion toll is one where price remains less than social marginal cost. A toll on the z road that set price equal to marginal cost would induce relatively too many people to travel on the x road, resulting in relatively too high congestion levels on the x road.

3. EXTENSIONS OF THE MODEL

A number of other constraints and situations can be investigated in our model. We mention two here.

Budgetary Limits. Suppose public budgetary considerations reduce the amount of money available for transportation to a nonoptimal level. For example, there could be a limit on the deficit a transport authority may have. This deficit constraint could be added to equation (7.4) through the constraint $p_x X + p_z Z + D = K_x + K_z + XC + ZC'$ where D is the allowable deficit. The need for a deficit would exist even in a world of complete congestion pricing if there were nonconstant returns to scale in road services, since with nonconstant returns to scale optimal tolls do not cover capital costs. Road construction is viewed as having two components, the variable number of lanes and then components fixed in size, such as shoulders, buffer zones between roads and housing, and median strips. Therefore, the average cost curve for capacity declines as capacity increases, indicating increasing returns to scale and the fact that tolls will not cover capital costs. Then government subsidization is needed but may be limited to some inefficient level such as D in the constraint above. With this type of constraint one can work through the welfare maximization model to show that one simply raises prices above social marginal costs to make up the deficit. The optimal investment rule still is to invest until the last dollar brings forth a dollar's reduction in total variable costs.

Gasoline Tolls

Gasoline tolls are a prevalent part of transportation policy. In addition to raising revenue, they raise the price of road travel above private cost and, as such, partially price externalities, such as air pollution and congestion. However, they are a very inadequate substitute for congestion tolls. Within a speed range of 25–50 mph, gasoline consumption per mile is nearly constant (Johnson, 1964), so a gas tax simply raises the cost of travel within this speed range by the same amount per mile. On the other hand, congestion levels vary considerably in this speed range and thus desired congestion tolls also vary. Therefore, the problem for a policymaker is how to use the gasoline tax, which raises travel price on different roads by the same amount, whereas what is desired is a set of taxes that raises travel prices by different amounts according to congestion levels on different roads. In examining what the optimal gasoline toll is, we follow Mohring's discussion (1970, pp. 699–701).

In our model we let x and z be two types of road trips that are imperfect substitutes in consumption. Travel on the x road is very congested while on the z road it is relatively less congested. The gasoline toll T is effectively the same on both roads; therefore, $p_x - C = T = p_z - C'$ where gasoline tolls are the only way to raise price above average cost. This relationship may be incorporated into the maximization problem in equation (7.4) by adding the constraint

$$\theta((p_z - p_x) + (C(X, K_x) - C'(Z, K_z))). \tag{7.10}$$

Redoing the maximization problem yields new investment criteria

$$-\frac{\partial C(X, K_x)}{\partial K_x} X = 1 - \frac{\theta}{\lambda} \frac{\partial C(X, K_x)}{\partial K_x} > 1,$$

$$-\frac{\partial C'(Z, K_z)}{\partial K_z} Z = 1 + \frac{\theta}{\lambda} \frac{\partial C'(Z, K_z)}{\partial K_z} < 1. \tag{7.11}$$

Here $\theta = \partial V^1/\partial(p_z - p_x) = -\partial V^1(\partial(C - C')) > 0$ or as the gap between average cost levels on the two roads declines, utility rises. Therefore, the optimal investment criteria say we should stop investing in the x road when marginal investment benefits $((-\partial C/\partial K_x)X)$ still exceed marginal cost ($1) and vice versa for the z road. That is, we should "underinvest" in the x road and "overinvest" in the z road, which should help induce consumers to travel on the less congested road and should offset price distortions (discussed next).

The new pricing criteria are[5]

$$p_x - C_x = T - X\frac{\partial C}{\partial X} = \frac{\theta}{\lambda} \frac{(S_{zz} + S_{zx} - (\partial C/\partial X)|S|)}{|S|} < 0,$$

$$p_z - C_z = T - Z\frac{\partial C'}{\partial Z} = -\frac{\theta}{\lambda} \frac{(S_{xx} + S_{xz} - (\partial C'/\partial Z)|S|)}{|S|} > 0. \tag{7.12}$$

Providing $S_{zx} (=S_{xz})$ is relatively small, the numerators of the two equations are negative, given $S_{xx} < 0$ and $|S| > 0$. Then the optimal gasoline toll is one where the toll exceeds the congestion externality $(Z(\partial C'/\partial Z))$ on the less congested road and falls short of the congestion externality on the more congested road. That is, the toll must necessarily be set at a compromise level, trading off the costs of overpenalizing z users against the costs of underpenalizing x users.

In summary, the optimal transport policy where gasoline tolls are the only way of pricing congestion on different roads is a two-pronged one. The toll overprices [underprices] travel on less [more] congested roads but this relative penalization is offset by a more favorable investment policy toward

---

[5] In equations (a)–(c) in footnote 2 we add terms due to the new constraint and then perform the same operations.

less congested roads. This suggests an argument for overinvestment in rural as opposed to urban roads, given that gasoline tolls probably underprice urban congestion and travel while overpricing rural travel.

4. THE ALLOCATION OF LAND TO ROADS IN AN URBAN AREA

One area of theoretical concern in the urban economics literature is the question how the amount of land devoted to roads should vary with distance from the city center. Consider a monocentric model of a city where everyone commutes to the CBD. As we approach the CBD, the number of commuters passing through each residential ring increases, because the number of commuters is an accumulation of all people who live farther from the CBD plus the people in the current ring. If travel time is a function of the number of travelers, or there is congestion, this would suggest that the absolute amount of land devoted to roads might increase as we approach the CBD, so as to relieve congestion as the number of travelers increases.

However, as we saw in Chapter 1, the opportunity cost of land rises as we approach the CBD, indicating increased marginal costs of investing in roads. Therefore, in allocating land to roads, the policymaker has to trade off the rising marginal costs of investment as one approaches the CBD against the potentially rising marginal benefits caused by additional travelers and potentially increased congestion. The general conclusion is that the relative amount of land devoted to roads in each ring increases as we approach the CBD (noting that the total amount of land in each ring is simultaneously declining). The absolute amount of land devoted to roads also probably increases as we approach the CBD, particularly in small cities. In larger cities with a higher opportunity cost of land near the CBD, the absolute amount of land devoted to roads may decline at some points as we approach the CBD, especially near the CBD. Mills and de Ferranti (1971), Oron, Pines, and Sheshinski (1973), and Solow and Vickrey (1971) all have extensive discussions of this topic.

5. CONCLUSIONS

In this chapter we first examined the nature of congested systems, such as roads, and derived the usual optimal pricing and investment rules for congested roads. We then turned to the issue of whether rapid transit should be subsidized. Transit capital facilities may need to be subsidized because with declining total average costs of provision, marginal cost pricing will not yield sufficient revenue to cover total costs. However, it was pointed out that public subsidies per se may not be needed. The transit authority could employ a two-part pricing scheme where travelers pay a fixed annual fee to use the transit facilities and then pay the marginal cost price for each trip. The annual fee is set so as to cover any deficit.

It may also be desirable to subsidize transit fares so they are less than marginal costs. This situation arises if transit is a reasonable substitute for roads, and if congestion on roads is unpriced so the private cost of road travel is less than the marginal cost. Thus road travel is implicitly subsidized and hence overused relative to other modes. Then the urban policymaker has a two-pronged policy. One prong is to underinvest in roads and the other is to subsidize rapid transit fares. Both prongs are designed to discourage road travel.

Finally, we examined the implementation of a gasoline toll which raises the per mile cost of travel by a fixed amount, essentially independent of the speed of travel. Gasoline tolls tend to overprice uncongested roads, on which no toll is needed, and underprice very congested roads, where a very high toll is needed. To offset these price effects and encourage movement to uncongested roads, it is optimal to overinvest in lightly congested roads and underinvest in heavily congested roads.

8

Transportation and the Peak-Load Problem

In this chapter we examine the phenomenon of peak-period travel, such as the morning or evening rush hour for commuters. Peak periods of travel such as the rush hour are usually characterized by low traffic volume and congestion at the start of the period, a steady buildup of traffic and congestion until almost the end of the period, and then a sharp decline in traffic volume as the peak period ends. At the height of the peak period, roads are usually heavily congested and traffic moves very slowly. This is a phenomenon of popular concern because of the heavy time costs (and frustration) involved in traveling at that time.

To understand the nature of the peak period, it is essential to examine how and why individuals choose to travel at different times during the peak period. Once we understand the individual's decision when to travel, we can derive an aggregate peak-period pattern of traffic, demonstrating the buildup of traffic flows and congestion during the peak period. We can also show that congestion tolls or other forms of regulation could be used to eliminate the heaviest congestion at the height of the peak period, to efficiently alter the peak-period pattern of traffic flows, and to lower travel costs for all commuters.

The individual's decision when to travel from origin to destination during the peak period is based on the cost of travel at different times during the period. The cost of travel is a function of (a) road congestion, and hence travel costs, at these different times; and (b) the cost of arriving at the destination at the most desired time versus less desirable times. This inclusion of the cost of arriving at times other than the most desired time is very important when a large number of people are trying to get to (leave from) the same place at the same time. Road capacities are such that not only is it impossible for everyone to arrive together, but some people prefer to arrive late or early to avoid the traffic jams incurred by those people who arrive at the most desired time. For example, in going to a football game, concert, or work, some people arrive early (late) to avoid the heavy congestion and higher travel or time costs incurred by the bulk of people arriving just before starting time. In addition to avoiding road and parking congestion, early arrivals may enjoy talking and drinking coffee before work or drinking beer and watching the pregame show before a football game. It is this property of arriving at a destination at times other than the most desirable one that is an important and somewhat unexplored aspect of peak-period travel.

Since these types of situations probably account for the majority of intraurban trips, modeling and analyzing them is critical to the understanding of urban transportation problems. This decision when to travel and the nature of peak-period traffic has been examined by Vickrey (1969) in the context of a pure queuing or bottleneck problem and by Henderson (1974b) in a more general commuting context. The discussion that follows is adapted from Henderson. Although the presentation here is very similar to Henderson's, traffic flows and congestion are modeled somewhat differently to be more consistent with the properties of congested systems discussed in Chapter 7.

Modeling a Peak-Period Situation

We model a particular peak-period situation, where a large number of people are trying to arrive at a particular destination at the same time. We consider the commuting trip to work where commuters all leave from the same point, say a suburb, and travel on the same road a given distance to work in, say, the Central Business District (CBD). For simplicity it is generally assumed that work starts at the same time for all commuters. In general, although not always, commuters are assumed to have identical time preferences and wages.

With a group of consumers ideally wishing to arrive at the same destination at the same time, there will evolve an actual pattern of different departure and arrival times. This pattern and the actual choices of departure times will be consistent with a stable equilibrium where all commuters are satisfied that their departure times minimize their travel costs. Corresponding to the pattern of departures is a pattern of traffic flows and congestion on the road where the sum of flows during the peak period equals the total number of commuting trips. Given the array of departure times, many commuters will arrive at work early, avoiding the heaviest congestion at the peak of the rush hour but incurring costs of waiting for work to start. It is assumed people cannot consistently arrive late or they will be fired. Allowing commuters to arrive late can be incorporated into the analysis, but is confusing and demonstrates no new principles.

In analyzing peak-period traffic, we use the first model of a congested system discussed in Chapter 7. Groups or flows of cars from the start of the peak period are continuously leaving the suburb and moving onto the road, traveling the road as a group, and then exiting in the CBD. For an entrant, the speed of travel is solely a function of the number (flow) of cars entering the system at the same time he does and this speed of travel is constant throughout the journey. Although the flow of cars onto the road is continuous, given that different groups of cars travel at different speeds according to the size of the group, the flow of cars exiting the system may not be continuous.

As discussed in Chapter 7, this model of congested systems inherently limits the possible solutions and peak-period traffic patterns that can be considered. Given an equilibrium array of departure times, it must be the case that people leaving at time t will not catch up to people who left at time $t - 1$ and people who leave at time $t + 1$ will not catch up to people who left at time t. Otherwise, the speed of travel for an entrant can no longer be constant throughout the journey and no longer just a function of the number of people entering at the same time he does. It must be true that if traffic departure flows [speed] onto the road are increasing [decreasing] continuously, people leaving at time t never encounter travelers from other departure times. Those ahead of them travel faster, those behind slower. During peak-period traffic flows, for the journey from home to work, this is generally the case. If, however, the opposite is true, we must ask if those behind catch up to those ahead. This can be determined by examining exit times, where if people who leave at time t exit after those who left at $t - 1$, then those behind do not catch up. Travel time on the road is T_r and the exit time for people leaving at t is $t + T_r$. If $|dT_r/dt| < 1$, the reduction in travel time for those traveling later is not enough for them to catch up given the difference in departure times. In our model parametric values will be such that $|dT_r/dt| < 1$ in equilibrium and we may treat the flows and speeds of each departing group independently of other groups. Note from this discussion that we have assumed that speed is a unique function of flow. In the traditional characterization of congested systems in Figure 7.1, this means we never operate beyond the point of maximal flow.

1.   EQUILIBRIUM TRAFFIC PATTERNS

1.1   The Individual's Travel Cost Function

To solve for an equilibrium we must first examine individual behavior. The behavioral assumption underlying the model is that consumers seek to maximize the total value of time. Time costs of travel are the only travel costs considered, other than costs of road capacity or provision. Automobile operating costs can be incorporated easily but for expositional simplicity are excluded. T is time, valued at W, spent in all activities other than commuting. T_r is time on the road, valued at W_r, and T_0 is time at the office before work starts, valued at W_0. W_r and W_0 are measures of the enjoyment (marginal utility) or marginal product of time (in producing leisure services) in driving and waiting activities. We assume that $W_0 < W$ and $W_r < W$, or that activities other than driving and waiting, such as being at home or working (both valued at W), are more desirable. Driving and waiting are simply a necessary part of holding a job, although we assume they bring positive pleasure. We also assume that $W_r < W_0$, or waiting is preferred to driving (in congested conditions). It is this parametric assumption that $W_r < W_0$ which rules out the case where $|dT_r/dt| \geq 1$, discussed in the previous paragraph.

Consumers seek to maximize $WT + W_0 T_0 + W_r T_r$ where $T + T_r + T_0 = 24$ hr (ignoring the evening commuting trip, which is discussed later). Therefore, consumers seek to maximize $W(24 - T_0 - T_r) + W_0 T_0 + W_r T_r$ or alternatively to minimize costs C where

$$C = T_r(W - W_r) + T_0(W - W_0); \qquad (8.1)$$

$(W - W_r)$ is the opportunity cost of time on the road, and $(W - W_0)$ is the cost of time waiting for work to start. Note that it is assumed the values of time W_r and W_0 are constant over the range of variation in T_r and T_0. W_r could be a function of T_r, or the amount of time spent on the road, both due to the length of travel time itself and due to the fact that longer travel times reflect lower travel speeds, heavier congestion, and more aggravating travel conditions.

For a commuter the total time spent traveling and waiting for work to start is the time work starts at, $\bar{t}$, minus the time people leave home at, t. Therefore, in equation (8.1), the time spent waiting T_0 equals the total time spent waiting and traveling, or $\bar{t} - t$, minus travel time. The distance people travel is m (miles). The speed of travel for people departing at time t is $S(t)$ in miles per hour. The time it takes to travel 1 mile is $1/S(t)$. Thus, the time people take to travel m miles is $m/S(t)$. Therefore, we may write

$$T_r(t) = m/S(t), \qquad T_0(t) = \bar{t} - t - m/S(t). \tag{8.2}$$

Given equation (8.2), equation (8.1) may also be written as

$$C = (W - W_r)m/S(t) + (W - W_0)(\bar{t} - t - m/S(t)). \tag{8.1a}$$

1.2 Properties of Equilibrium Traffic Patterns

The peak-period departures start at time i and end at time n, where i and n are endogenous variables solved for later. $F(t)$ is the number of people entering the road from the suburban homes at any instant. Therefore, total commuting trips during the peak period are

$$M = \int_i^n F(t)\, dt. \tag{8.3}$$

The speed of travel for entrants $F(t)$ is a function of the number of entrants and road capacity, R. Therefore,

$$S(t) = S(F(t), R), \qquad \partial S/\partial F(t) \leq 0, \qquad \partial S/\partial R \geq 0. \tag{8.4}$$

Given equations (8.1)–(8.4), we can now depict the properties of a stable equilibrium traffic pattern. Because commuters have the same values of time in all activities, for a stable equilibrium to be sustained these identical commuters must all incur equal total commuting costs, or have the same C in equation (8.1). Thus, for a stable equilibrium, if people with the same values of time depart home at different times, they must be indifferent between starting times, or their travel costs must be the same. Otherwise, people incurring higher costs will change their starting times to those with lower costs. Therefore, in equilibrium, from equation (8.1a)

$$\begin{aligned} dC/dt = {} & -(W - W_r)m/S(t)^2(dS(t)/dt) - (W - W_0) \\ & + (W - W_0)m/S(t)^2(dS(t)/dt) = 0. \end{aligned} \tag{8.5}$$

Rearranging terms, we have

$$m/S(t)^2(dS(t)/dt) = (W - W_0)/(W_r - W_0) < 0, \qquad \text{given} \quad W_0 > W_r. \tag{8.6}$$

Given that people have the same $(W - W_0)/(W_r - W_0)$, $m/S(t)^2(dS(t)/dt)$ is a negative constant and hence $dS(t)/dt < 0$ and it can be shown that $d^2S(t)/dt^2 > 0$. Speeds decline for people who have later departure intervals. The relationship between S and t is graphed in Figure 8.1 by curve A.

From equation (8.4), since speed is a unique decreasing function of flow, the way in which the continuous reduction in speed is accomplished is

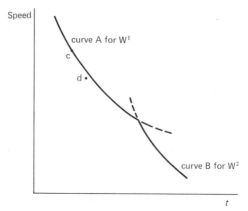

FIGURE 8.1 Speed and departure times.

through a continuous increase in departing flows. That is, since $dS(t)/dt = (\partial S(t)/\partial F(t))(dF(t)/dt) < 0$ and $\partial S(t)/\partial F(t) < 0$, then

$$dF(t)/dt > 0. \tag{8.7}$$

These equilibrium properties are the key to the whole analysis. People who leave earliest travel at high speeds in light traffic but wait longest at the office for work to start. Those who leave later and arrive just before work starts travel in heavier traffic and spend longer on the road (at a higher opportunity cost than waiting at the office). In this way identical people who leave later or earlier incur the same total commuting costs as is needed for a stable equilibrium. There are three important comments on this equilibrium and Figure 8.1. First, as illustrated later, the height and interval of curve A are dependent on the total traffic flows. As the number of commuters increases, the curve shifts down and the peak period increases, with i and n both declining (where $|\Delta i| > |\Delta n|$).

Stability

Second, the attainment and stability of equilibrium for identical commuters has certain conceptual problems. People must somehow order themselves so that some people leave early and others leave later in the specific pattern implied by curve A in Figure 8.1. Usually, goods or times in simple economic models are allocated through the "as if" model of the Walrasian auctioneer where full information is assumed and trading only occurs at equilibrium prices. In our situation it is less plausible than usual to envision the "as if" model with the Walrasian auctioneer at the morning breakfast tables allocating starting times. In Figure 8.1, it is true people have no incentive to switch planned departure times on a given morning, *given* the shape of A and its implied costs. However, the question is how commuters know ex ante the shape of A so as to make their correct departure time decision. A day-to-day stable commuting pattern must arise, with some people leaving consistently early and others consistently later. One cannot have all people daily switching travel times, since then a stable commuting pattern and curve A in Figure 8.1 will be unlikely to arise.[1] Once there is a day-to-day stable commuting pattern, individual equilibrium is stable. Then if a person who normally leaves early (at, say, point c) leaves later one day, he will find his commuting costs are higher by the amount he increases congestion at this later time (e.g., he will be at point d). Therefore, the next day he will switch back to his normal time.

Different Values of Time

The third comment concerns what happens to curve A and departure times if people have different values of time. Suppose there are two groups of people—one with wage rate W^1 on curve A and a second with a higher wage W^2. A number of assumptions about how W_0 and W_r might differ for these two groups of people could be made, but for simplicity it is assumed they are the same. (For high-priced executives with flexible work times W_0 might also rise; for higher-wage union or assembly line workers there is no reason to assume W_0 rises.) Intuitively, it would seem that if W is higher for a group of people, they will spend more time at activities valued at W and less at those valued at W_0 and W_r. In that case, they would leave home later than those people with a lower W, spending more time at home and less in total on the road and at the office before work starts.

We can demonstrate this proposition and the nature of the equilibrium with two groups of commuters as follows. In equation (8.1) low-wage people incur C_1 in costs. For these people to be indifferent between departure intervals *within* their own group, they must all incur C_1 in costs, or equation (8.6) must hold. The dS/dt relationship for C_1 is given by curve A in Figure 8.1. At some point of overlap, high-wage people start to depart and join the

---

[1] To formally arrive at a day-to-day stable pattern, we could postulate information cost functions and loss functions from switching times. Alternatively, we could assume people have slightly different values of time, as discussed later. A similar situation arises in the attainment of spatial equilibrium in residential choice models where people of identical tastes and income commute daily to the CBD. We know that there is a pattern of land rents consistent with a stable equilibrium. The mechanics of how equilibrium evolves, with identical people choosing to live at different locations, is a decidedly more difficult phenomenon to model. See Alonso (1964).

traffic stream. Two points can be made about the overlap. At the departure time at the point of overlap the two groups of people travel in the same congestion and at the same speed. Second, for high-wage people to be indifferent between departure intervals *within* their own group they must all incur the same commuting costs C_2. Therefore, they have an equation (8.6) that must hold; but in their equation (8.6) the right-hand side, $(W - W_0)/(W_r - W_0)$, has risen in absolute value. If $(W - W_0)/(W_r - W_0)$ has risen, then on the left-hand side of equation (8.6) in the period of overlap when S is the same for the two groups of people, $|dS/dt|$, must be higher for high-wage people. Therefore, high-wage people have curve B in Figure 8.1 where curve B is steeper than A at the point of overlap. The dashed parts of the A and B curves indicate speeds that would have to persist for low-wage and high-wage people in order for C_1 and C_2 to be maintained, if they were to shift into, respectively, later or earlier departure times. These dashed parts of the curves are the key to arguments that can be used to show that this equilibrium is the only stable one.

Stability within groups exists given a stable day-to-day commuting pattern as indicated by curves A and B. In addition, W^1 people have no incentive to travel in the later departure intervals of W^2 people. The speeds of the W^2 group indicated by curve B are lower than the speeds indicated by the dashed part of curve A needed to hold costs at C_1 for W^1 people. For similar reasons W^2 people would not travel earlier. Therefore, as argued intuitively, W^1 people leave before W^2 people and this is a stable equilibrium. If W^2 people leave before W^1 people, by rearranging the curves in Figure 8.1 we can show that, at the point of overlap, equilibrium is unstable. W^2 people would be better off switching to the times at which W^1 people travel and vice versa.

1.3 Solving for Equilibrium

Having determined the properties of a stable equilibrium, we now examine how to solve for a particular equilibrium. First, we must solve for i and n, the times at which the peak-period departures start and end. For i, the first person(s) to leave the suburb travel at maximum speed, $S(\text{max})$, on an uncongested road with minimum flows. $S(\text{max})$ is assumed to be a technical parameter. i is found by substituting $S(\text{max})$ into the cost function (8.1a) and solving to get

$$i = \left[\bar{t} + \frac{m}{S(\text{max})} \left(\frac{W - W_r}{W - W_0} - 1 \right) - \frac{C}{W - W_0} \right]. \qquad (8.8)$$

Time i is then a function of C, the equilibrium level of costs. As C rises, i declines. n is the last time people can leave for work and arrive on time.

n is solved by setting waiting time at the office, or $(\bar{t} - t - m/S(t)) = (\bar{t} - n - m/S(n))$, equal to zero and solving (8.1a) for the travel time to work where $m/S(n) = C/(W - W_r)$. Then substituting this expression into $(\bar{t} - n - m/S(n)) = 0$, we get

$$n = \{\bar{t} - [C/(W - W_r)]\}. \tag{8.9}$$

Again as C rises, n declines. However, as C rises the decline in i relative to n is greater, since by assumption $|\Delta C/(W - W_0)| > |\Delta C/(W - W_r)|$ in equations (8.8) and (8.9). Therefore, as C rises, $n - i$ or the length of the peak period increases.

How do we determine per commuter costs C and total commuters M? In general, there should be a unique relationship between C and M. As total commuters increases, so do congestion levels and hence costs. This may be argued as follows. From equation (8.1a) as C increases $S(t)$ declines for any t, which implies from equation (8.4) for any t that $F(t)$ increases as C increases. We have also just shown in the previous paragraph that as C increases, $n - i$ increases. Therefore, in the expression $M = \int_i^n F(t)\, dt$, as C increases, so do the individual $F(t)$, as well as the interval of integration (although the interval shifts). Thus we expect[2]

$$C = C(M), \qquad dC/dM \geq 0. \tag{8.10}$$

To actually illustrate an equilibrium traffic pattern we need to specify a functional relationship between $F(t)$ and $S(t)$. Then we can define total commuters M as the integral of an expression defined in terms of $S(t)$ rather than $F(t)$. Into this expression we can substitute for $S(t)$ from a rearranged equation (8.1a). In the resulting expression the integrand would be defined in terms of parameters and C. The limits of the integral from equations (8.8) and (8.9) can also be defined in terms of parameters and C. Therefore, we would have an equation defining M as a function of C. This is illustrated later.

2. OPTIMAL TRAFFIC PATTERNS AND INVESTMENT

Section 1 described an equilibrium traffic situation where congestion tolls are not imposed. In this section we derive a traffic planner's optimal solution to the peak-load traffic situation. The basic components of the solution necessitate the imposition of congestion tolls and the building of a road that is optimal in capacity. The traffic planner seeks to minimize the costs of getting a given number of people to work. Costs include the capital costs of building the road as well as operating costs or the value for all

---

[2] To prove this, it is desirable to specify the form of the $S(t)$ and $F(t)$ relationship.

commuters of time on the road and time spent waiting for work to start. Therefore, the planner seeks to

$$\min \int_i^n F(t)[T_r(t)(W - W_r) + T_0(t)(W - W_0)] \, dt + Rmk \qquad (8.11)$$

subject to

$$M - \int_i^n F(t) \, dt = 0.$$

The first part of the cost function is the summation over all departure times of the costs of travel and waiting multiplied by the traffic flow associated with each departure time. The second part is the capital cost of the road. R is a measure of road width, m the length of the road, and k the cost of building the road per unit width. The constraint is simply that the total number of commuters equals the sum of all departures. The cost function implies that the only use of the road is this journey to work. If the road is used for the return journey home or in off-peak hours the investment criterion developed below will be affected as will be discussed.

Minimizing (8.11) with respect to $F(t)$ and R, we find that the first-order conditions where λ is the multiplier are

$$\lambda = T_r(t)(W - W_r) + T_0(t)(W - W_0)$$
$$+ F(t)(W - W_r)(\partial T_r(t)/\partial S(t))(\partial S(t)/\partial F(t)), \qquad (8.12)$$

$$-\int_i^n (W - W_r)F(t)(\partial T_r(t)/\partial S(t))(\partial S(t)/\partial R) \, dt = mk. \qquad (8.13)$$

In equation (8.12), λ is the social marginal cost of transporting an additional traveler and this marginal cost should be equalized across all departure times. Otherwise it would be efficient to shift travelers from high to low marginal cost departure times. Commuters privately only incur $T_r(t)(W - W_r) + T_0(t)(W - W_0)$ in costs and to raise the price to λ for all travelers it is necessary to impose a congestion toll for entry onto the road that varies with the time of departure. From (8.12) the toll equals the value of the externality, or the amount by which an additional traveler raises the costs to other travelers by increasing congestion and reducing speed of travel. Therefore,

$$\text{toll}(t) = F(t)(W - W_r)(\partial T_r(t)/\partial S(t))(\partial S(t)/\partial F(t)). \qquad (8.14)$$

With the imposition of a set of optimal tolls, the allocation of travelers among departure times will be efficient.

Equation (8.13) describes the optimal investment criterion. This states that the marginal cost of expanding capacity, mk, should equal the marginal benefits from expanding capacity. The benefits are the summation over all departure intervals and travelers of the value of travel time savings due to increased speed of travel from increased road capacity. If the road is used at other times during the day, the travel savings at these times from expanding capacity should be added to the left-hand side of equation (8.13).

To describe the equilibrium properties of an optimal traffic pattern, we would redo the analysis in Section 1 using equation (8.12) to define individual operating costs, rather than equation (8.1a). In equation (8.12), given $T_r(t) = m/S(t)$, $T_0(t) = \bar{t} - t - m/S(t)$, and $\partial T_r(t)/\partial S(t) = -m/S(t)^2$ from equations (8.2) and (8.3), individual costs for an optimal solution which are denoted by $\overset{*}{C}$ are

$$\overset{*}{C} = (W - W_r)m/S(t) + (W - W_0)(\bar{t} - t - m/S(t))$$
$$+ F(t)(W - W_r)m/S(t)^2(-\partial S(t)/\partial F(t)). \qquad (8.12a)$$

The equations in Section 1 defining traffic flows and speeds are unchanged. However, in working through solutions since the relationship between C and $S(t)$ in equation (8.1a) is changed to that in equation (8.12a), the relationship between C and total commuters M will be altered relative to that in equation (8.10).

The expression defining the first departure time is unchanged. $S(i)$ always equals $S(\max)$, and at $S(\max)$, because $F(i) \to 0$, there is no congestion toll, or toll $(i) \to 0$. The new expression for the last departure time when waiting time is zero is

$$n = \bar{t} - m/S(n) \qquad (8.15)$$

where $S(n)$ must be solved as a function of $\overset{*}{C}$ from equation (8.12a).

To compare an optimal traffic pattern with an equilibrium pattern where congestion is unpriced, the easiest thing to do is to use an example. An example will also allow us to illustrate the general properties of peak-period traffic patterns. Given that congestion pricing will raise the costs of traveling at heavily congested times relative to less congested times, we should expect there to be a shift of travelers away from the height of the peak period. The congestion pricing should tend to spread travelers more evenly over the peak period, eliminating the heaviest congestion levels.

3. AN EXAMPLE

In this example we want to answer the following questions for a situation where a fixed number of commuters are going to the CBD. (1) For a road of an initial fixed capacity, what is the nature of the equilibrium that would result without congestion pricing? (2) For the *same* road capacity, what is the nature of the equilibrium that would result with congestion pricing and how does it compare with the no-pricing equilibrium? (3) If the initial fixed road capacity is optimal for the no-pricing equilibrium, how will optimal road capacity change with congestion pricing? This optimal change in road capacity will result in a somewhat different congestion pricing equilibrium than in question 2. (4) What are the differences in total resources expended among these three equilibria—no congestion pricing with optimal capacity, congestion pricing with the same initial but now nonoptimal capacity, and congestion pricing with optimal capacity?

To solve an example we need to specify a functional relationship between speed $S(t)$, flow $F(t)$, and road capacity R. We use the familiar relationship between travel time or $1/S(t)$ and flow $F(t)$ postulated by Vickrey (1965). This relationship is

$$1/S(t) = a + bF(t)^\gamma. \qquad (8.16)$$

Therefore,

$$F(t) = (1/S(t) - a)^{1/\gamma} b^{-1/\gamma} \qquad (8.17)$$

where $F(t)$ is measured in equivalents of flow per hour. a equals $1/S(\max)$ where $S(\max)$ is maximum speed on an uncongested facility. We set $S(\max) = 60$ mph or $a = 0.016$. Vickrey suggests γ lies between 1 and 2, so we specify $\gamma = 1.5$. b is a variable that is a function of road capacity. We postulate a constant returns to scale situation, where b is defined such that a doubling of inputs (a doubling of R road capacity and $F(t)$) will leave $S(t)$ and travel costs unchanged. Therefore,

$$b = R^{-\gamma} \quad \text{or} \quad R = b^{-1/\gamma}. \qquad (8.18)$$

Given the functional relationship between $F(t)$ and $S(t)$ in equation (8.17), from equation (8.3) for total commuters we know

$$M = \int_i^n b^{-1/\gamma}(1/S(t) - a)^{1/\gamma}\, dt. \qquad (8.19)$$

The other parameters of the model are as follows. Distance from the suburb to the CBD is $m = 15$ miles. The wage rate is \$2.00 per hour, value of time on road $W_r = \$0.60$, and value of time at the office before work starts $W_0 = \$1.20$. For simplicity, it is assumed there is one commuter per car. If it is assumed there are, say, two commuters per car, this just doubles all opportunity costs. The time work starts or $\bar{t}$ is 9:00 A.M.

Question 1.   The Equilibrium No-Toll Situation for 955 Commuters

To solve for an equilibrium traffic pattern, we set b equal to 10^{-7}, or set road capacity R equal to $10^{7/1.5}$ from equation (8.18). We then solve for total flows M as a function of per person costs C and of the parameters whose values have been specified. Rearranging equation (8.1a), we have $S(t) = (W_0 - W_r)m/(C - (W - W_0)\bar{t} + (W - W_0)t)$. Substituting into equation (8.19), we find

$$M = \int_i^n b^{-1/\gamma} \left[\left(\frac{C - (W - W_0)\bar{t}}{(W_0 - W_r)m} - a \right) + \frac{W - W_0}{(W_0 - W_r)m} t \right]^{1/\gamma} dt. \quad (8.20)$$

For the example, we choose a (somewhat arbitrary) value for per person costs C of \$1.00. To solve for the interval of integration, parametric values and $C = \$1.00$ are inserted into equations (8.8) and (8.9). Solving these equations yields $i = 7.94$ hr A.M and $n = 8.29$ hr A.M. Therefore, the length of the peak in terms of departure times is 0.35 hr. Given values for i and n as well as our parametric values, we integrate (8.20) to find that $M = 955$ when $C = \$1.00$. (We could have specified an initial M and solved for the corresponding C, but this is more tedious since we have to experiment with different C in equation (8.20) until we find the C that yields the particular M.)

The equilibrium pattern of flows and speeds for $M = 955$ and $C = \$1.00$ is depicted in Figure 8.2. The first person(s) who depart at $i = 7.94$ hr travel at maximum speed, taking 0.25 hr to get to work; and they wait 0.81 hr for work to start. Travel flows increase and speeds decline continuously until the end of the peak. The last people leave at $n = 8.29$ hr, take 0.71 hr to travel to work, and arrive exactly on time at 9 hr.

The results for no-toll peak-period traffic pattern are summarized in column 1 of Table 8.1. Some of the results in the table are not discussed until later.

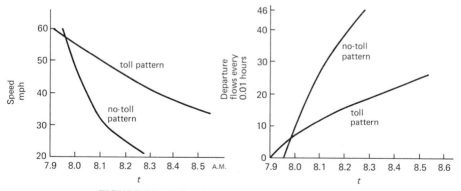

FIGURE 8.2   Toll and no-toll equilibrium traffic patterns.

TABLE 8.1

	(1) No Toll Optimal Investment	(2) Toll Nonoptimal Investment	(3) Optimal Solution: Toll Optimal Investment
Private travel cost (C or λ)	$1.00	1.01	1.27
Average per person toll revenue	n.a.	0.25	0.35
Per person tax to cover capital costs	0.61	0.36	0.0
Total per person costs	1.61	1.37	1.27
Total resources costs ($955 \times$ line above, or equation (8.11))	1538.00	1309.00	1217.00
Capital costs Rmk	582.57	582.57	331.07
Time of first departure i	7.94 hr	7.93 hr	7.41 hr
Time of last departure n	8.29 hr	8.56 hr	8.49 hr
Length of peak $n - i$	0.35 hr	0.64 hr	1.08 hr
Minimum speed during peak ($S(n)$)	21.00 mph	34.20 mph	29.20 mph

Value of externality at time n
   (equals toll, if tolls are in force,
   or equation (8.21))
	0.98	0.40	0.55

Marginal benefits of increased road capacity	0.0126	0.0051	0.0126

Question 2.   *The Equilibrium Toll Situation for the Same Capacity and Commuters*

How do the foregoing results compare with a traffic planner's optimal pricing solution for 955 commuters? A traffic planner would impose a toll on entrants to the road where from equations (8.14) and (8.16) the optimal toll is

$$\text{toll}(t) = (W - W_r)m\gamma(1/S(t) - a). \tag{8.21}$$

Therefore, per person variable commuting costs from (8.12a) are now

$$\overset{*}{C} = (W - W_r)m/S(t) + (W - W_0)(\bar{t} - t - m/S(t))$$
$$+ (W - W_r)m\gamma(1/S(t) - a). \tag{8.22}$$

Solving this for $S(t)$, we substitute into equation (8.19) to get

$$M = \int_i^n b^{-1/\gamma}\left[\frac{\overset{*}{C} - (W - W_0)\bar{t} + (W - W_r)m\gamma a}{(W_0 - W_r)m + (W - W_r)m\gamma} - a\right.$$
$$\left. + \frac{W - W_0}{(W_0 - W_r)m + (W - W_r)m\gamma}t\right]^{1/\gamma} dt. \tag{8.23}$$

The interval of integration is given by equations (8.8) and (8.15) for any value of $\overset{*}{C}$. To solve for the $\overset{*}{C}$ that corresponds to $M = 955$ we try different $\overset{*}{C}$ in (8.23) until we find the correct one.

With the toll, in this example with 955 commuters, the variable costs of travel $\overset{*}{C}$ rise slightly from \$1.00 to \$1.01. However, toll revenue is collected where total tolls equal $\int_i^n F(t) \, \text{toll}(t) \, dt$ or from equations (8.21) and (8.17)

$$\text{total tolls} = \int_i^n b^{-1/\gamma}(W - W_r)m\gamma(1/S(t) - a)^{1/\gamma + 1}. \tag{8.24}$$

Total tolls collected in this example are \$237 or an average of \$.25 a commuter. If this money were redistributed to commuters, the effective variable per person costs of travel would fall from \$1.00 to \$.76 with the imposition of congestion pricing.

This potential benefit of reducing per person costs occurs because of the efficient regulation of traffic flows. This can be seen in the results in column 2 of Table 8.1. The toll, which is heaviest in the peak minutes, tends to spread out travel times of commuters, since the cost of peak-time travel rises *relative* to earlier travel. The heavy congestion levels at the height of the peak period are eliminated. The result is an efficient reordering of traffic flows. This reordering involves the lengthening of the traffic period from 0.35 hr to 0.64 hr with the first commuters leaving only slightly earlier than before. Therefore, the big change is that the last commuters now leave at a much later time and travel at a much higher speed. This is possible, as illustrated in Figure 8.2, because flows during the peak period are now more evenly distributed.

It is possible to do examples where the *direct variable costs of travel including the toll or $\overset{*}{C}$ fall with the imposition of tolls.* For example, in the model suppose we raise the congestion parameter γ from 1.5 to 2 with other parameters unchanged. For $C = \$2.10$ we have a no-toll equilibrium of 570 commuters ($i = 6.56$ and $n = 7.50$). With the imposition of tolls for 570 commuters the direct variable costs of travel fall or $\overset{*}{C} = \$2.00$ ($i = 6.69$ and $n = 8.38$). If the toll revenues of \$376 collected in this example are redistributed to commuters, their effective variable costs will fall even more (to \$1.34). (Note that there is no back-bending flow–time cost relationship here, given the form of equation (8.17).)

Finally, we note that in terms of moving from the equilibrium without tolls to the equilibrium solution with tolls, the analysis is straightforward. If the initial tolls are set at the externality values in the no-toll equilibrium, they are very high at the peak, as indicated in Table 8.1 by the value at n. These tolls spread out the flows and starting times, removing the incentive to travel in the old peak minutes. A new pattern emerges where there is a new set of *relative* prices and optimal tolls determining the optimal set of travel time–waiting time allocations. Given the new relative prices, the

optimum is stable since any commuter by changing commuting patterns
only raises his costs, as argued previously.

Question 3.   Optimal Capacity Considerations

So far, we have held road capacity fixed. However, optimal road capacity
will vary according to whether congestion tolls are imposed or not. We
assume the initial road capacity is optimal for 955 commuters when there
is no congestion pricing. In other words, $b = 10^{-7}$ and $R = 10^{7/1.5}$ are
optimal when there are no tolls. Optimal investment in capacity implies
that equation (8.13) is satisfied or the marginal benefits of investment equal
the marginal costs. Equation (8.13) can now be written as

$$mk = \int_i^n (W - W_r)m\gamma b^{(\gamma + 1)/\gamma} F(t)^{\gamma + 1}\, dt. \qquad (8.13a)$$

In the no-toll situation for $b = 10^{-7}$, by substituting in equation (8.17)
for $F(t)$ and then equation (8.1a) for $S(t)$ and integrating, we can see that
equation (8.13a) can only be satisfied if $mk = 0.0126$. Therefore we define
$mk = 0.0126$ to be the marginal costs of investment for the current analysis.
For $mk = 0.0126$ and $R = 10^{7/1.5}$, total (rental) expenditures on capacity
per day are $582.57.

Once we impose congestion tolls for 955 commuters, equation (8.13a)
is no longer satisfied. If we integrate the right-hand side of equation (8.13a)
given the parameters and functions pertaining to the toll solution, we find
that the marginal benefits of additional investment are $0.0051. Since these
fall short of the marginal costs of $0.0126, this implies the initial road capac-
ity is now too large.

To find the planner's solution that is optimal in terms of both pricing
and investment we proceed as follows. Using equation (8.23) for $M = 955$
and equation (8.13a) for optimal investment where $mk = 0.0126$, we have two
equations in two unknowns, $\overset{*}{C}$ and $\overset{*}{b}$. Solving, we find that $b = 2.334 \times 10^{-7}$
and $\overset{*}{C}$ is $1.27. Optimal expenditures on roads fall from $583 a day to $331 a
day. Given optimal expenditures on capacity and constant returns to scale
in providing road capacity, the tolls raised exactly cover capital costs.
Because of reduced investment and the efficient increase in the direct costs
of travel, the minimum speed declines and the length of the peak period
increases relative to the overinvestment situation. The actual changes are
presented in Table 1.

Question 4.   Differences in Resource Usage among the Three Equilibria

The first equilibrium we examined was one without congestion pricing
but with optimal investment. In this case the per person nominal variable
costs of travel equal the per person variable resource costs of travel equal

$1. Therefore, in equation (8.11) for total resource costs, the value of the integral which equals total variable resource costs is $955. Capital costs were previously calculated to be $583. Therefore, the total resource costs of providing the journey to work are $1538, which represents a per person cost of $1.61.

With congestion tolls but unchanged (and now nonoptimal) capacity, the person nominal variable costs of travel are $1.01 or $963 for all commuters. However, nominal variable costs now exceed variable resource costs in equation (8.11) by the amont of congestion tolls. Total congestion tolls are $237 and hence total per person variable resource costs are $726. Capital costs are still $583. Therefore, total resource costs are $726 plus $583 or $1309 for a per person cost of $1.37. Another way of viewing the calculation is to state that since $237 in tolls are raised from total per person nominal variable costs of $963, only $346 more is needed in (tax) revenue to cover capital costs of $583. Or total per person nominal costs ($963) plus the planner's nominal costs ($346) equal social resource costs of $1309. The switch to congestion pricing results in substantial resource savings or a drop in costs from $1538 to $1309.

Finally, with congestion tolls and optimal capacity, total per person nominal variable costs are $1.27. The tolls included in these nominal variable costs exactly equal capital costs. Therefore, total resource costs in equation (8.11) for 955 commuters are simply $1217. The switch from $583 to $331 of road capacity provides further substantial resource savings.

These results are all summarized in Table 8.1.

4. EXTENSIONS

Two extensions of the model are very straightforward. One is to examine the journey home in the evening peak period. If values of W, W_r, and W_0, where W_0 is the value of time waiting at the office after work has ended, are unchanged, the solution should be perfectly symmetrical to the one presented above. People will be going in the opposite direction, with the greatest number leaving initially at 5:00 P.M. and then tapering off until the last people leave.[3] A second extension is to introduce modal choice. The introduction is superficially easy in that people are allowed to choose between, say, roads and transit, with their choices based on amenity and travel cost differences. However, as is apparent in the foregoing, the calculation of changes in the marginal cost of travel in response to changes in traffic volume M is more tedious than in Chapter 7.

---

[3] As long as $W > W_0 > W_r$, there is no problem of later departures overtaking earlier departures.

There is a third extension of particular interest. This is the introduction of work staggering in the CBD. The commuting cost benefits of having work start at a variety of times rather than just at $\bar{t}$ are obvious, in that departure times and traffic flows would be spread out much more evenly. The costs of work staggering are harder to model. For the firms in the CBD there would be a loss of intrafirm efficiency if people in the same firm arrive at work at different times, with an extreme example being assembly line efficiency. There is a loss of interfirm efficiency if different firms start work at different times, with an extreme example being the financial industry and operation of the bond and stock markets. For commuters there is obviously a limit to how early or how late they want to start work due to both preferences and problems in coordinating family activities. It would appear that the marginal benefits of a small amount of work staggering are great but decline as the extent of staggering increases, whereas the marginal costs of a small amount of work staggering are small but increase with the amount of staggering.

Therefore, there should be some optimal level of staggering. Two interesting questions arise about the nature of this optimum. First, can it be achieved through the uncoordinated activities of different firms in the CBD, given that firms do not account for the effect of expanding their work staggering on reduced congestion for commuters to other firms. Second how do wages vary among workers with similar skills within or between firms, given that workers who start (and leave) work early may be less [more] efficient than other workers and that they must be equally well off in a stable optimum with offsetting differences in commuting costs and wages?

5. CONCLUSIONS

In this chapter we examined the phenomenon of peak-period travel. Given a group of commuters trying to arrive at work at the same time, we showed that there will evolve an equilibrium travel pattern where some commuters leave early, travel in light traffic, and upon arrival wait for work to start. The majority of commuters leave later, travel in heavy traffic, and arrive close to the time work starts. In this situation, optimal congestion pricing raises the cost of traveling at the most congested times and spreads out traffic flows so that there is a more even flow of traffic. The result is a lengthening of the peak period, an elimination of the heaviest congestion, and substantial savings in resources devoted to transportation. Also, with congestion pricing, the optimal level of road capacity is reduced, since the heaviest congestion has been eliminated and the road system is less crowded.

9

Issues in Urban Public Economics

In the next two chapters four topics of both recent and long-standing interest in the field of urban public economics are examined. Although the discussion is primarily focused on theoretical and conceptual issues, it is prompted by very practical and critical questions about the current and future fiscal problems of cities. In this chapter we examine the incidence of the property tax, fiscal federalism, suburbanization, and the impact of inter-governmental grants such as revenue sharing on local government decision making. In the next chapter, we examine various models of the suburbanization process. Although the four topics are treated separately, they are all closely linked and these links will be emphasized.

1. THE PROPERTY TAX

The property tax is used extensively in American cities to finance local public expenditures. As a tax on housing services, it is nominally a very heavy tax relative to taxes on other consumer goods, with tax payments ranging from 10% to 30% of annual rental payments. It is also a comprehensive tax, covering not only residential land, structures, and improvements, but also commercial land and structures and often commercial capital formation, inventories, and some consumer durables. In fact, excluding capital in the agricultural sector of the economy, the tax covers most of the private physical wealth of the nation.

In analyzing the property tax we are concerned with two interrelated sets of questions and issues. The first concerns the distortions created by the property tax and the costs of these distortions. The property tax on residential housing may be viewed as an excise tax that raises the price of housing and lowers the return to producing housing. This distorts the consumption level of housing relative to other goods. As a tax on commercial capital and land, the property tax may raise the price of these inputs relative to other inputs, such as labor, and distort producer choices of production inputs. This tax on inputs of goods produced in urban areas should also raise the price of urban goods relative to goods not affected as much by the property tax, such as agricultural products and imports.

The second set of issues relates to the question what is the incidence of the property tax, or who effectively (as opposed to nominally) pays the property tax and bears its burden. Do property taxes primarily come out of the pockets of consumers in the form of higher gross housing prices (producer price plus tax) or are they passed back to owners of capital and land in the form of lowered returns to these factors? Of course, if housing is owner occupied, this distinction between residents and owners of factors is basically eliminated. However, there remains the question in a dynamic context under what conditions current permanent increases in property taxes are borne by past, current, or future owner-occupiers through changes in property values. Finally there is the question whether tax payments on capital and land in commerical areas primarily come out of the pockets of capital owners and landowners, or whether they are passed forward to consumers in the form of higher retail prices.

The answers to these questions determine whether the property tax is basically a progressive or regressive tax. Under the traditional view in the literature, consumers of housing and retail goods tend to bear the burden of the part of the tax that falls on capital, and landowners tend to bear the burden of the part that falls on land. Given this analysis, the property tax is usually estimated to be quite regressive. Under the new view in the literature, capital owners tend to bear the burden of the tax on capital. In this case, since lower income people tend to rent rather than own housing while middle and upper income people tend to be owner-occupiers and since ownership of business capital is concentrated in the upper income brackets, the property tax is estimated to be proportional or mildly regressive up to a family income of $15,000 (in 1966 dollars) and then quite progressive thereafter. Aaron (1975) presents a variety of calculations illustrating these statements. Since the new and old views reach different conclusions, it is useful to examine how their results are derived. To isolate the differences in the two views, we present them in their *simplest* and boldest forms, without going into the more sophisticated extensions that have been made. Both views are based on static models where the housing market is viewed as a rental market and only long-run effects and solutions are considered. The same results follow if housing is owner occupied, but their interpretation is altered, since capital owners and landowners are then the same people as residents.

Before proceeding with the comparisons, we should note that the incidence of the property tax is only half of the story. The other half is the incidence of benefits of government expenditures made from property tax revenue. Combining these two halves would tell us the incidence of the total fiscal system. Unfortunately, there is very little evidence on and analysis of this second incidence question.

1.1   The Traditional View

The traditional view examines the incidence and welfare questions in a partial equilibrium framework, usually concentrating on an analysis of the property tax on residential housing. By partial equilibrium we mean that the property tax is analyzed by only examining equilibrium in the residential sector of a single city, whose use of capital is negligible relative to the capital stock of the economy. In the long run, capital is perfectly mobile, so that the city faces an infinitely elastic supply curve of capital at the fixed rental rate set in the national market. The other factor in housing production is land, where the supply of land to the residential sector is viewed as fixed, or completely inelastic.

The long-run effect of the property tax is pictured in Figure 9.1a. The tax shifts back the demand curve for housing, raises the gross price of housing to $p_t + t$, and lowers the price received by producers to p_t. The supply curve is upward sloping, reflecting diminishing marginal returns to capital applied to the fixed quantity of urban land. The welfare cost of the tax is the shaded triangle. Producers pay $p - p_t$ of the tax per unit of housing in terms of a lower price received on housing and consumers pay $(p_t + t) - p$ per unit. The burden borne by consumers increases as demand becomes less elastic or supply become more elastic.

For producers, the reduced return to producing housing lowers demand for both inputs. However, since the price of capital is fixed to the city, in the long run, capital owners do not bear any of the burden through a reduced return on capital. The immobile factor, land, bears the entire burden on the production side; and the return to holding land declines. The assumption that the reduced demand for capital in this city does not affect the national

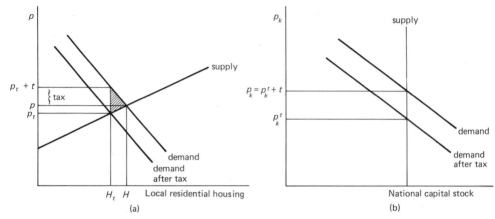

FIGURE 9.1   The burden of the property tax.

demand and return on capital is critical. Because only a small fraction of the nation's capital is used to produce housing in this city, the exodus of capital from the city can be absorbed into other sectors and cities of the economy with no affect on the return to capital.

1.2   The New View

The new view as developed by Mieszkowski (1972) takes an entirely different perspective, particularly with respect to the role of capital. Mieszkowski employs a general equilibrium framework, which recognizes that property taxes are imposed in all cities in the economy, not just one city. Moreover, the tax covers almost all forms of private urban wealth. Since most capital in the nation is taxed, capital in any one city cannot escape the burden by being absorbed in an untaxed sector with only a negligible effect on the return to capital.

The Primary Effect.   Consider a polar case where the property tax is imposed at an equal rate in all localities on all capital in the nation. Capital is perfectly mobile and is fixed in quantity nationally. With the imposition of the tax, the local and hence national demand for capital usage in production of housing and other goods falls. Since the national supply is fixed and all capital is taxed, capital cannot escape the burden of the tax. The net return on capital falls by the full amount of the tax assessed on capital, while the gross return is unchanged. This is pictured in Figure 9.1b. If we combine this analysis with the assumption that the supply of land is fixed in each city so that landowners bear the burden of the tax on land, under these polar assumptions consumers do not bear any of the burden. More-over, since consumer prices are unchanged and gross input prices are un-changed, the tax creates no distortions in consumer and producer choices. There is no welfare loss from the tax. Of course, if one relaxes the assump-tions of a fixed supply of capital or allows for an untaxed sector of the economy, these conclusions must be adjusted and the results are not quite so simple. As the relative size of the untaxed sector of the economy increases we are forced back toward the traditional model of property tax incidence.

Variations among Cities in Property Tax Rates

Effective property tax rates vary among cities either because desired per person consumption of public services varies or because some cities produce public services more efficiently than others and hence require lower tax rates for a given level of services. What effect do variations in the property tax rate have on our analysis? To examine this question, we first consider an example.

Suppose that one city raises its tax rate relative to the equal tax rates prevailing in the rest of the nation. This increase will result in a decline in the demand for capital in the residential and commercial sectors of the city and an outflow of capital from the city. Since the city is small relative to the nation, this outflow is absorbed into the rest of the economy with a negligible impact on the net return to capital. Capital owners will not bear any of the burden of the increase in the property tax rate. This reasoning leads Mieszkowski (1972) to state the following proposition. While capital owners bear the burden of tax payments according to the national average tax rate, local deviations about this rate are borne locally.

If that is the case, then who bears the burden of deviations from the national rate in a particular city? The situation we are examining is very similar to the situation considered in the discussion of the traditional view of the property tax. If in Figure 9.1a we redefine the tax rate t to be the amount by which the local tax rate exceeds the national average, the analysis in Figure 9.1a and in Section 1.1 describes the basic impact of deviations in the local tax rate. However, it is useful to consider the incidence of deviations in local tax rates in a spatial model of a city where we allow some adjust-ment in the supply of land and also consider the tax effects on the business sector of the city.

In Chapter 2, we examined such a situation in a spatial model where labor is imperfectly mobile and land is available to the city at a fixed rent in agriculture. In the analysis in Chapter 2 we assumed output prices of the city's goods are fixed; land rents in the city are redistributed equally to city residents, rather than going to a separate group of people, or rentiers; and the tax revenue is redistributed to city residents so that there are full benefits from public expenditures in the sense that tax dollars are not wasted. We call this the neutral benefit case, since although the tax dollars accrue to residents, they are not a separately demanded good. Note, however, that businesses get no direct benefits from the property taxes they pay.

Under these assumptions, in the residential sector of the city, the increased tax rate causes gross housing and land rents to rise and the residential demand for capital and land to fall. Net land rents decline at all points and at the city edge the return to land falls below the return in agriculture. Consequently, the city shrinks in size as urban land is converted back to agricultural land. In the commercial sector of the city, because the prices of output and capital are fixed and the increased taxes bring no productivity benefits, to pay increased taxes on land and capital, the wages and land rents offered by firms decline. Combining the price effects in the two sectors of the city, we see that city residents have reduced wages and land rental income and increased housing costs. However, since the tax revenue is returned to city residents, the basic impact of the change in the whole fiscal system on the welfare of residents is not a loss of income but the distortions created by the increased taxes. The utility of city residents declines and there is an exodus of people from the city, along the supply curve of population to the city. City area and population decline. Thus the initial city residents bear the burden of the increase in the tax.

How does the analysis change if we alter the assumptions made in Chapter 2? If we relax the assumption of fixed prices of the city's output and assume the city faces a downward-sloping demand curve for its product, the increased tax in the commercial sector will raise the price of the city's output. Then consumers of the city's goods will bear some of the burden of the increased taxes and part of the property tax will be "exported" to consumers in other cities and/or countries.

If we assume land rents are paid out to rentiers rather than city residents, the analysis is somewhat changed. First, since net land rents will decline due to the reduction in city size and demand to live in the city, rentiers will bear some of the burden of increased taxes. Moreover, since the revenue raised is returned to city residents, it is possible residents could benefit from increased taxes on land. Although the land taxes distort consumer and producer choices, they also result in a transfer of income from rentiers to city residents. (This is different from the Henry George proposal discussed in Chapter 4, which would tax the land rental income of rentiers rather than land per se.)

Finally, the assumption of neutral benefits from public expenditures means that generally increased property taxes will make residents worse off because of the distortions created, even if their incomes are virtually unchanged. Suppose the benefits are not neutral. If the increased revenue is wasted, this increases the loss to city residents and the decline in their welfare. On the other hand, suppose the revenue is spent on local public services where the services cannot be provided in other cities or residents in this city just prefer greater expenditures. In this case the increased expenditures may make the city more fiscally attractive and cause an in-migration to the city. In that case if there are rentiers, they are likely to bear less or none of the tax burden, since there will be an increased demand for land in the city. Housing consumers or city residents, because they demand these increased expenditures, will bear most of the burden of the increased taxes in the form of higher gross housing prices or lower wages. The lower wages reflect the assumption that for businesses the increase in taxes brings no direct benefits although the hypothesized increase in city population may result in positive scale economy effects; and hence to finance the tax payments, given fixed output and capital rental prices, firms may have to offer lower wages and land rents. Through higher housing costs and reduced wages and land rental income, residents pay for their increases in public expenditures, although of course they benefit from these expenditures.

Comparison with Other Taxes. Based on the new view, our conclusions are that capital owners bear the burden of the national average tax rate on capital, whereas local deviations in the rate of taxation on capital are borne by residents and possibly landowners. Suppose that the property tax is either replaced or supplemented by a wage tax. This is a common proposal that is based on the notion that wage taxes tend to be more progressive than property taxes. However, this notion is questionable.

If wage taxes replace property taxes in all cities, in a model with a fixed national supply of mobile laborers, the analysis of incidence is pictured in Figure 9.1b, except that labor rather than capital is the subject of discussion. The wage tax reduces the national demand for labor. Given a completely inelastic supply curve of labor, labor bears the entire burden of the tax. In short, it is not to the advantage of laborers to substitute a wage tax for a property tax nationally. Even if housing is owner occupied, so residents tend to bear residential property taxes, they do benefit from property taxes raised on commercial capital, whereas an equal revenue wage tax would be borne entirely by wage earners. Finally, we note that if one city substitutes a wage tax for the property tax at the margin to raise additional revenue, it is unlikely that labor will benefit from the substitution. Just as local increases in the property tax rate are borne by local residents, so are local increases in wage taxes. Mieszkowski (1975) examines the effects of substitution of these taxes.

1.3   Variations in the Property Tax Rate
within Cities and Capitalization

The final consideration involves the burden of variations in tax rates, particularly residential tax rates, *within* a metropolitan area. Wages, capital rentals, and traded good prices within the urban area are everywhere the same. Hence, internal variations in tax rates must be borne by housing consumers or landowners through variations in housing and land prices. We examine two reasons why effective tax rates may vary internally in a metropolitan area and the effect of these variations on housing and land prices.

Assessment Practices

The first reason tax rates may vary within a metropolitan area is institutional in nature. Although the official property tax rate may be the same in a metropolitan area, the effective rate may vary because the assessed value of housing relative to the market value may vary. For example, as general housing values inflate over time assessment practices may be such that the assessed value of housing is unevenly updated. In that case, houses whose assessed values have declined the most relative to their market values are lightly taxed compared to other houses. This would appear to be an inequitable situation that should be changed.

For the initial owners, who may be either occupants or rentiers, it is true that those whose assessed values fall the most relative to market values benefit from being lightly taxed. Moreover these lighter taxes mean that buyers would be willing to pay a premium to purchase these houses relative to more heavily taxed houses. This premium arises because market prices will adjust so that the gross price of equal-quality houses will be equalized across the metropolitan area, where this price is the purchase price plus the present value of future expected tax liabilities. Any lighter tax burden which is expected to persist is fully capitalized into a higher purchase price of a house. Therefore initial owners benefit from both the light taxes in each period they occupy the house and a capital gain when they sell the house.

However, because people who purchase these homes from initial owners pay the same gross price for housing as those who purchase relatively heavily taxed homes, any unexpected movement to change the situation and update and equalize assessment practices will only *create* (not eradicate) inequalities among newer owners. If assessments are changed to current market prices, those people who paid high net of tax housing prices because of previously low taxes will suffer both higher taxes and a capital loss when they sell and those with previously high taxes will benefit from both lower taxes and a potential capital gain. In this case equity rests on maintaining the status quo or meeting expectations. (Of course, regular announced reassessment is equitable, since it is expected and fully reflected in housing prices.)

Differing Fiscal Jurisdictions in a Metropolitan Area and Capitalization

The second reason why property tax rates may vary within a metropolitan area is that the area may be divided into different fiscal jurisdictions with differing tax rates. These differing rates may affect housing and land rents within and between communities. This affect on rents has implications discussed in Chapter 10 for the efficiency of land use, as well as for assessing the burden of property taxes. We illustrate this problem with a simple example taken from Hamilton (1976).

Suppose there are two types of consumers in a metropolitan area, high housing consumers (h people) and low housing consumers (*l* people). There are three communities: homogeneous high housing, homogeneous low housing, and mixed housing communities (h, *l*, m communities). Because of zoning or developers' strategies in the provision of housing, h people consume the same level of housing h_h in the h and m communities and similarly for *l* people who consume h_l housing in the *l* and m communities. Due to institutional factors or because h and *l* people have the same demand for public services, the level of public services is the same in each community. These two assumptions allow us to isolate the pure effect of property tax differences on housing prices, without having to consider the effect of housing or public good consumption differences.

What differences in housing and land prices will arise in the metropolitan area? Comparing the h and m communities, in the m community the average tax base, or average housing consumption, is lower, due to the presence of *l* people, and to finance the same level of services requires a higher tax rate. High-income people are perfectly mobile between the two communities and hence must have the same level of utility. Given that they consume the same level of public services and housing in the two communities, in order for them to have equal utility, their expenditures on all other goods must be equalized between the communities. Given the same incomes and expenditures on all other goods, the gross expenditures on housing must be the same, or $p_h^m h_h(1 + t^m) = p^h h_h(1 + t^h)$ where p_h^m is the unit price of h housing in the m community, p^h is the price in the h community, and t^m and t^h are the corresponding tax rates. Therefore

$$p_h^m = p^h \frac{(1 + t^h)}{(1 + t^m)}.$$

Given $t^h < t^m$, $p_h{}^m < p^h$ by the amount needed to exactly compensate h people in the m community for their higher taxes. To express this in asset, as opposed to rental, prices, one simply adds up the current and future discounted rental prices. Comparing the m and l communities, l people in the m community benefit from the presence of h people, relative to l people in the l community. Using the same type of reasoning as above, we can show where p^l, $p_l{}^m$, and t^l are respectively the prices of low level housing in the l and m communities and t^l is the tax rate in the l community that

$$p_l{}^m = p^l \frac{(1 + t^l)}{(1 + t^m)}.$$

Since $t^l > t^m$, $p_l{}^m > p^l$. These price differences between the same quality housing in different communities maintain a stable equilibrium with respect to residential movements. They reflect the fact that through capitalization housing prices adjust with tax rates to maintain the same gross price of housing for equal quality housing and thus fiscal differences are fully capitalized into housing prices.

While this makes sense these equations only describe *relative* price differences between the same type of housing in different communities. We need to determine absolute prices as well, which brings out several problems in the analysis. To determine absolute prices, we first assume that the price of housing in the homogeneous communities is the same, or $p^l = p^h$; and it equals the opportunity cost of housing in its alternative use such as agriculture. Developers must be paid this price before they give their land to residential use in the l or h communities. If $p^l = p^h$, this implies from the above equations that

$$p_l{}^m > p^l = p^h > p_h{}^m$$

If housing is malleable and lot size can be redesigned in the long run, this implies that some type of zoning will be needed to maintain this solution and stop the conversion in the m community of high level housing into low level housing. If there are competitive developers in the m community, not only will the owners of high housing land be receiving a price below opportunity cost, but they will profit by switching their land to low housing use, until prices are equalized in all uses. Given the derivation of the housing price equations (and even allowing housing consumption to vary between similar people in different communities), this equalization can only occur when the mixed community becomes homogeneous in one or the other of the land uses. This suggests that without zoning, these types of capitalization solutions cannot be maintained in the long run, since the basis for capitalization cannot be maintained.

However Hamilton (1976) points out that with respect to the actions of developers, the solution is stable without zoning if there is only *one* developer in the mixed community or if transfer payments among developers are feasible. This occurs because it can be shown that the average price of housing in the m community remains the opportunity cost of housing, which equals p^l and p^h.[1] However even if the developer could be happy with the solution, it still may not be stable with respect to the actions of renters. Renters have an incentive to recontract, where h people in the m community would benefit by renting out portions of their low priced housing to l people. Therefore even if there is just one developer, zoning may still be needed to prevent renters from converting one type of land use to another.

2. FISCAL FEDERALISM

The federal government intervenes in the affairs of local governments by transferring tax money among regions and cities and also by transferring tax money within regions and cities. In this section we examine the economic reasons behind such transfers. In Section 4, we examine the impact on local decision making of certain types of transfers.

Transfers among Cities and Regions

In the literature there is an extensive discussion of equity and efficiency reasons for transferring money among regions and by implication among cities (see Oates, 1972, for a review of the literature and issues). The efficiency grounds in a situation where labor is perfectly mobile are considered in the analysis of externalities in Chapters 4 and 5. Other efficiency considerations as well as equity considerations deal with a situation where labor is imperfectly mobile between regions, and real wages and employment rates are lower in some regions than others. National policies may be designed to encourage employment in depressed areas, on the efficiency grounds that this will increase regional and national output, as well as on equity grounds of redistributing income and resources towards depressed areas.

With respect to these depressed areas, the usual scenario is that at one time investment and employment rates in these areas were high. However,

---

[1] The proof of this is simple but tedious; we outline one way of proving the proposition. We make use of expressions for each community stating that taxes collected equal public service expenditures. Into the taxes equal dollar expenditures expression for the m community we substitute for p_l^m and p_h^m from the equations in the text. Into the result we substitute for t^l and t^h from the taxes equal expenditures expression for the homogeneous communities. If we simplify the resulting expression, substitute in for expenditures from the original taxes equal expenditures expression for the m community, and rearrange terms, the resulting expression states that the average price paid in the mixed community equals the opportunity cost of housing.

over time with technological and other economic changes, real wages and
employment rates in a large spectrum of occupations declined in these regions
relative to other regions as it became unprofitable to invest there. This type
of situation in an area may reflect one or more of several problems. There may
be currently insufficient demand for its natural resources. Labor may be
unskilled in the production of currently demanded goods. The region may
be far from current national product markets and at a transport cost disadvantage given current transport technology. Combined with one or more
of these other factors population growth (net internal and migratory changes)
in the region may be relatively low or negative and the absolute population
level may be too low to offer sufficient scale economies in production. Any
one of these factors may make the region unattractive to invest in, keeping
real wages down.[2]

To reduce unemployment in depressed areas, one strategy is to encourage
investment, by reducing the costs to firms of employing other inputs, in
particular labor. If this investment leads to employment of the unemployed,
it will be efficient because national output will rise, Investment itself will be
efficient because capital will only be invested if it earns a competitive rate of
return. The gain in output arises because, although labor costs are partially
subsidized, those people who previously had zero marginal products will
now have positive marginal products. We note two policies which encourage
investment and hence employment.

(a) Wage sudsidies. For incoming or expanding industries the national
government pays a certain fraction of the wages of each new employee, making
labor even cheaper in depressed areas relative to other regions. Wage subsidies
can be direct transfers, business tax reductions per employee, training subsidies, etc. Wage subsidies are preferred to sudsidies on plant and equipment
since they encourage the location of labor intensive industries which help
sop up unemployment, as opposed to capital intensive industries which may
have little impact on regional unemployment.

(b) Subsidies to investment in public facilities. High investment in
facilities such as transportation networks may encourage investment in
depressed areas by reducing firm production costs related to these facilities.

The strategy of trying to encourage the employment of the unemployed
is designed to provide employment for people in their home region, allowing

[2] Factor price equalization, which results in simple regional models through trade, does
not occur here between regions for several reasons. One is transport costs; another is regional
specialization because of natural resource factors; and a third is scale economies. The considerations also mean that there can be equilibrium unemployment in some regions, given that labor
is imperfectly mobile (Henderson, 1972).

them to preserve their existing social structure and cultural life. In some circumstances where a region is at a very bad competitive advantage, even in a broad sense accounting for the costs of social upheaval, it may be most efficient to encourage out-migration of the population to high employment areas. While individuals can migrate on their own to improve their employment opportunities, migration sudsidies may be needed to offset the non-migration incentive effects of income redistribution programs. Income redistribution tends to equalize incomes between regions, thus reducing the private benefits from migrating.

Income Redistribution

Income redistribution is the transfer of income among individuals aimed at providing income for people who have low earning capacities. It is concerned with individual equity as a public good. In the past in the United States, income transfers among individuals were basically a local public service. A primary question is whether income redistribution should remain a local good or whether some type of federal intervention is needed to provide efficient levels of this good. There are definite reasons for maintaining it as a local, as opposed to a national, service. First, local provision allows for the expression of local preferences and the determination of redistribution levels that local voters want in their region. Federalization of income redistribution would impose the same level of transfers and consumption of charity on all regions regardless of their preferences. Local provision also accounts for the fact that localities will generally be more concerned about their own poor. Under a national redistribution program, particularly in richer regions, people may be less likely to vote for adequate redistribution levels given that only a fraction of the money raised locally is spent locally.

However, local redistribution presents certain externality problems because of population mobility. First, if a region raises its level of transfers, it may attract poor people from other regions. This raises the cost of giving to one's indigenous poor above the basic cost. This problem of attracting the unwanted poor of other regions should lead regions to underprovide redistribution services to their own poor (although stiff eligibility requirements can remove much of this problem). It is also possible that some regions will deliberately keep redistribution services low in an attempt to induce their poor to emigrate to other regions. Second, because regions have different compositions of rich and poor, the cost of a given level of redistribution per person, or the cost of giving, varies among regions. By moving to a richer region, a wealthy person can consume a given level of giving more cheaply. Moreover, poor regions do not have the tax capacity to finance adequate redistribution programs. This problem of varying capacities of regions to make redistribution payments suggests that some type of federal intervention in the process is needed.

If federal intervention could provide some base level of redistribution, removing gross regional inequalities, it would remove most of the incentive for the rich and poor to move around to better their transfer position. Room could be left for expression of local tastes, by allowing regions to add to this base level on their own. This partial federalization would also be efficient to the extent that people in a locality have preferences defined not just over their own poor, but over the poor in all regions.

Federal Policies and Implicit Transfers
within Regions or Metropolitan Areas

Money is sometimes transferred to regions to bring about a redistribution of the tax burden of financing expenditures within regions. Suppose the local tax system is regressive whereas the federal tax system is progressive. By raising federal taxes and redistributing the money to localities so that their dependence on local taxes is reduced and they reduce their local taxes (see Section 4), we replace a regressive tax system by a progressive one. These federal transfers redistribute the tax burden of financing local expenditures from lower-toward higher-income people. Of course, this result only occurs if the local tax system is less progressive than the federal tax system. In America, where local taxes are primarily property taxes, given the discussion in Section 1, it is unclear which tax system is more progressive, especially in the upper-income ranges. Therefore, reducing local dependence on property taxes may or may not redistribute the tax burden away from lower-income groups.

The second consideration involved in transferring money to regions concerns suburbanization. Before we can discuss and analyze the reasons for monetary transfers because of suburbanization, we need to describe the suburbanization phenomenon. Then we will examine reasons for intra-regional transfers.

3. SUBURBANIZATION

There has been tremendous suburban population growth in the last 25 years, combined with a leveling off of or even a decline in core city population in metropolitan areas. The people who have suburbanized have tended to be higher-income people, whereas lower-income people have tended to remain behind in the core cities.[3]

---

[3] See Bradford and Kelejian (1973) on suburbanization patterns.

One explanation of the greater propensity of higher-income people to suburbanize is that as cities grow, over time higher-income people move out simply to take advantage of the cheaper land prices at the edge of the metropolitan area. This idea was discussed in Chapter 1. Federal tax loopholes connected with home ownership (the incidence of which rises with income) and the desire of higher-income people for newer homes are also reasons suggested for this phenomenon. However, the suburbanization process seems to be more complex than is suggested by these reasons, particularly given that suburbanization of high-income people has occurred only in some American cities and has, for example, not occurred to the same extent in Canadian cities. Second, these reasons do not explain why suburbanization is also linked with a process of fiscal separation, where higher-income people usually form fiscally independent communities, rather than remaining part of the core city. Moreover, if we examine the phenomenon more carefully, we see that there are several odd features to it which support the notion that suburbanization represents a desire for fiscal separation on the part of higher income people. First, the spreading out is not always spatially continuous. Sometimes there is a spatial gap of unused land between where residential housing ends in the core city and where suburban housing starts at the fiscal boundary of the core city and suburb. This suggests suburbanization represents not just a desire to spread out in which case the gap would be filled, but also a desire to fiscally separate. Second, suburbs seem to be internally relatively homogeneous in terms of income of the residents, whereas there are variations in income between suburbs. The homogeneity may reflect a desire for people to live with others of similar incomes and tastes. However, as in the core city this desire could be realized through different homogeneous neighborhoods in a suburb, without homogeniety of the whole suburb. As we will see below total homogeniety has certain fiscal advantages. These considerations suggest that higher-income people tend to suburbanize for fiscal reasons, as well as all the other reasons suggested above.

The fiscal reasons for suburbanization are based on the following notions. If there are public goods in a core city financed through a property tax, higher-income people are fiscally disadvantaged for two reasons. First, the level of public goods as determined by majority vote is usually less than that desired by high-income people. Second, higher-income people have a higher tax base, or value of housing, and they pay proportionately more in taxes than lower-income people. They can avoid this disadvantage by moving beyond the legal fiscal boundary of the core city and forming a homogeneous suburb that is fiscally independent of the core city.

Some of the restraints on the suburbanization process are the increase in commuting costs, given that the suburb must form beyond the core city fiscal boundary, and the reduction in the relative price of core city to new suburban housing as the demand for the core city housing stock falls with the exodus of people. If we have a core city with no suburbs, there are three things that will start suburbanization. Probably all of these have been important in American suburbanization. One is growth in the public sector, increasing the fiscal benefits of moving. Another change is reduction in commuting costs, reducing the costs of suburbanization. This reduction may occur because of technological change in the transportation sector or because of investment in highways. It could also occur because of decentralization of production activity in the city away from the CBD into the suburbs. The third change is simply city growth, reducing the gap (if any) between the legal fiscal and effective residential edges of the core city or the increment in commuting costs resulting from moving beyond the fiscal boundary to a suburb.

In Chapter 10 we will argue that when suburbanization involves stratification of the population into homogeneous communities, there are certain desirable efficiency properties of this stratification. These properties pertain to the efficient provision of public services, where through stratification people reveal their preferences for public services. In homogeneous suburbs all people get to consume their most preferred level of public services rather than some nonoptimal level, given the social marginal costs of providing public services. However, suburbanization has also presented some other efficiency and equity problems involving the disruption of public services in core cities. We now look at some of these problems and try to determine to what extent they can be solved through federal government intervention. If they can be solved, under certain conditions, suburbanization is an efficient way to provide public services and perhaps to spatially arrange the population.

Federal Government Intervention and Suburbanization Problems

As suburbanization in a metropolitan area occurs, the loss of higher-income people and businesses from the core city means a reduction in not just the total but also the average tax base in the core city. This decline in the average tax base in the core city may result in lower per person public expenditures in the core city and a loss in welfare for lower-income people. However, whether public expenditures for lower-income people actually fall when higher-income people leave depends not just on the change in tax base, but also on the distribution of public expenditures among the population that existed before higher-income people left. This distribution may have heavily favored higher-income people, in which case the loss of higher-income people may result in no losses in net fiscal benefits for lower-income people. If there is a loss, it may be socially desirable to compensate lower-income people for their fiscal losses. This could be accomplished by redistributing federal tax dollars, which tend to be raised in greater proportion among higher-income suburbanites, to core city treasuries.

A second problem with suburbanization is that after high-income people leave the core city they may continue to use the public facilities of the core city, such as roads, police protection, art galleries, and libraries, when commuting to work or recreation in the core city. In general, they may not pay for the cost of these services. If this is so, this represents the traditional spillover, or externality, situation where public service benefits of a government extend beyond its fiscal boundary. For example, if public services are provided by the core city such that marginal costs equal internal marginal benefits, this means that social marginal benefits, including the spillovers, exceed marginal costs of providing core city services. In this situation if the recipients of the spillovers can be taxed and the money used to subsidize provision of the goods that spill over, everyone can be made better off. Recipients of spillovers would be taxed according to their marginal benefits from spillovers and this money would be used to subsidize public service provision at the margin so that in effect social marginal benefits are equated with marginal costs. Whether the suburbanites benefit from this program to some extent depends on whether they have to pay taxes on intramarginal units of public services that are already provided and that they have been consuming for free, or whether they only pay taxes to subsidize the increases in services. The subsidization could be effected by using federal taxes raised in greater proportion from the middle- and upper-income suburbs to subsidize provision of those public services in core cities whose benefits spill over into suburbs. Connally (1970) and Pauly (1970) present analytical examples of tax-subsidy programs that would lead to optimal provision of services under varying assumptions about whether the public services are pure public goods, pure private goods, or congested goods. Note that there is a presumption that suburbs on their own will not bribe, or subsidize, the core city to increase public services. The problem is that there are many suburbs that will collectively benefit from such an increase. Hence, the usual free-rider and organizational problems in suburbs getting together to make joint decisions will stop any individual suburb from voting to adequately subsidize core city services.

It is not clear how important the spillover problem is. Bradford and Oates (1974) present a strong case for the view that suburbanites contribute more to the core city fiscally than they take out. Some of the core city services consumed by suburbanites are paid for by user fees. Second, when shopping in the core city suburbanites contribute to the local treasury by paying any local excise taxes; and when working in the core city, they contribute through any local wage taxes. Moreover, usually the core city has a higher proportion (relative to the population) of the metropolitan area's industrial and commercial base. Hence, the core city benefits from property taxes on productive capital not found in suburbs. Alternatively viewed, by suburbanites commuting to work in the core city and thus contributing to the core city labor force needed to maintain and attract the industrial base of the core city, these suburbanites confer a fiscal benefit on the core city in terms of a greater industrial base. On the other hand, these suburbanites also avoid environmental disamenities connected with industries locating in or near their residential areas.

4. THE IMPACT OF FEDERAL GRANTS ON LOCAL JURISDICTIONS

If transfers are made among regions or cities for any of the reasons suggested in the preceding sections, one important question to investigate is the effect of these transfers on the internal allocation of resources. In this section we examine the effect of transfers made to local governments on the provision of local public services and the well-being of different local residents. We first review some of the general discussion of grants in the literature (Fisher, 1976; Bradford and Oates, 1971; Heins, 1971; Wilde, 1968), and then turn to a discussion of revenue sharing taken from Fisher's (1976) work.

4.1 The Partial Equilibrium Approach

The first approach to the intergovernmental grants problem is a partial equilibrium one. By this is meant that the grants that local governments receive are free in the sense that the size of their grant does not affect their local taxes. This assumption is consistent with two descriptions of the grant program. First, we could assume that the program only results in grants to a few communities out of the many in the nation, so that the national tax increase used to finance the grant is tiny and has a negligible impact on the taxes of the benefiting communities. Other communities effectively pay for the benefits going to the few recipients. Second, we could assume that the grants are financed by shifting money out of certain categories of federal government expenditures into the grant programs. For example, the program could be financed by reducing military expenditures in foreign countries and shifting the reduction into the grant program, with perhaps no perceived loss in federal government services.

Given that the grants are free, the basic analysis has focused on the types of grants that are made and their impact on local government spending. We note three general types of grants.

(1)   Lump-sum grants.   The federal government transfers a lump sum to be spent on local public goods. In general, we will assume there are no restrictions on the way these grants may be used. In practice, the federal government may impose limits on the cutback in local expenditures or restrictions on the type of services that the money may be used to finance. As suggested in Sections 2 and 3, the purpose of such grants may be to help fiscally disadvantaged communities or to replace local government taxes that may be raised from regressive types of taxes with federal taxes.

(2)   Open-ended matching grants.   The federal government agrees to subsidize local expenditures on certain categories of public expenditures by paying a fixed fraction of each dollar of local expenditures. This type of grant has the feature that, given the federal rate of subsidization, local not national decisions on the level of local expenditures actually determine the total amount of federal expenditures on grants. Such grants might be designed to encourage local expenditures on public services whose benefits spill over into other communities. Alternatively they might be used to encourage the provision of services the federal government feels local governments should be providing that they are not providing, at least in the quantity deemed fit by the federal government.

(3)   Closed-ended matching grants.   These are the same as the second type of grant except that the federal government restricts the total amount of dollars it will pay out in subsidies.

Before outlining the impact of these types of grants, we note the following assumptions. For diagrammatic simplicity, in what follows it is assumed that public services are pure public goods. Local tax shares, which are the proportion of local taxes paid by each resident, are exogenously given but may differ among individuals. We assume the level of community public services is determined by majority vote in a political system where voters are fully knowledgeable (Public services can also be determined through a community indifference curve model.) The equilibrium level of services chosen will be that which is demanded by the median voter. Under the median voter hypothesis, if we rank community members according to their desired level of services, the median voter is the median person in the ranking.[4] The median voter determines the level of public services since that is the only stable electoral outcome. If public services are higher [lower] than that demanded by the median voter, a majority including the median voter will vote to decrease [increase] public services. The political system may be either a two-party system with each party competing for the center of the road or a referendum system where people vote and revote on the level of

---

[4] An assumption of single peaked preferences for public services is needed here; but that simply is equivalent to assuming that utility functions are monotonic and strictly quasi-concave.

public services until voting no longer changes the level chosen. If individuals have identical preferences and if tax shares are a monotonic function of income, the median voter is the median-income person (Barr and Davis, 1966).

The Impact of Intergovernmental Grants

In Figure 9.2, we illustrate the impact of intergovernmental grants. On the horizontal axis is community consumption of public goods g. On the vertical axis is the median voter's consumption of private goods x. The median voter's initial budget line is ef and the initial level of each good chosen is x_a and g_a. The slope of the median voter's budget line is given by the unit tax cost (in terms of x) to the median voter of public services. Where p_g is the unit production cost of g (in terms of x) and t_m is the median voter's tax share, the slope is $t_m p_g$.

The federal grants take the form of units of the pure public good or of dollars earmarked for this good. However, given the transfer, the community can vote to reduce its local taxes and increase each member's disposable income, according to the size of the tax cut and each member's local tax share. Therefore, the transfer implicitly directly affects individual budget lines, increasing the opportunities for x and g consumption, given the transfer and the reduction in local taxes. The extent of the increase in income for each person is derived below.

We first illustrate the impact of an open-ended matching grant. The federal government agrees to supplement public expenditures at a rate s and hence the slope of the budget line of the median voter becomes $(1/1 + s)t_m p_g$. Given that the median voter in effect determines the level of public services, the new equilibrium is at point b. The median voter's consumption of private goods rises by $x_b - x_a$, the amount in x units by which his local taxes fall; or $x_b - x_a = (g_a - g_c)t_m p_g$. Community consumption of public services rises by $g_b - g_a$ given a government transfer of public

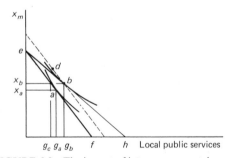

FIGURE 9.2   The impact of intergovernmental grants.

services equal to $g_b - g_c$. Since local expenditures on g have fallen, each consumer i has an increase in disposable income equal to $(g_a - g_c)t_i p_g$. (In the next section we more fully detail the effects of grants on citizens other than the median voter.) In summary, in this illustration the subsidy has the effect of lowering local public expenditures and raising consumption of both public and private goods.

How does a matching grant compare with a lump-sum grant of equal magnitude? To see this, we draw in a budget line parallel to ef passing through point b. This budget line implies a federal transfer of g equal to $g_b - g_c$. The new equilibrium is at a point such as d. Since in terms of increasing public services, there is only an income effect and not a substitution effect, the increase in private [public] good consumption is greater [less] than under a matching grant program. For the same expenditures, the median voter reaches a higher indifference curve under a lump-sum grant. This may suggest a superiority of lump-sum grants. However, if the reason for the matching grant is spillovers of public service benefits into other communities (which are not represented in the diagram), and if the rate of subsidy corresponds to the magnitude of the spillover externality, from the perspective of the federal government the matching grant program will be superior.

We can also examine the effects of closed-ended matching grants in this framework. Starting from point e on the vertical axis, the slope of the budget line would initially be $1/(1 + s)p_g t_m$, as with the open-ended grant. However, as we move down the new budget line, there will be a kink in the line when the level of potential federal government transfers, which equals the horizontal distance between the new and the pretransfer budget lines, reaches the maximum allowed. After the kink the slope of the new budget line will equal the slope of the old line. Whether the median voter will view this program as a subsidy or income-type grant depends on which segment of the budget line his highest indifference curve will be tangent to.

4.2 A General Equilibrium Approach

In contrast to the partial equilibrium approach in Figure 9.2, the general equilibrium approach assumes that all localities receive grants and that these grants are directly financed out of federal taxes. Therefore, an average increase of $1 in grants in all regions means an average increase in taxes of $1 in all regions. Grants cannot change the totality of resources available to the aggregate of local communities. However, they can redistribute money among regions, increasing the incomes of those regions where federal grants exceed taxes raised to pay for the grant program. Similarly, the grants can redistribute money locally, given that the cost of the program to an individual is proportional to his federal tax share and, as we saw earlier, the benefit of the program in terms of an effective increase in income is proportional to the individual's local tax share. Then, for example, if the federal tax system is progressive and the local tax system is regressive, a grant program will tend to favor lower-income people.

In examining the net impact of federal grants on a locality, again we initially examine the impact on the median voter. The median voter is initially at point a with budget line $x_a g_a$ in Figure 9.3. The federal taxes used to finance the program reduce his income by $t_m{}^f T$ where T are federal taxes raised from this locality and $t_m{}^f$ is the median voter's share in federal taxes raised in this region. The reduction in income is pictured by the shift in the budget line back to $x_b g_b$ and hence $t_m{}^f T = x_a - x_b = t_m P_g(g_a - g_b)$. As before, grants are analyzed as implicitly entering the pockets of local consumer-voters, given their control over local expenditure decisions. The grant effectively results in a forward shift of $t_m E$ in the post federal tax budget line, where E is the size of the grant and t_m is the median voter's local tax share. In Figure 9.3, we show a shift out to $x_c g_c$ in the budget line, or $E = p_g(g_c - g_b)$. The net effect of the grant program in this locality is to effectively increase the median voter's income. The new equilibrium is at point c. This increase

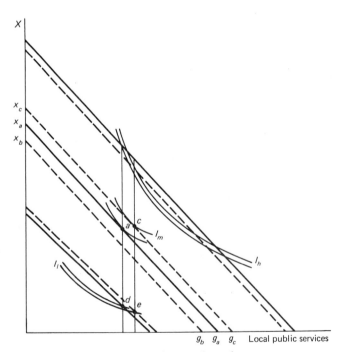

FIGURE 9.3   The net impact of transfer programs.

in income occurs if $t_m E > t_m^f T$, which requires that either $t_m > t_m^f$ or $E > T$. Therefore, the median voter can benefit if $t_m > t_m^f$ even if the region as a whole loses income under the program.

For other voters in the community, their effective income increases if $t_i E > t_i^f T$. However, an increase or decrease in effective income for people other than the median voter does not always guarantee an increase or decrease in welfare (although normally it will). The possibility of income gainers being made worse off is pictured in Figure 9.3. The higher- and lower-income people in the diagram experience, respectively, a loss and a gain in income. However, they respectively experience an increase and decrease in welfare because public services demanded by the median voter increase, where this increase is desired by higher-income people but not by lower-income people. For example, consider a lower-income person who is originally consuming at the nontangency point d. Although the net impact of the grant is to shift out his budget line, because the median voter imposes even higher elevels of public expenditure on him, at his new equilibrium position e he is worse off. A similar argument shows that higher-income people may be made better off.

Revenue Sharing

The basic impact of revenue sharing may be analyzed using the foregoing framework. Revenue sharing programs contain different rules for redistributing the federal tax dollars raised for the program. In the United States, these rules indicate that money should be redistributed on the basis of origin, of population, of per capita income, and of local tax effort. What are the impacts of these different allocation rules on regional income and on the incomes of individuals in the regions?

In terms of regional income, if federal revenue is allocated on the basis of tax origin alone, by definition the net change in total regional income is zero. If federal revenue is allocated by population or the money raised is divided exactly in proportion to regional share in national population, each region in the country effectively gets the same or average per capita grant. Then poorer regions will have an increase in total regional income because they contribute less than average taxes. Similarly, if taxes are allocated according to the inverse of per capita income, poorer regions gain. However, this information does not tell us how individuals in the regions fare.

Whether an individual gains or loses income from revenue sharing depends on whether the amount taken out of one pocket in federal taxes exceeds or falls short of the amount of money put back in the other pocket. This in turn depends both on the individual's relative local and federal tax shares and on whether the region in total gains or loses income. For example, if the amount of federal tax dollars paid by the region equals revenue sharing transfers to the region, the federal tax system is progressive, and the local tax system is regressive, high-income people should be income losers and low-income people income gainers. As earlier, except for the median voter, net increases in income do not always imply increases in welfare.

In revenue sharing programs there is also a positive relationship between federal transfers and local tax effort. This relationship provides an incentive for localities to increase their taxes so as to increase the size of their grants. To demonstrate this, Fisher (1976) develops a model with two regions competing for a fixed pot of transfers. The level of transfers is determined by relative local tax effort, where relative (to the other area) increases in local taxes lead to increased public expenditures, constrained by the fact that there is a fixed sum of federal money to be split among the regions. Under the Cournot behavioral assumption that each region takes as given the other region's tax effort, the two regions will raise their local expenditures to compete for the pot. Suppose the two regions are of identical equal size and income. *Before* federal intervention they are providing an *optimal* level of public services. After federal intervention, by competing for federally raised money in an attempt to increase their transfers, they increase public services. Since nothing else has changed in the economy—there are the same resources, after transfers there is the same total regional and national income, and the regions always achieve identical equilibria—they are made worse off because local expenditures rise above the optimal level.

Essentially, in this case revenue sharing is a mirage. The two identical regions by competing for a fixed pot cannot gain anything from the competition; yet if one region does not compete it will lose out. However, if the regions are nonidentical, one region can gain in net while the other loses.

10

Suburbanization: The Jurisdictional Fragmentation of Metropolitan Areas

In the first part of this chapter, a static model of suburbanization is presented which illustrates and analyzes the phenomenon of urban residents stratifying into suburban communities that are each homogeneous in terms of people's demand for public services. This is similar to the phenomenon originally analyzed by Tiebout (1956); our presentation of it is to some extent based on Ellickson's (1971) model and refinement of Tiebout's work. Besides illustrating stratification, we examine the exclusionary role of various types of zoning, methods of exclusion other than zoning, the role of scale effects, and reasons for imperfect stratification. In our model public services are financed by a property tax, which in general leads to distortions in the choice of housing and hence nonoptimal consumption levels of all goods. As an extension we consider the Hamilton (1975) model, where with a certain hypothetical type of zoning the provision of all goods is optimal.

In the second part of the chapter we adapt the static model to a dynamic situation in which suburbs are growing over time. In this context, we analyze conflicts among initial residents, later residents, developers, and excluded residents. We also outline a theory of the intertemporal determination of land prices in suburbs.

1. A STATIC MODEL OF JURISDICTIONAL FRAGMENTATION

In developing a model of suburbs, we make the following assumptions, some of which are relaxed later. Consumers in a metropolitan area or region are divided into discrete groupings, each containing identical-income people, starting from the lowest income level y_1 and going to the highest level y_n. These incomes are exogenous to the problem. People choose to live in suburbs for the purpose of jointly consuming public services, where the demand for public services varies with income. The number of people in each income group is potentially large enough to support a separate suburb. Housing capital is perfectly mobile and malleable and the array of suburbs may be costlessly designed and redesigned before formation takes place. Commuting cost differences among suburbs are ignored in the model. (One could conceive of suburbs forming a ring about the core city where each suburb is equidistant from the CBD.) Therefore, the net price of land in suburbs is initially assumed to be equal to the opportunity cost of land in agriculture.

Potential suburbs are designed and offered as places of residence by land developers who own the undeveloped metropolitan area land. Within a suburb, the land may be owned by one developer or by a group of developers. If by a group of developers, it is assumed that they can effectively act collectively, or as a single decision maker. Between suburbs there are sufficient developers in the metropolitan area competing for residents to join their suburbs so that the suburbanization market is competitive. Developers offer suburbs for potential residents, usually specifying possible land prices, taxes, and public service levels. Fiscal characteristics of any suburb are confirmed by a majority vote of its residents. Given the opportunity cost of land in agriculture or other uses, the size of suburbs is endogenously determined by developers, as is the total land devoted to all suburbs in a metropolitan area, given the opportunities for investing land in suburbs. As discussed later, in the model there is a tâtonnement process by which we costlessly grope for a stable equilibrium solution. In a stable solution no new suburb can be designed and sustained that offers a more attractive fiscal and housing package to any group than they currently experience (given the fiscal tools we assume are available to the developer and the community).

Before discussing stratification solutions, we develop the consumer choice mechanism and conditions defining the technology and financing of public services.

Consumer Side

Consumers in the area maximize identical utility functions defined over housing h, public services g, and all other goods x, subject to a budget constraint where income, denoted by y, equals $x + (1 + t)ph$. p is the rent on housing where housing is competitively produced with inputs of land and capital and a constant returns to scale technology. t is the effective property tax rate (the multiple of the tax and assessment rates), defined for rental as opposed to asset prices. We define the gross or total price of housing as $\overset{*}{p} = p(1 + t)$. It is $\overset{*}{p}$ that the consumer views as the opportunity cost of housing to him, as opposed to p, which is the opportunity cost of housing to society. Given that the consumer views $\overset{*}{p}$ rather than p as the price of housing, his choice of housing will be distorted and he will generally under-consume housing to avoid some of his property tax liabilities.

Maximizing the utility function with respect to market goods and rear-ranging terms we find that the usual marginal rate of substitution equals the private marginal cost condition for housing, or

$$\frac{\partial V'/\partial h}{\partial V'/\partial x} = \overset{*}{p}. \tag{10.1}$$

From the first order conditions we can also specify demand equations for market goods, which when substituted back into the direct utility function yield the indirect utility function

$$V = V(y, \overset{*}{p}, g). \tag{10.2}$$

V is increasing in income and public services and decreasing in g. Note in the derivation of equation (10.2) that it is assumed the consumer can choose any level of h at the going $\overset{*}{p}$. This implies that we are assuming there is no zoning of housing services per se (although there may be other kinds of zoning).

We want to determine which suburbs consumers will choose to live in so as to maximize utility, given the $\overset{*}{p}$ and g combinations offered. The problem is somewhat similar to allocating consumers to their optimal loca-tions in Chapter 1. We first examine how much consumers are willing to pay to live in different suburbs offering different levels of g. Inverting equa-tion (10.2) we get a bid rent function where

$$\overset{*}{p}{}^0 = p(V, y, g). \tag{10.3}$$

$\overset{*}{p}{}^0$ is the amount consumers are willing to pay for housing in a particular suburb given their income y and the level of g offered them. To find the properties of this function, we differentiate equation (10.2) holding income and utility constant. Differentiating, we get

$$\frac{d\overset{*}{p}}{dg} = -\frac{\partial V/\partial g}{\partial V/\partial \overset{*}{p}} > 0.$$

Recalling Roy's identity, where $\partial V/\partial \overset{*}{p} = -h(\partial V/\partial y)$, we can substitute in for $\partial V/\partial \overset{*}{p}$. Defining p_g to be the marginal evaluation of a unit of g or

$(\partial V/\partial g)/(\partial V/\partial y)$, we can then rewrite the expression above as

$$dp/dg = h^{-1}p_g. \tag{10.4}$$

Equation (10.4) is the slope of a bid rent function showing the trade-off between p^0 and g for utility held constant. In Figure 10.1, we present a set of indifference or bid rent curves I_1 whose positive slope at each point is given by equation (10.4). As indifference or bid rent curves shift down, utility *increases*. In Figure 10.1, we also show a convex opportunity locus S, which is derived later. Bid rent curves are assumed to be more concave than the opportunity locus to ensure a well-behaved equilibrium.

Before turning to the supply side, we need to determine the effect on these bid rent curves of income differences. Differentiating (10.4) with respect to income, we get

$$\frac{\partial(dp/dg)}{\partial y} = h^{-1}p_g y^{-1}[\eta_{p_g,y} - \eta_{h,y}] \quad 0 \tag{10.5}$$

where $\eta_{h,y} = y(\partial h/\partial y)h^{-1}$ and $\eta_{p_g,y} = (\partial p_g/\partial y)yp_g^{-1}$. If the income elasticity of the marginal evaluation of public services is positive and if it is greater than the income elasticity of demand for housing, then the slopes of the bid rent curves increase with income. (See a similar discussion in the context of leisure evaluation in Chapter 1.) To narrow our discussion, we will assume this is the case, and note that our basic results are unchanged if (10.5) is negative. Accordingly, in Figure 10.1, we show a second set of bid rent curves I_2 for a higher-income person, where these bid rent curves are steeper at the point of overlap than those for lower-income people.

Supply

In any suburb that forms, all residents consume the same quality and quantity of public services g. Throughout most of the discussion, to simplify the algebra we assume that the community can produce or purchase units

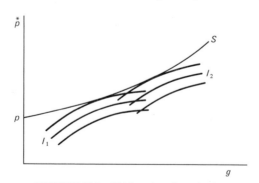

FIGURE 10.1   Bid functions for suburbs.

of g at constant unit cost. Publicness in the consumption of g arises because the cost of providing a unit of g to *all* residents is $c(N)$ where N is suburban population and $dc/dN \geq 0$. Total community cost of providing g to all residents is $g \, c(N)$. If g is a pure public good, $dc/dN = 0$. If g is a mixed or congested good, $dc/dN > 0$, with the special case $dc/dN = c/N$ when g is a pure private good. The usual presumption is that dc/dN is small for low levels of N but increases as a suburb grows, reflecting perhaps increasing administrative costs, difficulties with supplying services to a spatially diffused population, or some forms of congestion.

The total cost of services must equal tax revenue raised. Total taxes are tpH where H is the sum of the N individuals' housing consumption in the suburb. Equating costs and revenues, we have that

$$t = g \cdot c \cdot p^{-1} H^{-1}. \tag{10.6}$$

Substituting this into the expression for the gross price of housing where $\overset{*}{p} = p(1 + t)$ we then have a supply relationship between $\overset{*}{p}$ and g, or

$$\overset{*}{p} = p + H^{-1} g c(N). \tag{10.7}$$

In a stable solution in a static model, p is the same across suburbs. Otherwise suburbs will arise offering land at opportunity cost. For a given population, or a fixed $c(N)$, $\overset{*}{p}$ is an increasing function of g, or

$$d\overset{*}{p}/dg = c(N)H^{-1} > 0$$

$\partial^2 \overset{*}{p}/\partial g^2 > 0$; or as we increase g, t and hence $\overset{*}{p}$ must rise at an increasing rate because the tax base H is declining due to the normal price effect on demand as $\overset{*}{p}$ rises. For any N, given the intercept p and a slope defined in (10.8) we have a supply relationship between g and $\overset{*}{p}$. How does the relationship vary with N?

To answer this question, we must examine the question of optimal suburb size. In doing this, we assume suburbs are homogeneous, since that will generally be the case in the solutions we consider. Optimal suburb size for any g is that which minimizes gross housing costs $\overset{*}{p}$. Therefore, at an optimal N

$$\frac{\partial \overset{*}{p}}{\partial N} = g c H^{-1} N^{-1} \left[-\frac{N}{H} \frac{\partial H}{\partial N} + \frac{dc}{dN} \cdot \frac{N}{c} \right] = 0. \tag{10.9}$$

Since within each suburb residents all have the same income, average housing consumption H/N will equal consumption of a new resident, or marginal consumption $\partial H/\partial N$. Then $N/H(\partial H/\partial N) = 1$; and from (10.9) optimal suburb size occurs when $(dc/dN)N/c = 1$ or the marginal cost of providing a unit of g equals the average cost (i.e., average costs are minimized). If $(dc/dN)N/c = 1$ is uniquely satisfied, that implies all homogeneous suburbs

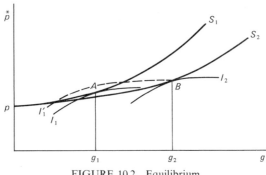

FIGURE 10.2   Equilibrium.

have the same optimal size regardless of income level and amount of g. (This only holds because unit costs are specified to be a function of N and not g. If they are a function of g, optimal suburb size is the same for each level of g but will vary with g.) For simplicity we assume $(dc/dN)N/c = 1$ (or there are constant costs in providing g to the population) over a wide population range, beyond some initial critical population level. Therefore, for homogeneous suburbs, optimal size for much of our analysis is effectively any N beyond some critical level.

In Figure 10.2 for a suburb population beyond the critical level, we show a supply relationship whose slope is given by (10.8). (Note that the slope at any point is then invariant with respect to N, since $c(N)$ and H change in the same proportion as N changes.) Everyone in this suburb has the same income level. What happens to the supply curve if community income level changes? Differentiating (10.7) with respect to y holding g constant and assuming H is a normal good, we find

$$\partial \overset{*}{p}/\partial y = -gcH^{-2}(\partial H/\partial y) < 0. \qquad (10.10)$$

Because as income rises the average tax base in the community rises, the tax rate and $\overset{*}{p}$ needed to finance any g decline. Therefore, in Figure 10.2, the supply curve is depicted as rotating down as income rises.[1]

---

[1] If we were to include spatial dimensions in the cost function, $\partial \overset{*}{p}/\partial y$ might be greater than zero. For goods such as sewers, side roads, sidewalks, and water mains, the cost of provision is a function of lot frontage, which rises with income. In determining if $\overset{*}{p}$ and t are lower as income rises we must see if the now relevant tax base, the value of housing per unit lot frontage, rises with income. This depends on whether the income elasticity of demand for lot frontage is greater than that for other housing components. (Comparing demand for land in general versus structures, Beck (1963) suggests that the income elasticity of demand for land is greater than for structures, whereas King (1974) and Muth (1971) suggest the opposite.) If it is greater, the value of property per unit lot frontage and the relevant tax base fall with income and the tax rate rises.

Community Choice of g. The level of g in any community is determined by majority vote and under a median-voter hypothesis g will equal the level demanded by the median voter. Since in a homogeneous community all voters are identical, each voter votes for and gets his most desired level of services, given prices and income.

1.1 A Stratification Solution

Given the foregoing model and assumptions, we can describe the equilibrium pattern of suburbs, housing consumption, and level of public services provided. In solving for equilibrium in terms of a tâtonnement process, one could conceive of two markets in each potential suburb, a housing market where people bid for housing and a "market" where people vote for public services. Equilibrium in the metropolitan area is achieved when suburbs are designed such that all markets in all suburbs clear simultaneously and in the resulting solutions land developers are renting land and housing to the highest bidders and consumers are living in the suburb that has the best $\mathring{p}$ and g combination for them.

In general, the tâtonnement process should lead to a solution where consumers stratify into different homogeneous suburbs, according to their income level. A solution for individuals in income groups y_1 and y_2 is illustrated in Figure 10.2 at points A and B, where consumers are at a tangency point of their indifference and supply curves. At a tangency point by equating equations (10.4) and (10.8) and rearranging terms, we see that

$$Np_g = c(N). \tag{10.11}$$

This is simply the Samuelson condition for the consumption of public services, where the sum of the marginal rates of substitution in consumption equal the marginal cost of provision. In a homogeneous suburb, this level of services will be unanimously confirmed by majority vote. In the solution, suburbs will be of optimal size, since if any suburb does not satisfy equation (10.9), a land developer will set up an optimal size suburb and attract the residents of the inefficient size suburb by offering them a higher utility level (the same comment can also apply to equation (10.11)). This also offers the land developer a potential profit equal to some portion of the monetized difference in utility levels of the two suburbs, but of course various land developers competing for the population of the inefficient size suburb will dissipate any profits through offering higher and higher utility levels.

Therefore, except for housing consumption, suburbs should have optimal characteristics. To see this we can derive the optimal characteristics of any suburb by maximizing the utility of a representitive suburb resident with respect to N, g, x, and h. Where p is the opportunity cost of housing and

$c(N)g/N$ is the per person cost of public services, maximizing

$$V'(y - ph - c(N)g/N, h, g)$$

with respect to g and N yields respectively equations (10.11) and (10.9). Note that in the process of suburb formation, consumers reveal their preferences for public services, a main point of Tiebout's (1956) article. Maximizing with respect to h yields

$$\frac{\partial V'/\partial h}{\partial V'/\partial x} = p. \tag{10.12}$$

This differs from equation (10.1) describing equilibrium housing consumption when public services are financed out of a property tax (as opposed to some optimal tax such as a head tax or fee per unit service).

So far we have presumed that suburbs will be homogeneous. This presumption is based on the following reasoning. Providing their suburb exceeds the critical size at which scale economies are exhausted, higher-income people would never want to admit lower-income people to their suburb. This occurs because of conflicts over desired levels of public services and because lower-income people would purchase a lower-valued house, hence would have a lower tax base, and for the same property tax rate would provide less tax revenue. Therefore, higher-income people would always choose or want to live in a developer's suburb that excludes lower-income people. However, because the reverse may not be true, exclusion may not be realized automatically in free-market solutions.

Lower-income people could benefit from joining a higher-income suburb. Although higher-income people consume a higher level of public services than lower-income people desire, because of the higher average tax base (value of housing) in the community, lower-income people face lower tax rates for any level of g than in a purely low-income suburb. Given the relative positioning of the I and S curves in Figure 10.2, we show that a lower-income person moving into a type 2 suburb and consuming g_2 would be worse off than at A, or on a higher indifference curve I'_1. Later (in Figure 10.3) we redraw the curves so that this is not the case.

If the relationship where both higher- and lower-income people are worse off with mixing holds for all income groups, then a tâtonnement process should yield stratification given profit maximization behavior of developers. Any mixing solution is unstable and would result in an exodus of higher- or lower-income people or both. It should also be noted that any mixing solutions are always inefficient (regardless of the shape of indifference curves), providing publicness or scale economies in the provision of g have been exhausted. Even if we forced a mixed tax base (through fiscal transfers among communities) on higher-income and lower-income people, so that all people have the same tax base, everyone would still be better off being fiscally separated. If still fiscally separated, the two groups each get to consume their desired and differing levels of public services. If forced into the same community, either some compromise level of services too high for one group and too low for the other would be provided or the politically dominant (numerically) group would force the other (through majority voting) to consume at its level.

An alternative proposition is that forcing communities to mix in order to redistribute income from high- to low-income people through the fiscal system is inefficient. It would be better to explicitly redistribute income through a direct income tax and supplement policy, and to allow consumers to stratify for the purpose of consuming public services.

1.2   The Possibility of Mixed Solutions and Methods of Exclusion

In Figure 10.3, indifference and supply curves are drawn such that if a lower-income person moved into the higher-income suburb, he would be better off, even given he consumes at g_2. Stratification can only be maintained if the higher-income suburb can exclude lower-income people. Assuming direct or discriminatory exclusionary laws are illegal, exclusion can still be effected in several ways.

Explicit or Implicit Zoning

Theoretically, the community could pass zoning laws requiring all residents to consume the level of housing demanded by higher-income people. Then lower-income people will not want to enter the suburb because, first, they are forced to consume more housing than desired, and second, their tax

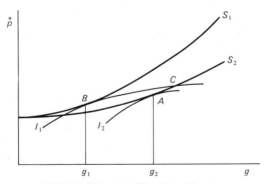

FIGURE 10.3   Stability of stratification.

base is raised such that they must pay their full share of providing g_2. This latter consideration is sufficient to exclude lower-income residents, since they only want to consume g_2 at less than cost (otherwise they want g_1). In practice one does not see this solution because it is difficult to design zoning laws that legislate a given (or minimum) level of housing services. Housing is produced with land and a vector of capital inputs identifying everything from floor space to quality and quantity of building materials to types of bathrooms and facilities. Zoning housing consumption to be a certain level would require specifying levels and qualities of each type of construction input. This not only is technically complex but obviously would also limit the diversity and types of homes higher-income people are allowed to build. Thus communities do not generally attempt to legislate zoning housing services to be at a certain level. One way to avoid these technical difficulties is to zone housing *values*; but legal constraints usually rule out this possibility. Thus, in practice, one or both of two other zoning policies result.

Developers can effect implicit zoning on the level of housing services by renting or selling houses of only a certain type in a particular suburb. In our model this would be sufficient to effect stratification. Although in practice this happens to some extent, there are certain real world problems attendant on this practice. It means the developer must build all housing in the suburb before any sales accur (so that first entrants are guaranteed later entrants will not consume lower levels of housing). This requires the developer to get involved in the home construction business rather than just selling lots and leaving construction to residents and contractors. It involves a much greater financial commitment on the part of the developer. It means the developer must know and offer the various types of homes demanded by higher-income people. Moreover, in a more complicated dynamic model where housing is not perfectly malleable and mobile, the developer must incur the risk of building homes that may never be purchased (at least at a positive profit). Finally, as we will see in Section 2, the developer may maximize profits over time by not maintaining the homogeneity of the community.

As a result of these considerations, rather than leaving stratification to the developer, the community usually makes explicit zoning ordinances. However, these ordinances deal with only one or two inputs into the production of housing, such as lot size or floor space. We consider a case where minimum lot size is zoned. We will show that although appropriate zoning should be sufficient to exclude lower-income people, it may not raise their consumption of housing services, which is the usual presumption.

In Figure 10.4, we illustrate the housing situation facing a lower-income person about to enter a higher-income suburb. With no zoning the purchase price of housing is $\mathring{p}_2$ and a lower-income person would purchase land and

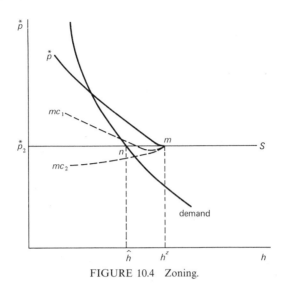

FIGURE 10.4   Zoning.

a vector of construction inputs at levels $\hat{l}$ and $\hat{K}$. Equilibrium would be at n in Figure 10.4. Suppose zoning raises minimum lot size to $l^z > \hat{l}$. Unless capital inputs and housing production rise proportionately to the increase in l for the same factor prices, the average cost of housing will rise because zoning forces inefficient factor proportions and overuse of land relative to capital. For example, in Figure 10.4 to the right of point m housing production is sufficiently high so the same factor proportions are used (and zoning is essentially ineffective). To the left of m, $\overset{*}{p}$ rises as we reduce h, as graphed by the $\overset{*}{p}$ curve. Essentially inefficiency increases as we move away from efficient factor proportions, or $\partial p / \partial h < 0$. The marginal purchase price of housing is $mc = p + h(\partial \overset{*}{p} / \partial h)$. For factor prices unchanged, $mc \lessgtr \overset{*}{p}_2$, the original price, depending on the size of $\partial \overset{*}{p}/\partial h$.[2] If the zoning restrictions introduce minor production distortions, then $\partial p/\partial h$ is small and $mc > \overset{*}{p}_2$ over some range of h, as graphed by mc_1. If production distortions are severe, as when many inputs are zoned to some minimum level, $\partial \overset{*}{p}/\partial h$ will be large and $mc < \overset{*}{p}_2$, as graphed by mc_2. For the same factor prices, if $mc > \overset{*}{p}_2$ at the point of intersection with the demand curve, then housing consumption will decline, not rise, with zoning, If $mc < \overset{*}{p}_2$, housing consumption *may* rise, although the higher average price $\overset{*}{p} > \overset{*}{p}_2$ will have a negative income effect on demand, shifting the demand curve back (not shown). Clearly, zoning may not raise the tax base of incoming residents.

---

[2] Robert Sinche pointed out to me that the mc curves must approach point m from below $\overset{*}{p}_2$, just as any mc curve must approach the average cost curve from below.

However, the zoning should be sufficient to exclude lower-income people, since the resulting inefficiencies from zoning raise the effective cost of housing, as illustrated by the $\hat{p}$ curve in Figure 10.4. In Figure 10.3, the supply relationship facing lower-income people entering the type 2 suburb then rotates up. Beyond some minimum lot size and upward rotation in the supply relationship, lower-income people will no longer want to enter the suburb. If the necessary minimum lot size for exclusion is less than or equal to that desired by higher-income people, the supply relationships facing them will be unchanged.

Other Methods of Exclusion.   Since the use of any type of zoning to exclude lower-income people has been questioned in the courts in recent years, it is useful to consider other exclusionary tactics that higher-income residents could employ. First, they could "oversupply" public services, raising the tax rate beyond what low-income people are willing to pay. Such a situation is illustrated by point C in Figure 10.3. Second they could "bribe" lower-income people not to move into the suburb by subsidizing from their own budget the provision of public services in lower-income communities. This would raise the supply curve in the higher-income community and lower it in the lower-income community, making the lower-income community a more attractive place to live and the higher-income community a less attractive place to live. At some level of subsidization a lower-income person would not want to enter. This subsidization is in effect a mixing of the tax bases of the high- and low-income communities. However, the subsidization solution maintains stratification and allows higher-income people to retain political control of their community and both groups to consume their desired level of services. Thus it can be shown to dominate a solution where low-income people enter and the higher-income suburb becomes a mixed suburb.

1.3   Extensions of the Static Model

The suburbanization model presented earlier ignores a vairety of interesting considerations. In the discussion above we divided consumers into homogeneous groups, each sufficient in size to support a suburb. Suppose instead that either consumers are not discretely grouped, so that there is a continuum of consumers ranked by income, or the size of any one group is not sufficient to support a suburb. Then suburbs will not be perfectly homogeneous. The level of public services will be determined by the median voter, who will be the only person consuming at a tangency point in Figures 10.1 to 10.3. However, we should expect suburbs to contain people of similar incomes, since they have similar tax bases and demands for public services.

This will minimize political conflicts and fiscal disparities, allowing residents to consume at "almost" a tangency point. In determining their size, suburbs will be concerned with choosing the lowest income level at which they are willing to admit people to the suburb. In deciding whether to admit the next person down the income scale, they will want to know if his tax payments (which, given his housing consumption, will be the lowest in the community) will equal the marginal cost of providing him with public services (where, for this to be possible, $dc/dN < c/N$). The community will also be concerned with his impact upon political decision making.

So far we have assumed all suburbs are entirely residential and all have equal job access. The location of industrial activities in suburbs has potential costs and benefits as analyzed by Fischel (1975). The benefits are the increase in tax base and easy work access for residents. The costs are environmental disamenities imposed by commercial activities. In suburbs deciding whether to admit industrial activities or not, there is a potential spillover problem among suburbs. If one suburb allows for industrial activity, in return for increased taxes it endures disamenities but its members also have increased work access. However, all the neighboring suburbs benefit from increased work access (presumeably without the disamenities), for which the industrializing suburb is not compensated. This raises the possibility that there will not be sufficient industrialization in suburbs, since individual suburbs are not compensated for the full benefit of suburbanization.

1.4 The Welfare Benefits of Perfect Zoning

In the presentation in Section 1.2, although suburbs are of optimal size and people consume their desired level of public services, the solution is not Pareto optimal because of the use of the property tax to finance public services. This distorts the choice of housing consumption such that equation (10.1) rather than (10.12) is satisfied. As Hamilton (1975) has demonstrated, perfect zoning of housing services can move us to a first best world.

To accomplish this, developers would offer suburbs where the *only* level of housing available is that suggested by equation (10.12), and equations (10.9) and (10.11) are satisfied. People will choose to live in this type of suburb because it offers them a higher utility level than any other solution. By offering *only* the optimal level of housing in a suburb, the developer eliminates the free rider problem of people reducing housing consumption to avoid taxes. Essentially fixing housing consumption converts the property tax to a head tax. (The zoning rule can be relaxed to state that housing should be greater than or equal to the level that satisfies equation (10.12). Residents would never choose to live in communities where their housing exceeds the minimum zoned level satisfying equation (10.12), since that would only increase their taxes as well as resulting in overconsumption of housing.)

While perfect zoning is potentially a very useful tool, we have already noted problems connected with developers trying to fix consumption of housing services throughout a suburb, as well as with suburbs zoning to accomplish the same purpose. There is an additional problem with perfect zoning which is an information problem of how developers know what level of housing satisfies equation (10.12). Unlike the housing level satisfying equation (10.1), it is not revealed in the market place through consumer choices of housing given private marginal costs. Only by developers experimenting repeatedly with various g and h combinations in potential suburbs will the optimal combination be revealed and shown *experimentally* to dominate all other combinations.

In a subsequent paper, Hamilton (1976) points out a very relevant potential role of perfect or nearly perfect zoning in metropolitan areas. Suppose preferences differ such that there are people with identical demands for public services but differing demands for housing. If these people group into the same suburb can this be a stable solution and will such a solution be efficient? That is, is it necessary for people to stratify on the basis of both housing and public service demands or only public service demand, to achieve an efficient or nearly efficient provision of local public services in metropolitan areas? This is a most relevant question since it is unlikely that in many metropolitan areas groups of people with similar demands for both housing and public services are sufficiently large to adequately exploit economies of scale or Samuelson publicness in the provision of public services within a suburb. However suburbs composed of people with similar demands for public services but varying demands for housing increase the possibility that scale economies will be adequately exploited, and thus our stratification solutions presented above would be likely to be realized in more metropolitan areas.

We have already presented the basis of the Hamilton model in the discussion of capitalization in Section 1.3 of Chapter 9. There we considered a situation with two types of consumers, high housing demand and low housing demand consumers (h and l people), who had the same demands for public services. We assumed the existence of three types of communities of suburbs, homogeneous high housing, homogeneous low housing, and mixed housing (h, l, and m suburbs). We showed that if we zoned housing consumption of h and l people in the m suburb to be that level demanded by h and l people in the h and l suburbs, the solution with a mixed suburb could be stable with respect to both the actions of developers and residents, with housing prices adjusting to reflect capitalization of the fiscal benefits and disadvantages for respectively l and h people of living in the m suburb. The mixed suburb solution can be stable, without the actual existence of the homogeneous suburbs, as long as such suburbs could potentially arise, so that prices in the

m suburb reflected capitalization relative to potential competitive suburbs.[3]

If housing in the h and l suburbs is zoned to satisfy equation (10.12) and similarly for the two types of people in the mixed suburb, then providing equations (10.9) and (10.11) are satisfied, the solution in Chapter 9 will be Pareto optimal. Even without perfect zoning, if housing can be provided by developers so that generally equation (10.1) is satisfied, mixed housing suburbs could be stable, dominating all other realizable solutions.

2. EXTENSION INTO A DYNAMIC WORLD

So far the suburbanization phenomenon has been analyzed in a static model. Our understanding of the phenomenon can be greatly enhanced by extending the analysis to a dynamic situation. Initially in extending the model we simply add a second period to our first period. For expositional simplicity, particularly in the use of diagrams, we redefine the nature of the housing good so that housing services are produced only with land. Moreover, we assume lot sizes purchased in the first period are fixed and cannot be adjusted in the second period. This assumption implies that suburbs cannot readily be redesigned and restructured once they have formed. Also, the consumer is locked in and cannot adjust his land consumption without selling his current lot, moving, and purchasing a different size lot.

Homogeneous suburbs form in the first period by the process described in Section 1.[4] In the second period the suburbs grow internally in population, as new people of similar incomes arrive in the metropolitan area or leave the core city to live in a suburb. In the interests of maximizing profits from the sale of vacant land and to allow for greater exploitation of scale efficiencies in providing public services, developers set aside vacant land in the

---

[3] Of course if the m suburb forms because of inadequate scale economies in potential homogeneous h and l suburbs, such competition will only result in partial capitalization. The positive and negative premiums paid by l and h people respectively would be relative to the actual potential situation in possible homogeneous suburbs.

[4] Technically, the consumer maximization problem in the first period must be restated. Consumers entering the suburb in period 1 maximize $V = V'(x(1), x(2), l(1), g(1), g(2))$ subject to $y(1) + y(2)(1 + r)^{-1} = x(1) + x(2)(1 + r)^{-1} + \overline{l(1)}(p_l(1)(1 + (1 + r)^{-1}) + a(1)t(1) + a(2)t(2)(1 + r)^{-1}$. $x(i)$ and $g(i)$ are consumption levels of x in period i, r is the discount rate, $y(1)$ and $y(2)$ are incomes in period 1 and 2, $l(1)$ and $p_l(1)$ are fixed lot size and fixed unit land rent for the two periods and $a(i)$ and $t(i)$ are, respectively, assessment prices and tax rates in period i. The indirect utility function becomes $V = V(y(1) + y(2)(1 + r)^{-1}, g(1), g(2), p_l(1)(1 + r)^{-1}) + a(1)t(1) + a(2)t(2)(1 + r)^{-1})$. If the consumer expects $a(1) = a(2)$, $g(1) = g(2)$, $t(1) = t(2)$, then in Figure 10.2 we get the same type of trade-off between $g(1)$ and $t(1)$ as before. Note that this specification assumes the world evaporates at the end of period 2. Then for consumers entering the analysis in period 2 there is no need to distinguish between income and wealth nor between rental and purchase prices.

first period to allow for this internal growth. It is assumed that the developers own all the vacant land and hold it costlessly during the first period—they pay no taxes on it and continue to rent it to farmers.

In acting to maximize profits in the second period, a developer may be able to control the unit price of land and plot sizes. In selling land to new residents the developer will basically want to implement policies that will ensure the price received per unit of vacant land and hence total revenue are maximized. This may involve a policy of selling a little land to a lot of people at a very high price.

The developer's policies will conflict with what is best for initial residents of the community, who are best off maximizing the fiscal surplus to be attained from selling to new residents. In general, maximizing fiscal surplus will involve a strategy of selling a lot of land to a few people, thus benefiting from high per person taxes at the expense of a small increase in total public services provided. In setting any policies, the community is restricted by several laws. The community must set a uniform tax rate on all residents new and old. The assessed price per unit of housing services may also have to be uniform, although we will consider situations where housing is assessed according to market price paid, which will differ between new and old residents. The community can zone lot sizes subject to various restrictions considered in the following analysis and it may be able to impose a lump-sum entry fee on new residents.

Potential residents wanting to live in a suburb in the second period will live in the suburb that offers them the best fiscal package. For several reasons, this should turn out to be a suburb with similar-income people. The resident is likely to find his best public service–tax package there. He is unlikely to want to enter a lower-income suburb, where his tax base is greater than average and public services are less than he wants. Moreover, he will probably be excluded from higher-income suburbs by both the initial residents there, who would find him a fiscal burden, and the developers, who may make more profits by selling to only higher-income people.

A basic presumption of the following analysis is that after a suburb forms in the first period it holds a monopolistic position in the second period in that for potential similar-income residents this suburb dominates all other existing or potential suburbs. Incoming people are willing to pay a premium to live in this suburb where this premium reflects capitalization of excess fiscal benefits for these residents of living in this suburb as opposed to other suburbs. Incoming people also probably pay a rental premium relative to initial residents. In period 1 when suburbs form the situation is competitive, with developers competing for potential residents to form suburbs. Hence initial residents should pay relatively low land prices. In period 2, the spectrum of suburbs is given and each suburb has a monopolistic position in that no other suburb offers the same set of services. Later residents should pay relatively high monopolistic prices. Underlying these statements is the idea that the scale economies and publicness in the provision of public services require a fairly large critical population to be exhausted. The local metropolitan area may not be able to support more than one suburb for people in a particular income bracket. Even if it can support two suburbs, we assume it is difficult for the second suburb to find a sufficiently large startup population to exploit scale economies and compete with the first suburb. After the first suburb forms, the influx of potential residents in the second period is not large enough to support a suburb (and people already residing in the first suburb will not move because they are locked in by their fixed-size lot, which they could only sell at a loss to lower-income people). A second similar-income suburb would only be likely to form if the initial suburb has exhausted its vacant land or does not want new similar-income residents.

A new resident about to enter a suburb is willing to pay a price for land based on the level of g in the suburb and on his opportunities in other (lower-income) suburbs. In this suburb his utility is determined from the optimization problem of maximizing $V = V(x, \bar{g}, l)$ subject to $y - T = (p_l + at)l + x$, where T is any community lump-sum charges, $\bar{g}$ the fixed level of public services, p_l the unit land price received by developers, a the assessed price of land, t the tax rate, and l lot size. He can obtain utility level $\bar{V}$ in his best alternative suburb and hence we may expect the developer and/or community to pursue policies in terms of raising p_l, a, T, or t to reduce his utility level to near $\bar{V}$. Utilizing the indirect utility function we may state $\bar{V} = \bar{V}(\bar{g}, y - T, p_l + at)$ and, inverting, we can define the maximum unit land price that developers can charge where $p_l = p(\bar{g}, y - T, \bar{V}) - at$. This specification assumes the resident can buy as little or as much land as he wants at the offered price, whereas we also wish to consider situations where the resident is not offered free choice in land consumption but is offered a preset lot size. Moreover, for diagrammatic purposes in this section, it is useful to utilize a different diagram than before. Accordingly, we simply use the direct form of the utility function where

$$V = V(x, \bar{g}, l) = V(y - T - l(p_l + at), \bar{g}, l). \quad (10.13)$$

In Figure 10.5 we show the trade-off between x and l for a resident, *given* the level of g in the suburb he is about to enter. Indifference curve I defines the trade-off between x and l for a given g that yields the person utility level $\bar{V}$, his highest utility level in his best alternative suburb. ox on the axis representing all other goods defines his money income before taxes and expenditures on l. Given this situation, there are two sets of questions.

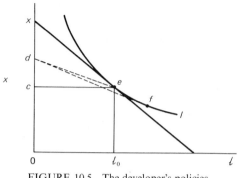

FIGURE 10.5   The developer's policies.

What policies in terms of setting p_l or l will maximize the developer's profits, and what policies in terms of influencing l will maximize the fiscal surplus of the community from new residents? The discussion of the developer's and community's strategies is partially based on Edelson (1975) and White (1975).

The Developer's Policies

In deriving the developer's optimal policies where he is not constrained by community restrictions on his actions, we consider two situations. In the first situation the developer has more equal-income customers than he would be able to sell land to, given the amount of land he has. In the second he has a limited number of customers. We assume in general that $T = 0$, although we will consider the effect on a developer's profits of the community raising T and lowering t for a given level of tax collections.

If the developer has effectively "unlimited" customers, his best policy is simply to set the highest possible gross price per unit of land that leaves each customer on indifference curve I in Figure 10.5. He need not set lot size, since he is getting the highest price possible when allowing residents to choose their own lot size. The maximum gross price consumers will pay is given by the slope of the budget line xb in Figure 10.5, where the gross price $\overset{*}{p}_l = p_l + at$. For a given $\overset{*}{p}_l$, if the community raises t, the developer must lower p_l to maintain the same $\overset{*}{p}_l$, with lot size chosen by residents unchanged. Given expenditures on all other goods, the resident spends xc on land in Figure 10.5. Suppose the tax and assessment rates are such that the developer nets dc of this expenditure. Therefore, the average net price per unit of land is given by the slope of the line ed.

For tax collection xd, the developer would be better off if this money were raised through a lump-sum tax rather than a unit tax. A lump sum tax

xd in Figure 10.5 would reduce disposable income to od. From od the consumer would be willing to pay a gross land price (equals net price for $t = 0$) equal to the slope of the line df. df is steeper than de, representing a higher average unit price received by the developer. This suggests that the developer would, for example, prefer community expenditures on capital facilities per lot to be raised through an initial lump-sum tax, as opposed to being financed by regular property taxes.

If the developer has a limited number of customers of similar incomes, and due to community zoning ordinances or other restrictions he cannot rent to lower-income residents, his best policy is to increase lot size beyond l_0 as long as his profits rise. Define $R(\bar{V}, l)$ as the total revenue received by the developer for a lot of size l. For a limited number of entrants the developer seeks to maximize per entrant profits. These are $R(\bar{V}, l)$ minus atl going to the community minus $\bar{p}_l l$. $\bar{p}_l$ is the opportunity rent of the developer's land in agriculture; and by renting to an entrant he foregoes $\bar{p}_l l$. Per entrant profits are maximized when $\partial R/\partial l - at - p_l = 0$. However from equation (10.13), given the fixed $\bar{V}$, $\partial R/\partial l = (\partial V/\partial l)/(\partial V/\partial x)$. Therefore profits are maximized when $(\partial V/\partial l)/(\partial V/\partial x) = \bar{p}_l + at$. In Figure 10.6 this occurs at l_1 where the slope of the line tangent to I at l_1 equals $\bar{p}_l + at$. If he can, the developer in this situation will try to sell land to lower-income residents. Although they will not be willing to pay as high a maximum price for land, they may be willing to pay a price equal to or exceeding that at l_1 in Figure 10.6.

If the community does not intervene in the process and allows the developer to freely pursue profit-maximizing policies, a relevant question is whether the community gains or loses from the addition of new residents. If scale economies are exhausted, for the same t facing all residents, the only way in which the community can benefit is if new residents have a higher

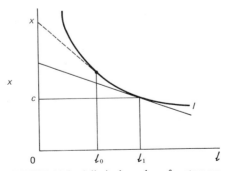

FIGURE 10.6 A limited number of customers.

tax base than old residents. We argued earlier and will demonstrate later that new residents pay higher gross per period rental prices and have lower second period utility levels than initial residents. Therefore it seems likely that new residents have a lower tax base. To see this we examine the case where there are unlimited customers.

If new and old residents are assessed equally in terms of unit prices (not quantity), then entering residents will definitely have a lower tax base. Since new residents pay a higher price, they buy less housing and hence have a lower assessed value. (Note that it does not matter whether assessed prices are new or old market prices, since for the same g the tax rate will vary inversely with the level of assessed price.) However, residents are often assessed de facto differentially, which is usually to the advantage of initial residents.

For example, all residents may be assessed at their initial per period rental price, so that initial residents are assessed at period 1 rents and later residents at period 2 rents. Then the question is whether later residents have a higher per period rental value of housing with their higher price than initial residents. For similar-income people, if the (money income held constant) price elasticity of demand η^D is less than 1, then later residents have a higher value. However, if $\eta^D > 1$, they have a lower assessed value.

If the developer has only a limited number of customers, the chances that new residents will have a higher tax base than initial residents are greater. Under equal assessment, because the developer increases lot sizes, the tax bases of new residents will rise relative to a situation with unlimited customers. Similarly, under purchase price assessment practices, as the developer increases lot sizes, people's expenditures on land increase and hence so do their tax bases.

Community Policies

If the community is not well organized and is unable to act offensively to maximize the fiscal surplus arising from the entry of new residents, it may still act defensively to ensure that it is not made worse off by the entry of new residents. The simplest policy is to zone minimum lot sizes to raise the tax base of incoming residents. This should also have the effect of excluding lower-income people, if the developer should want to sell to them. Another policy is to zone such that the developer is forced to supply certain public services. For example, a policy that forces the developer to provide public services such as parks or shopping centers in return for the (unhindered) right to develop a certain part of the suburb would act as a lump-sum tax. These policies would expropriate some of the developer's profits and improve the fiscal situation in the community.

If the community acts aggressively to maximize the fiscal surplus from the entry of new residents, its optimal policies depend on its assessment restrictions. Suppose tax and assessment rates are fixed. Then the same amount of revenue per unit of land is raised, no matter how the land is divided up. To maximize its fiscal surplus, the community should minimize the number of entrants, and hence the increase in public service expenditures, subject to the fact that $ta + \bar{p}_l$ cannot exceed the gross price of land (given $\bar{V}$, if $ta + \bar{p}_l$ exceeds this price, that implies the net price received by the developer is less than $\bar{p}_l$, in which case the developer would not sell any land.) In Figure 10.7, the community sets lot size l_1 where the slope of xb approaches $ta + \bar{p}_l$ and the developer's net revenue on land sales approaches zero. l_1 is the maximum lot size the community can set given the fixed tax and assessment rates, indifference curve I, and nonnegative profits to the developer. If assessment is not fixed and is according to purchase price, then there is a cost to increasing lot sizes which the community must account for in its calculus. The cost is the loss in taxes is caused by the reduction in *average* unit purchase prices and hence average assessment prices that entering residents will pay as lot size is increased. In this situation it can be shown that optimal lot size will be less than l_1.

In the discussion of both the developer's and the community's strategies, we did not explicitly discuss the community's determination of g and t. If initial residents benefit from the entrance of new residents, they are likely to both increase g and reduce t. Our analysis implicitly assumes that the g and t specified are the new equilibrium ones given the prices paid by new residents and a balanced fiscal budget of the community. The equilibrium level of g is chosen by initial residents, assuming they remain a majority. This level will differ somewhat from the level demanded by new entrants.

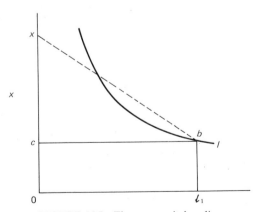

FIGURE 10.7   The community's policy.

Equilibrium Policies

So far we have developed the policies that will make first developers and then residents best off under a variety of different circumstances. Which policies will prevail in an equilibrium solution? The answer to that question depends on the legal and political situation in the community, as well as on the expectations of developers and residents and the information available to them. There are many possible outcomes and we only examine the outcomes that might occur under one set of institutional factors. This will serve to illustrate the problem and the types of solutions that can occur.

We assume the community is organized politically such that it is able to pursue policies designed to maximize the fiscal surplus of incoming residents. The community can zone lot size without restrictions on the size chosen. By law, however, it must choose that size at the beginning of period 1 and the regulations cannot discriminate between initial and later residents. That is, any minimum lot size zoned applies to all residents. Otherwise the community would always choose to set lot size at l_1 in Figure 10.7 in period 2. We assume the community must apply the same tax and assessment rates to all residents, and it cannot lump-sum tax. The developer is not restricted in its design of plot sizes, except through zoning regulations set at the beginning of period 1.

Suppose both the developer and the community are naïve and do not perceive the monopolistic situation that will arise in the second period and assume prices on land will remain time invariant. Then the community may perceive no reason to impose any zoning regulations, which would leave the developer completely free to pursue his revenue-maximizing policies in the second period. However, the community may impose a minimum lot size equal to first period lot sizes as a type of insurance policy against the average tax base being reduced for unforeseen reasons.

If the developers but not the residents foresee the second-period situation, they will try to set up suburbs without zoning regulations, so as to have later freedom of action. However, as we will see in the next section, they may compete away future development profits.

If both developers and initial residents perceive the second-period situation, there are two possible outcomes. First, residents may zone all lots to be the same size and equal to their desired first-period size. Since assessment and tax rates are equal, residents will not zone any other size, since by doing so they would penalize themselves as much as future residents. However, a better solution for the community would be for developers to compete for initial residents by subdividing the community with one lot size for initial residents and larger lot sizes for later residents. This is legal under our assumptions, since it does not involve community action by zoning. The only question is whether at the beginning of the second period, the developer can reduce his originally designed second-period lot sizes to a revenue-maximizing level. If the community perceives that the developer can renege on his agreement, it will probably choose the first solution.

In the previous sections we examined how prices are determined within one suburb in the second period. We have yet to examine price differences among suburbs and between new and old residents of a suburb. We illustrate possible differences by examining particular situations.

Prices among Suburbs and across Time

A Naïve Model. Suppose the profits developers make in the second period are totally unexpected, and that developers are unconstrained by community zoning regulations and have unlimited customers in the second period. In the first period, prices are equalized to the opportunity cost of land across all suburbs. In the second period, given the monopolistic situation that develops, prices should not be equalized. The lowest-income, or y_1, suburb has the base price of land, which equals the price new y_1 suburbanites are willing to pay to live in that suburb as opposed to their best alternative, which may be the core city. In the next-income suburb y_2, the price of land equals the price y_2 people are willing to pay to live in the preferred y_2 suburb as opposed to the y_1 suburb. Hence $p_l^{y_2} > p_l^{y_1}$. Similarly, in the y_3 suburb, the price is what y_3 people are willing to pay to live in the preferred y_3 suburb as opposed to their best alternative, the y_2 suburb. Hence, $p_l^{y_3} > p_l^{y_2} > p_l^{y_1}$. This argument implies a scaffolding effect where prices rise continuously as we move up the income scale in suburbs.

A Slightly Less Naïve Model. Suppose that developers are still unconstrained by community zoning regulations and have unlimited customers but that profits from the sale of vacant land are anticipated by developers. This anticipation of profits will affect the prices developers are willing to sell at in the first period. In deciding at what price to sell to initial residents, developers have the choice of selling to suburbanites now and forming a suburb or renting to farmers at opportunity cost for both periods. The opportunity to form a suburb means that a developer can sell his vacant land at a higher than agricultural price in the second period. Accordingly, developers will compete for initial residents, so as to be able to form a suburb and get these higher second-period prices. To compete for initial residents, potential developers lower the price offered to initial residents below the agricultural price. In that case initial residents will capture some or all of the developer's future profits from the sale of vacant land. If profits are higher in higher-income suburbs due to the scaffolding effect, and suburbs are about the same size, then first-period prices will be lower in higher-income suburbs. One can take these arguments further in a general context and argue that farmers who sell the land originally to developers will get the profits. Developers will compete with each other for choice agricultural land and in doing so will drive up the prices offered to farmers.

The Model Extended to Many Periods.   There are two basic revisions that we should consider when extending the model to many periods. First, we may want to hypothesize that suburbs form sequentially as a metropolitan area grows, starting with the highest-income groups who have the greatest fiscal incentive to suburbanize. Second, the developer's problem of regulating the sale of vacant land must be extended to many periods, where the developer can spread out his land sales over a long time. Suppose in any one period he expects a limited number of potential similar-income entrants, he expects to be unrestricted by zoning regulations, and he expects the maximum price incoming residents are willing to pay to be the same in each period. If the discount rate is zero, in maximizing the present value of profits, the developer will plan to charge the maximum price possible to incoming residents in each period. However, if the discount rate is positive, the developer may maximize the present value of profits by lowering his current price below the maximum, so as to sell more land now rather than waiting to sell this land at a higher expected spot but lower discounted price later. (This is true as long as the price elasticity of demand for land is greater than 1; if it is less than 1, then of course lowering price will not increase total revenues.) Given these assumptions, he will plan for spot prices to rise strictly monotonically to that maximum price, which will be charged the period that the supply of vacant land is exhausted.[5]

---

[5] We can see this by solving the maximization problem

$$\max_{\text{w.r.t. } l(i),\, m} \int_1^m (p_l(i) - \bar{p})l(i)e^{-r(i-1)}\, di + \lambda\left(\bar{L} - \int_1^m l(i)\, d_i\right)$$

where $\bar{p}$ is the rent in agriculture and $l(i)$ is the quantity of land demanded in each period by all incoming residents. Only if the price elasticity of demand for land $\varepsilon < 1$, will prices always be set at their maximum level. If $\varepsilon \leq 1$, revenue will decline if price is lowered below the maximum.

References

Aaron, H. J. (1975), *Who Pays the Property Tax?* Washington: Brookings Institute.

Agnew, C. E. (1973), "The Dynamic Control of Congested Systems Through Pricing," Rep. No. 6, Stanford Univ. Center for Interdisciplinary Research.

Alonso, W. (1964), *Location and Land Use*. Cambridge: Harvard Univ. Press.

Arrow, K. J. (1968), "Optimal Capital Policy with Irreversible Investment," in *Value Capital and Growth, Papers in Honor of Sir John Hicks* (J. N. Wolfe, ed.). Edinburgh: Edinburgh Univ. Press.

Ayres, R., and A. V. Kneese (1969), "Production, Consumption, and Externalities," *American Economic Review* **59**, 282–297.

Bailey, M. J. (1957), "Note on the Economics of Residential Zoning and Urban Renewal," *Land Economics* **35**, 288–292.

Barr, J., and O. Davis (1966), "An Elementary Political and Economic Theory of the Expenditures of Local Governments," *Southern Economic Journal*, **33**, 149–165.

Baumol, W. J., and D. F. Bradford (1970), "Optimal Departures from Marginal Cost Pricing," *American Economic Review* **60**, 265–283.

Baumol, W. J., and W. E. Oates (1975), *The Theory of Environmental Policy*. Englewood Cliffs: Prentice-Hall.

Beck, M. (1963), "Property Taxation and Land Use," *Research Monograph 7*. Washington: Urban Land Institute.

Beckmann, M. J. (1968), *Location Theory*. New York: Random House.

Beckmann, M. J. (1974), "Spatial Equilibrium in the Housing Market," *Journal of Urban Economics* **1**, 99–107.

Bradford, D. F., and H. H. Kelejian (1973), "An Econometric Model of the Flight to the Suburbs," *Journal of Political Economy* **81**, 566–589.

Bradford, D. F., and W. E. Oates (1971), "Towards a Predictive Theory of Intergovernmental Grants," *American Economic Review* **61**, 440–448.

Bradford, D. F., and W. E. Oates (1974), "Suburban Exploitation of Control Cities," in *Redistribution Through Public Choice* (H. M. Hochman and G. Peterson, eds.), pp. 43–94. New York: Columbia Univ. Press.

Chipman, J. S. (1970), "External Economies of Scale and Competitive Equilibrium," *Quarterly Journal of Economics* **84**, 347–385.

Coase, R. H. (1960), "The Problem of Social Cost," *Journal of Law and Economics* **3**, 1–44.

Connally, M. (1970), "Public Goods, Externalities, and International Relations," *Journal of Political Economy* **78**, 279–290.

Davis, O. A., and A. B. Winston (1964), "The Economics of Complex Systems: The Case of Municipal Zoning," *Kyklos* **17**, 419–445.

Diamond, D. (1976), "Income and Residential Choice," Ph.D. thesis in progress, Univ. of Chicago.

Diewert, M. E. (1974), "Applications in Duality Theory," in *Frontiers of Quantitative Economics* (D. A. Kendrick and M. D. Intriligator, eds.), Vol. II, pp. 106–171, Amsterdam: North-Holland.

Dixit, A. (1973), "The Optimum Factory Town," *Bell Journal of Economics and Management Science* **4**, 637–654.

Edelson, N. M. (1975), "The Developer's Problem, or How to Divide a Piece of Land Most Profitably," *Journal of Urban Economics* **2**, 349–365.

Ellickson, B. (1971), "Jurisdictional Fragmentation and Residential Choice," *American Economic Review* **61**, 334–339.

Fischel, W. A. (1975), "Fiscal and Environmental Considerations in the Location of Firms in Suburban Communities" in *Fiscal Zoning and Land Use* (E. S. Mills and W. E. Oates, eds.), pp. 119–174. Lexington: D. C. Heath and Company.

Fisher, R. (1976), *The Theoretical Analysis of General Revenue Sharing Effects of Subordinate Government Public Expenditures*, unpublished Ph.D. dissertation, Brown Univ.

Fitch, L. C., *et al.* (1964), *Urban Transportation and Public Policy*. San Francisco: Chandler.

Flatters, F., J. V. Henderson, and P. M. Mieszkowski (1974), "Public Goods, Efficiency, and Regional Fiscal Equalization," *Journal of Public Economics* **3**, 99–112.

George, H. (1938), *Progress and Poverty*. New York: Modern Library.

Gould, J. P. (1968), "Adjustment Costs in the Theory of Investment of the Firm," *Review of Economic Studies* **35**, 47–55.

Hamilton, B. W. (1975), "Zoning and Property Taxation in a System of Local Governments," *Urban Studies* **12**, 205–211.

Hamilton, B. W. (1976), "Capitalization of Intrajurisdictional Differences in Local Tax Prices," *American Economic Review* **66**, 743–753.

Harberger, A. C. (1971), "Three Basic Postulates for Applied Welfare Economics," *Journal of Economic Literature* **9**, 785–797.

Hartwick, J. M. (1971), "Consumer Choice When the Environment is a Variable: The Case of Residential Site Selection," Discussion Paper No. 50, Queen's Univ., Canada.

Heins, A. J. (1971), "State and Local Response to Fiscal Decentralization," *American Economic Review* **61**, 449–456.

Henderson, J. V. (1972), "Increasing Returns to Scale, Free Trade, and Factor Mobility," *Canadian Journal of Economics* **5**, 293–298.

Henderson, J. V. (1974a), "The Sizes and Types of Cities," *American Economic Review* **64**, 640–656.

Henderson, J. V. (1974b), "Road Congestion: A Reconsideration of Pricing Theory," *Journal of Urban Economics* **1**, 346–365.

Henderson, J. V. (1977), "Externalities in a Spatial Context: The Case of Air Pollution," *Journal of Public Economics* **7**, 89–110.

Herbert, J., and B. Stevens (1960), "A Model for the Retail Distribution of Residential Activities in Urban Areas," *Journal of Regional Science* **2**. 21–35.

Johnson, M. B. (1964), "On the Economics of Road Congestion," *Econometrica* **32**, 137–150.

King, A. T., and P. M. Mieszkowski (1973), "Racial Discrimination, Segregation, and the Price of Housing," *Journal of Political Economy* **81**, 590–606.

King, A. T. (1974), *Property Taxes, Amenities, and Residential Land Values*. Boston: Balinger Press.

Kneese, A. V. (1971), "Background for the Economic Analysis of Environmental Pollution," *Swedish Journal of Economics* **1**, 1–24.

Kraus, M., and H. Mohring (1975), "The Role of Polluter Taxes in Externality Problems," *Economica* **42**, 171–176.

Kristoff, F. S. (1968), "Housing: Economic Facets of New York City's Housing," in *Agenda for a City: Issues Confronting New York* (L. Fitch and A. M. Walsh, eds.), pp. 297–348. Beverly Hills: Sage Publications.

Laurenti, L. M. (1960), *Property Values and Race*. Berkeley: Univ. of California Press.

Meade, J. E. (1952), "External Economies and Diseconomies in a Competitive Situation," *Economic Journal* **62**, 54–67.

Meyer, J. R., J. F. Kain, and M. Wohl (1965), *The Urban Transportation Problem*. Cambridge: Harvard Univ. Press.

Mieszkowski, P. M. (1972), "The Property Tax: An Excise or a Profits Tax," *Journal of Public Economics* **1**, 73–96.

Mieszkowski, P. (1974), "On Three Aspects of Urban Land-Use Regulation," mimeo, University of Houston.

Mieszkowski, P. M. (1975), "The Distributive Effects of Local Taxes: Some Extensions," mimeo, University of Houston.

Mills, E. S. (1967), "An Aggregative Model of Resource Allocation in a Metropolitan Area," *American Economic Review* **57**, 197–210.

Mills, E. S., and D. M. de Ferranti (1971), "Market Choices and Optimum City Size," *American Economic Review* **61**, 340–345.

Mirrlees, J. A. (1972), "The Optimum Town," *Swedish Journal of Economics* **74**, 114–135.

Mishan, E. J. (1971), "The Postwar Literature on Externalities, An Interpretive Essay," *Journal of Economic Literature* **9**, 1–28.

Mohring, H. (1970), "The Peak Load Problem," *American Economic Review* **60**, 693–705.

Mohring, H., and J. G. Boyd (1971), "Analyzing Externalities: 'Direct Interaction' vs. 'Asset Utilization' Approaches," *Economica* **38**, 347–61.

Montesano, A. (1972), "A Statement of Beckmann's Model on the Distribution of Urban Rent and Density," *Journal of Economic Theory* **4**, 329–354.

Muth, R. (1969), *Cities and Housing*. Chicago: Univ. of Chicago Press.

Muth, R. (1971), "The Derived Demand for Urban Land," *Urban Studies* **8**, 243–254.

Oates, W. E. (1972), *Fiscal Federalism*. New York: Harcourt.

Oron, Y., D. Pines, and E. Sheshinski (1973), "Optimum vs. Equilibrium Land Use Patterns and Congestion Tolls," *Bell Journal of Economics and Management* **4**, 619–636.

Pauly, M. V. (1970), "Optimality, Public Goods and Local Governments: A General Theoretical Analysis," *Journal of Political Economy* **78**, 572–585.

Rothenberg, J. (1967), *Economic Evaluation of Urban Renewal*. Washington, D.C.: Brookings Institute.

Schall, L. D. (1971), "Technological Externalities and Resource Allocation," *Journal of Political Economy* **79**, 983–1001.

Siegan, B. (1970), "Non-Zoning in Houston," *Journal of Law and Economics*.

Solow, R. M., and W. S. Vickrey (1971), "Land Use in a Long Narrow City," *Journal of Economic Theory* **3**, 430–477.

Stull, W. J. (1974), "Land Use and Zoning in an Urban Economy," *American Economic Review* **64**, 337–347.

Sweeney, J. (1974a), "Housing Unit Maintenance and the Mode of Tenure," *Journal of Economic Theory* **8**, 111–138.

Sweeney, J. (1974b), "A Commodity Hierarchy Model of the Rental Housing Market," *Journal of Urban Economics* **1**, 288–323.

Tiebout, C. (1956), "A Pure Theory of Local Public Expenditure," *Journal of Political Economy* **64**, 416–424.

Tietenberg, J. H. (1974), "Comment," *American Economic Review* **64**, 462–466.

Tolley, G. S. (1974), "The Welfare Economics of City Bigness," *Journal of Urban Economics* **1**, 324–345.

Vickrey, W. S. (1963), "Pricing in Urban and Suburban Transportation," *American Economic Review* **53**, 452–465.

Vickrey, W. S. (1965), "Pricing as a Tool in Coordination of Local Transportation," *Transportation Economics*, Washington, D.C.: Natl. Bureau of Economic Research.

Vickrey, W. S. (1969), "Congestion Theory and Transport Investment," *American Economic Review* **59**, 251–260.

Wheaton, W. (1974), "Linear Programming and Locational Equilibrium," *Journal of Urban Economics* **1**, 278–287.

White, M. J. (1975), "Fiscal Zoning in Fragmented Metropolitan Areas," in *Fiscal Zoning and Land Use* (E. S. Mills and W. E. Oates, eds.), pp. 175–202. Lexington: D. C. Heath and Company.

Wilde, James A. (1968), "The Expenditure Effects of Grant-in-Aid Programs," *National Tax Journal* **21**, 340–348.

Wilson, J. Q. (1966), *Urban Renewal*. Cambridge: MIT Press.

Wingo, L. (1961), *Transportation and Urban Land*. Washington, D.C.: Resources for the Future.

Worcester, D. A. (1969), "Pecuniary and Technological Externality," *American Economic Review* **59**, 873–885.

Yellin, J. (1974), "Urban Population Distribution, Family Income, and Social Prejudice," *Journal of Urban Economics* **1**, 21–47.

Index

A

B

C

236

236   INDEX

Neighborhood externalities
  housing upkeep, 136–138
  land assemblage, *see* Urban renewal
  land usage, 135, 136
  social externalities, 132–136
    inefficiency of market solutions,
      133–135

O

Oates, W. E., 100, 108, 113, 191, 197, 198,
  229, 230, 231
Oron, Y. D., 160, 231

P

Pareto-efficient city size
  comparison with market solutions, 90, 91
  failure of market solution, 94–96
  inappropriateness of partial equilibrium
    model, 96
  interpretation, 88–90
  public goods, 91–93
  in a system of cities, 72
Pareto-efficient resource allocation
  within a city, *see* Industrial air pollution,
    Water pollution
  neighborhood externalities, 132–138
  peak-load pricing, 171–173
  planning problem, 84–87, 93, 94
  road travel, 149–152
  in a system of cities, 83–98
    effect of public goods, 83, 84, 92, 93, 97,
      98
    effect of scale economies, 83, 91, 95
    government intervention, 95, 96, 97, 98
    industrial air pollution, 112–115
Pauly, M. V., 197, 231
Peak-load pricing
  effect on rush hour traffic patterns,
    175–178
  example of, 173–179
  optimal capacity, 172
  optimal set of prices, 172
  peak-load situation, 163, 164
  properties of equilibrium traffic patterns,
    167, 168
  resource savings, 178, 179
  stability of solutions, 168, 169
Pines, D., 160, 231

Pollution, *see* Industrial air pollution
Planning
  within a city, *see* Neighborhood,
    externalities
  system of cities, *see* Pareto-efficient
    resource allocation
Population density, 26
Population, residential, 30
Property tax, *see also* Capitalization,
    Suburbanization
  capitalization, 188–191
  comparison with wage tax, 187
  conversion to head tax, 217
  effect of rate variation, 185–187
  nature of, 181–183
Property tax incidence
  assessment practices, 188, 189
  new view, 184–186
  partial equilibrium model, 183, 184
  progressivity, 182, 183
  in a spatial model, 55–57
  tax increases, 185, 186
  traditional view, 183, 184

R

Rapid transit, *see also* Congestion, Road
    travel
  subsidization of construction, 152–153
  subsidization of fares, 153–157
  two-part pricing, 153
Rent control, 130–132
Rent gradient
  CBD, 34
    example, 35
  housing
    example, 20–22
    identical consumers, 11–14
    nonidentical consumers, 16–19
    relationship to land rent gradient, 24
  industrial air pollution, 111
  land, 15
    effect of population growth, 28
    example, 26, 27
  with a property tax, 54
  in a simplified city, 65
Residential sector
  aggregate relationships, 27–32
    example, 30–32
  characterization of, 8, 9